T0246734

ALL THE RAGE

Also by Josh Cohen

Not Working: Why We Have to Stop

The Private Life: Why We Remain in the Dark

How to Read Freud

Josh Cohen

All the Rage

Why Anger Drives the World

GRANTA

Granta Publications, 12 Addison Avenue, London W11 4QR

First published in Great Britain by Granta Books, 2024

A CIP catalogue record for this book
is available from the British Library.

1 3 5 7 9 10 8 6 4 2

ISBN 978 1 78378 945 0
eISBN 978 1 78378 947 4

Typeset in Bembo by M Rules

Printed and bound by CPI Group (UK) Ltd, Croydon, CR0 4YY

www.granta.com

MIX
Paper | Supporting
responsible forestry
FSC® C171272

In memory of my father, Edward Cohen

Contents

Note on the Clinical Cases

In the interests of preserving confidentiality, the cases discussed in this book are composites, drawn from my own consulting room and the work of clinical supervisees.

Introduction

Every morning, my inbox heaves with a new tranche of email alerts from Nextdoor, a social networking service for neighbourhoods where people in the local area post recommendations, enquiries, requests, offers, information. The tone can be chummy, jocular, kindly, anxious, but mostly the posts are angry. They include vituperative warnings about dodgy tradesmen; outraged reports of cruelty to animals witnessed by neighbours; snatches of grainy Ring camera footage purporting to show actual or attempted burglaries; complaints of junkies splayed on park benches and of predatory lone men approaching young girls; reports of vandalism, fly-tipping, charity muggers, phone scammers, poor restaurant service and late-night noise.

My heart sinks at each new set of notifications, festooned with rage emojis and opprobrium for *lowlifes, SCUM, animals!* Yet I've never been tempted to unsubscribe – and not only because the service is also a surprising showcase for human generosity and solidarity, reuniting desperate owners with their cats and wallets, offering help and advice to the hungry and infirm. Much as I appreciate these outbreaks of decency and kindness, it's the transmissions of rage that draw me to the posts. A batch of Nextdoor updates is a live window on the vexations of modern urban living, an electric chorus of sighs, growls and screams from the frontline of everyday reality.

I'm not on any other social media platforms, largely because I suspect they would ruin my life. I imagine being sucked down one or other virtual rabbit hole and remaining there indefinitely. On Twitter (now X), even upbeat sentiments like self-satisfaction, mutual affirmation and sincerity seem to have a tinge of anger about them; a subtext of enquiry as to why you haven't yet noticed the poster's unique wit and integrity, their fine creative output or charitable contributions or cookery skills.

The endearingly human anger on Nextdoor is lacking on X, characterized by its tones of righteous indignation and caustic sarcasm, high-handed contempt and gleeful cruelty. The times that I have looked at it, the trolling, shaming and piling on show it as a zone of freeform hate.

The social media giants promote the grandiose illusion that your smartphone is a global megaphone, blasting out your furious convictions on the social, ethical and geopolitical dilemmas of the moment to a potential audience of millions (even if your actual followers number in the low hundreds). It cultivates a mode of anger that is both impersonal and self-important, a style of slog-anizing that is grindingly repetitive, each post an echo of the last.

Nextdoor posts, in contrast, will reach (and likely interest) only those in your own neighbourhood, meaning there is less incentive to engage in performative provocation. The poorly styled, typo-ridden posts are genuine effusions of feeling, the sounds emitted by rubbing against the grain of life. Posters speak of wanting to vomit, to scream, to cry, to punch their antagonists. They remind us that anger, like all significant feelings, is experienced first of all at a bodily level, as a pressure towards discharge through the mouth or limbs.

Perhaps this is why these posts sometimes evoke for me a kind of makeshift psychoanalytic session. In my consulting room, one of the most common beginnings for a session is a launch by a patient into a full-throated rant against some individual (a teenage son, say, or a haughty barista), institution (a national bank or local gym) or situation (an unjust parking ticket or global heating). In moments like this, clinical psychoanalysis reveals itself less as communication between speakers as between bodies.

A raging patient will often induce in me mirror symptoms – contracted muscles, accelerated heart rate, grinding teeth, fluttering stomach – as I become not merely aware of their anger but possessed by it, experiencing the same overpowering congestion of bodily and psychic faculties, the same incapacity to think or feel anything but the object of their fury. In their very different ways, Nextdoor and a psychoanalytic consulting room offer a depository for dissatisfaction, a space in which to voice the frustrations of living in a world that forever fails to give us what we want.

Perhaps this gives us a clue about the nature of anger. We often associate, and sometimes even confuse, anger with aggression. But aggression, unlike anger, belongs to the domain of action. It is the effort to exert dominance over or hostility to some object outside oneself. Aggression can be channelled into hair-pulling, mockery or playing minor chords on a bass guitar, but it always manifests in the external world.

Anger, on the other hand, while it can certainly make itself perceptible to others, is first of all a feeling, a phenomenon of the mind and body. Unlike aggression, anger can be concealed from the world, and even from oneself. One of the most frequent and unsettling discoveries a person can make in psychoanalysis is just how much anger they're harbouring towards others in their past or present without having been aware of it.

We have a habit of thinking of anger and aggression in the terms Frank Sinatra speaks of love and marriage, a perfect couple in which one serves the other so seamlessly that you can barely tell them apart. Anger comes to be seen as aggression's head cheerleader, an agitating voice feeding the aggressive impulse with motive and impetus to act.

In *The Expression of the Emotions in Man and Animals*, Darwin argues that our common forms of emotional expression are vestiges of the actions they once accompanied, as when we mime the act of retching to express disgust. In anger, he observes, the impeded flow of blood can turn the face purple or white; our breathing becomes laboured, our teeth clench, our limbs may tremble, gestures that 'represent more or less plainly the act of striking or fighting with an enemy'.

On the one hand, this evolutionary perspective points to the Sinatran intimacy of anger and aggression; to be angry is to assume the physical attitude of a predator. But Darwin's theory equally implies that the angry stance is a kind of trace or relic of aggression, that while the link between the two once seemed organic and necessary, evolution has rendered it looser. An angry face may or may not anticipate an aggressive action.

Anger, in other words, lives a life quite apart from aggression, and aggression is only one of the ways we can express it. We can equally keep anger quietly to ourselves; turn it on ourselves; disguise it as sullenness, over-politeness or jocular teasing; or repress it to the point where we ourselves don't even know we're angry.

Each of these options raises the question of how I'm to live with my angry self, especially in a world so forbiddingly dense with angry selves. For at least the last decade, and perhaps especially since 2016, with its flashpoints of Donald Trump's election victory and the vote for Brexit, anger has felt like the defining colour and tone of our daily social and political lives, giving rise to a pervasive atmosphere of mutual fear, suspicion and accusation, in which any perception of difference – cultural, ideological, racial, sexual, class – shades quickly into the assumption of enmity. This public mood has seeped into our private lives and relationships. At the most immediate level, we can point to the well-documented divisions and resentments that Trump, Brexit,

Covid restrictions and so many other markers of cultural and political alignment have insinuated into the lives of families, friends,
couples and communities. In my consulting room, irritable talk
of these visible sources of division runs alongside more elusive
emanations of anger, perceptible in one person's clipped diction
and flared nostrils, in another's stiff, tightly guarded comportment
on the couch, in still another's coiled, withholding silence.

In short, I've found myself living in the shadow of the so-called
'age of rage' at every level of daily life, from the news headlines
blasting out of my phone and TV, to the feeling on the streets
around me, to the intimate space of the analytic session. Writing
this book has been a way of making sense of this experience,
of thinking through how and why anger drives us, both in the
universal experience of being human and in our own agitated
moment.

Any psychoanalyst's consulting room is a crucible of anger. Anger
is often directly expressed, but I also see it pressing through under
the cover of some other emotion – sadness, perhaps, or anxiety
or love. This clinical ubiquity has often led me to wonder why
psychoanalytic literature has so little to say about anger.

Sigmund Freud, founder of psychoanalysis, was more concerned with aggression, which he viewed as central to the life
of what he calls the drives, enigmatic entities situated on the
border between mental and physical life that impel us to satisfy our various needs and appetites. The drives are the region
of psychoanalytic theory which Freud revised more than any
other. In among numerous modifications and tweaks, there are
two major iterations of drive theory. In the first iteration, Freud
categorized the drives into a sexual drive and a self-preservative
or 'narcissistic' drive; he later considered that they consisted of a
life drive, directed towards the growth and expansion of the self,

and a death drive, directed towards self-erasure and unbound aggression. Spurned and doubted by his followers at first, and still controversial today, the death drive became one of the most famous of all Freud's ideas.

A drive is different from an emotion because its ultimate aim is to act rather than feel. While the impulse to love at the heart of the life drive, for example, makes itself felt at a bodily and emotional level, that feeling's primary purpose is as a spur to attain love in the external world. By analogy, we might say anger is what we feel (in technical language, the *affect*), and aggression is what we do about it (the drive).

These two levels of experience – feeling and action; affect and drive – are connected of course, but Freud says little about how. The one exception is in a curious paper from 1914: 'The Moses of Michaelangelo'. One of its oddities is that Freud chose to publish it anonymously in *Imago*, a journal founded by two of his disciples exploring various fields of cultural and social life from a psychoanalytic perspective.

Written in the guise of a submission by an amateur art enthusiast, the paper explores the question of what kind of relationship exists between anger and aggression, feeling and action. It begins by surveying various art-historical essays on Michaelangelo's great sculpture 'Moses' in Rome's San Pietro church. Each of the essays attempts to decipher the peculiar ambiguity of Moses' gait and expression as he sits with the tablets of the Ten Commandments and comes to quite different conclusions. Among these conflicting opinions, however, Freud finds one point of consensus: the idea that Moses' gaze is caught in the grip of an 'infinite wrath', 'which in the next instant will launch his great frame into violent action'.

Moses is captured, in this reading of the sculpture, at the moment he has caught sight of the idolatrous revels of the

Israelites before the golden calf, his body agitated with the immi-
nence of his action, which will be to spring up, raise the tablets
just received from God on Mt Sinai and hurl them to the ground
in fury.

This reading of the sculpture implies a seamless passage of the
drive: the aggressive impulse caught mid-flow on the way to its
full consummation in the action of smashing the tablets. The implied role of anger is as a kind of midwife to the aggressive drive,
the feeling that spurs and impels the act. Moses' 'infinite wrath'
with its imminent realization in the sublimely violent reproach to
his people is a model of the ideal harmony of feeling and drive,
based on the subordination of one to the other.

But the psychoanalytic conception of human drives implies
a different and more complex relationship between feeling and
drive. The distinction made by neuroscientist and philosopher
Antonio Damasio between feelings and emotions may be helpful
here. Damasio's definition of emotion follows that of Darwin as
the way an organism instinctively seeks to ensure its own preservation 'without conscious knowledge of the undertaking'.

Emotions are effectively stimulus responses to a given object
or event: I see a dangerous dog off its leash and cower in fear; I
smell roasting meat and am possessed by the irresistible urge to
devour it, or perhaps to vomit.

But feelings involve mapping these reactions to produce internal images of and ideas about them. Feelings creatively process
what emotions react to automatically, facilitating 'the possibility
of creating novel, nonstereotypical responses'. Anger, in this perspective, is of a higher order than aggression, a transformation
of reactive behaviour into a kind of self-reflection; feeling comes
after drive, not before it.

Damasio provides a fascinating illustration of this thesis from
clinical research at the Salpêtrière psychiatric hospital in Paris, in

the story of a sixty-five-year-old woman with Parkinson's whose symptoms were relieved by electrode contact with the affected parts of her brain. On one occasion, the electric current passed through a contact site just below the usual area. The patient very suddenly assumed an expression of sadness and began sobbing uncontrollably. A few seconds passed, and she spoke of how she could no longer go on living this way and wished fervently to die. The researchers immediately stopped the current, and the sobbing 'stopped as abruptly as it had begun'. Her behaviour returned to normal and she wondered good-humouredly what all that had been about.

Damasio's explanation was that the current had missed the 'general motor structures' it was intended to reach and instead made contact with brain stem nuclei that normally control action, including movements of facial musculature such as frowning and sobbing. His point is that these neural reactions occurred without any prior triggering thoughts of sadness, indicating that emotion, in the form of stereotype gestures such as crying, comes before feeling: 'Emotion-related thoughts came only *after* the emotion began.'

In a paper from 1971, the American psychoanalyst Hans Loewald offers a strikingly similar conception of feeling as belonging to a higher level of psychic function than emotion. In its most primitive form, a drive is a means to discharge instinctual energy by way of some action in the physical world. Human development involves the transformation of drives into 'psychic phenomena', that is, into feelings rather than programmed behaviours. This transformation is also a key aim of clinical psychoanalysis; for example, a patient might bring an inchoate unconscious aggression to the beginning of an analysis, which in the course of a treatment would become anger both felt and expressed.

In his ingenious reading of Michaelangelo's monumental sculpture, Freud tracks exactly this transformation. He suggests that Michaelangelo would have been aware of apparent anomalies of sequence in the Biblical text. For example, in Exodus Chapter 7, Verse 8, Moses intercedes for the idolators with God, after God tells him about the calf. And yet ten verses later, Moses appears to know nothing about the calf and is 'suddenly aroused to wrath' when told. Michaelangelo, Freud suggests, has mined these sequential inconsistencies to create a new version of the golden calf story, one that reverses its movement from anger to violent action.

In Freud's reading, Moses' wrath culminates not in the discharge but in the *mastery* of his rage. The strange bodily posture and expression of Michaelangelo's Moses is portraying not the imminent smashing of the tablets, but the agitated bodily stance of someone who has at once felt and overcome his wrath, who chooses to refrain from smashing the tablets and punishing his people.

This, writes Freud, is an exemplary Renaissance Moses, embodying a new and powerful emotional self-discipline: 'The giant frame with its tremendous physical power becomes only a concrete expression of the highest mental achievement that is possible in man, that of struggling successfully against an inward passion for the sake of a cause to which he has devoted himself.'

This sublime mental achievement complicates the sequential relationship between anger and aggression. Instead of anger being the signal that triggers an aggressive action, aggressive action is diverted towards a state of feeling. Instead of being discharged, the aggressive impulse is borne in the psychic and bodily interior.

The life of feeling, we might say, is a way of finding something to do with our emotions other than simply acting on them.

*

In his earliest formulations of the means and ends of psychotherapy, Freud was heavily invested in what we might call the hydraulic thesis, according to which human beings accumulate large reserves of tension in everyday life, inducing a permanent pressure on the nervous system and a consequent demand for its release.

In the context of psychoanalysis and its beginnings, this tension is commonly associated with the torrent of erotic desire and yearning which was heaving below the oppressively mannered surface of *fin de siècle* Viennese society. But in his early clinical practice, Freud was equally witness to frequent bottlenecks of anger and aggression in his patients.

One such intriguing instance is related in a brief clinical vignette from the 1893 'Preliminary Communication', co-written with his older colleague Josef Breuer, a Viennese GP, in which the pair outline their therapeutic innovations in the treatment of hysteria.

A man consults Freud at his newly established practice for the treatment of nervous disorders. He has been suffering from spontaneous hysterical attacks, during which he falls into frenzies of wordless rage. Under hypnosis, he reveals that he's been 'living through the scene in which his employer had abused him in the street and hit him with a stick'. Returning a few days later, the patient tells of a second attack, which is revealed under hypnosis to be a staging of the event that had triggered his illness: 'the scene in the law-court when he failed to obtain satisfaction for his maltreatment'.

Freud and Breuer tell us almost nothing about the man. He might be a factory worker or a waiter, but I always imagine him in the mould of an emerging stock type: the pinched, anxious clerk, soon to be immortalized in Franz Kafka's Josef K. or E. M. Forster's Leonard Bast, men whose apologetic façade conceals a quietly roiling anger and resentment.

These iconic fictional figures fit the classic neurasthenic profile that Freud was beginning to treat and to write about. A phenomenon of the rapidly urbanizing, industrializing society of the late nineteenth century, neurasthenia was the consequence of a sudden and excessive load of sensory and emotional stimuli bearing down on mind and body, inducing symptoms of irritability, fatigue and depression as well as headaches and spikes in blood pressure. The employee's silent pantomimic fury suggests a nervous system traumatized and overwhelmed, unable to bear the burden of humiliation induced by the public beating and the subsequent public repudiation of his legal case for compensation.

Freud's clinical interest in the nervous afflictions of the moment was accompanied by more fundamental enquiries into psychic life, equally relevant to the case of the beaten employee. In an unpublished text of 1895, known as the *Project for a Scientific Psychology*, Freud speculates on the baby's earliest experience of satisfaction, describing a being beset by excess internal tension brought about by hunger or some other vital need.

Unable to provide for herself, the baby cries, communicating her distress and drawing the attention of her caregiver. The circuit of tension, external intervention and relief constitutes 'an *experience of satisfaction*'. The efficacy of the baby's hungry scream leads Freud to the startling inference that 'the initial helplessness of human beings is the *primal source* of all *moral motives*'. That is, morality begins in the distress of the creature who calls on her carers to provide satisfactions she cannot supply for herself. For as long as they fail to do so, she screams her angry proto-moral protest.

The hypnosis of the beaten employee had revealed a similarly helpless scream, this time unvoiced, when he 'failed to obtain satisfaction for his maltreatment'. The verbal echo is more than coincidence. The humiliating incapacity to gain satisfaction puts the employee in contact with his original infantile helplessness. His reaction, like the baby's, is a wordless scream of rage, now driven into the silence of unconscious memory.

Hysteria, neurasthenia, infantile need: underlying these very different psychic phenomena is the same experience of helplessness. The baby's scream announces a gap between a need and its satisfaction, which becomes harder to bear the longer it is sustained. Ordinarily, our physical and emotional development removes us from this state of helplessness; as we grow in mental and bodily autonomy, we are able increasingly to help ourselves, to seek and find the food or love we crave.

But as the beaten employee's case reminds us, an experience of traumatic shock or humiliation can revive in us the desperate vulnerability of the infant. And as my psychoanalytic practice reminds me each day, even our much more ordinary experiences – real or perceived insults, slights, rejections, disappointments, frustrations – can bring us into contact with this primary layer of helplessness. Our persistent failures to remedy the insistent dissatisfactions of daily life give rise to that state of agitated enervation we call *anger*.

A hungry baby's cry is angry, an expression of raw physical and emotional need; but it is also a rudimentary form of aggression, what Freud calls a 'specific action' aimed at achieving real-world satisfaction. In his writings stretching from the 1930s to the 1970s, D. W. Winnicott, the British paediatrician and psychoanalyst, transformed our understanding of how the management of infantile needs shapes our subsequent development. He notes that the newborn infant has gestated in an environment in which all his needs have been satisfied before he could even become aware of them as needs. Expelled from the mother's body, exposed to the cold infinity of the new space around him, subjected to delay between hunger and feeding, the baby is made suddenly aware of himself as one who can lack what he needs.

According to Winnicott, the baby manages these traumatic intimations of a world of things and people outside himself by forging an illusion of his omnipotent control over it. When he cries, he causes the breast and its abundant supply of milk and love to appear. In the first weeks of life at least, his mother will be inclined to nurture this illusion by feeding and tending to her baby on demand. His total helplessness is thus inverted, such that every voice, every touch, every sensual emanation of the world around him becomes a projection of his own desire. It is, as the saying goes, his world – we just live in it.

The central task of development is the gradual and gentle dispelling of this illusion, and the concomitant acknowledgement of what Winnicott calls 'not-me' objects, a reckoning with a world of more than just one, in which the growing child must make room for others. And this is where the problems start, where his appetites for love, pleasure and power run up against the failure or incapacity or unwillingness of others to satisfy them, not to mention the scandalizing existence of the same appetites in others.

The lesson the child learns, in other words, is that his aggressive bids for one satisfaction or another are liable to fail, and that he is bound to carry the remnants of those failures within himself. When we describe a person's character as angry, we are saying that the weight of that burden is too heavy for them to bear.

The other lesson he learns, no less bitter but ultimately perhaps more productive, is that dissatisfaction, and by extension a certain quantum of anger, is endemic to living. This is why the hydraulic thesis, on which Freud based his 'abreactive' technique for treatment, is fatally flawed.

Under hypnosis, the beaten employee acted out the silent rage he had been forced to suppress, both in the street and in the court. The abreactive technique works on the premise that as the repressed memory rises to the surface of consciousness, so does its companion emotion, enabling the patient to describe the distressing experience and the feelings it aroused as fully as possible.

This is the psychotherapy of 'energetic reaction', which demands a release of emotion proportionate to the injury suffered. It is a technique whose rationale is implied in such idiomatic phrases as 'crying oneself out' or 'blowing off steam' (the German is *sich austoben*, literally 'to rage oneself out'), as well as in folk anger management techniques such as pillow bashing. Without hydraulic release, Freud posited, the distress and anger felt by the victim remain an ongoing burden on the nervous system.

The idea of a treatment directed at unmetabolized pain lodged in the deepest strata of mind and body has since been revived in various therapies, most famously in Arthur Janov's 'primal therapy', popularly known as primal scream therapy, which enjoyed a brief vogue in the early 1970s. Like Freud and Breuer, Janov saw psychic pain as located in suppressed traumas of early childhood. The proposed cure was to discharge the trapped reactive anger in uninhibited and spontaneous screaming and ranting.

The practice has occasionally been revived over the last fifteen years or so in the form of 'rage rooms', rented spaces in which customers wearing protective gear take metal poles to breakable objects – defunct electronic appliances, unwanted crockery, disused furniture – in an extended ritual of frenzied destruction which, as documented by *Guardian* writer Gaby Hinsliff, has become increasingly popular with young women as a hybrid health and leisure activity.

The problem with such cathartic extravagances is that they misrecognize the nature of rage. Abreaction assumes a set-up in which feelings are stored in finite quantities, to be cried out to the point of full discharge. But as he developed his thinking and gained clinical experience, Freud came to see his belief in abreaction as a mistake, albeit a productive one.

What it misses is the dogged persistence of feelings, their stubborn refusal to disappear on demand. The screams of the baby or the traumatized adult register a state of dissatisfaction, a gap between a need or desire – hunger, love, justice – and its fulfilment. But dissatisfaction is not simply a temporary state awaiting relief through appropriate action; it is an ineliminable condition of human life – and so, therefore, is anger.

The failure of the cathartic method ultimately comes down to the nature of human drives, one of the most basic but equally most enigmatic elements in psychoanalysis. In his definitive statement on the subject, his 1915 paper 'Drives and Their Vicissitudes', Freud notes first of all that a drive is a source of stimulus from within the organism, not outside it.

The difference is crucial in that the impact of an external stimulus – say, a bright light or loud noise – is always temporary. The stimulus exerted by a drive, on the other hand, is 'always a *constant* one'. And, because it issues from within, there is no escaping it.

Drives aim at satisfaction through the attainment of an aim. From the beginning of life, they teach us to love what satisfies us (the breast that feeds, the voice that soothes, the hands that hold us) and hate what frustrates us (hunger, inattention). These impulses are forever exerting themselves, calling on us – *driving* us – to obtain more of what we need and want.

A drive, Freud writes, lies 'on the frontier between the mental and the somatic'. It is the psychic representative of a bodily stimulus – what an itch might look like if it were a mental rather than dermal entity. Freud ascribes four components to a drive: *pressure*, the force it exerts in making its demand on us; *aim*, which Freud identifies as being 'in every instance satisfaction'; *object*, the thing required to achieve satisfaction (a breast, a touch, a voice); and *source*, the somatic location in which the drive originates (stomach, head, genital).

In concert, these four factors give rise to a predicament: the passage from the pressure of the drive to its satisfaction cannot be straight. Put simply, to be under pressure of the drive is to want something without knowing exactly what that something is. This distinguishes the drive from the more straightforwardly biological concept of an instinct.

An instinct is a mechanism at work in all life forms, such as the bee's gravitation towards honey and nectar, which ensures the attainment of vital needs. We might say that the newborn baby's rooting for the mother's breast is of the same nature, but the comparison would be both correct and incomplete. The French psychoanalyst Jean Laplanche points out that from the very beginning of life, our vital needs are inextricably tied up with our sexuality – not, of course, the genital sexuality of adulthood, but the sensual currents of tenderness and affection emanating from the mother's body. A breast feeds and fills the baby's hungry stomach, but also provides the more elusive pleasures that arise from the smell and feel of his mother's skin, the flood of abundant warmth that breaks over his lips with the flow of milk.

The aim and object of a drive, therefore, are both subject to infinite variation. Life almost never involves knowing what we want and getting it. The demands of the drive, Freud says, can be 'inhibited or deflected', diverted from the path they started down. Anyone who has spent significant time around a baby knows how frequently and frustratingly they can fail to be satisfied by, well, anything, how tormented they can seem by not knowing what they want, or perhaps by not having the means to tell us.

And anyone who has spent significant time around an adult, themselves included, knows how insistently this torment persists through the course of life. All those regions of life that arouse our deepest longings and desires – love, work, food, money, rest, meaning – are also those that arouse the most painful feelings of uncertainty and self-division.

The aggressive drive impels us to get what we want, but so often leaves us with the feeling that what we got wasn't quite what we wanted, if indeed we got it at all. We then cast around for something or someone to blame for this feeling, for standing in the way of the true fulfilment of our desire. We may try to tell ourselves that the one thing that eluded us – a longed-for birthday gift or lover or promotion – was the difference between happiness and misery.

Freud sees this malaise as rooted in the nature of childhood love, a first characteristic of which, as he writes in his 1931 essay 'Female Sexuality', is its boundlessness. A second, more surprising feature is that 'it has, in point of fact, no aim and is incapable of obtaining complete satisfaction; and principally for that reason it is doomed to end in disappointment and to give place to a hostile attitude'.

The aimlessness of the drive to love is destined to end in rage. This is the source of the complaint commonly heard in the consulting room, he goes on to say, that the patient's mother 'did not give her enough milk, did not suckle her long enough'. Freud initially offers a cultural explanation for this complaint, noting that in the highly regulated monogamous family of the modern West, breastfeeding tends not to last beyond six to nine months, where in traditional societies it is more likely to continue for two to three years.

But no sooner does he advance this theory than he rejects it, suggesting that the more likely explanation is 'the greed of a child's libido' renders her likely to make the same complaint regardless the length of her suckling period. The twin hungers for food and love become indistinguishable, and eventually a major source of eating disorders; unable to regulate her appetite for love, the child instead brings her appetite for food under tyrannical control.

Failure is endemic to the drive's quest to know what it wants and to obtain it. Put another way, to be governed by the drive is to be angry at two levels: the emotional level of the infant who discharges her anger in screams, and later at the feeling level of the older person – child, adolescent, adult – who can experience and elaborate her anger.

The theogonies and mythologies of the ancient world from Canaan to Greece, India to Iceland, abound with avatars of pure rage. Think of the *Erinyes*, the spirits of unbound fury who hound the matricidal Orestes, or of Lyssa, the goddess of rage who afflicts her victims with irremediable rabid frenzies. Hindu theogony tells of the goddess Kali, decorated with a garland of arms and weapons and a necklace of decapitated heads, springing from the body of Durga when the latter was assailed by demons, a terrifying embodiment of avenging rage. As represented in these figures, rage is less a feature of individual human psychology than an elemental force of the cosmos, unleashing limitless destruction on the world.

From early childhood, I was aware of this force presiding over the Hebrew Scriptures. Stupefied by the long Sabbath morning service, I would read a children's Bible, often turning to the story of the Flood. The telling of the story in sermons and Sunday morning classes would place all the emphasis on God's merciful preservation of a future human race – the ark, the dove, the rainbow! – skating over His more obviously destructive role in the story.

God enjoins Noah to build the ark which will preserve him, his family and his animals from the Flood He will soon be visiting on the earth 'to put an end to all flesh'. God is 'grieved at heart' by His own error in creating a race so irredeemably corrupt. 'I will blot out man whom I created from the face of the earth – man and beast and creeping things and birds of the air, for I regret that I made them.'

I remember the feeling of dismayed confusion I had on first reading these lines. Why punish the animals along with the people – what had *they* done? And *what about all the kids?* Could it really be that just one family merited saving? My mind's eye was assailed by the image of my own frenziedly waving hand rapidly disappearing beneath the rising flood waters.

But more frightening still than the wholesale drowning of life on earth was the image of a God who could erase the world he'd created as casually as a draughtsman rubbing out a pencil sketch. This God was nothing like a furious parent or stern teacher administering slaps or confiscations or issuing dire warnings, but a power of pure annihilation hovering menacingly over all existence.

The relief I felt on reading God's post-diluvian resolution to never again destroy all living beings was fleeting. While there was to be no reprise of the watery apocalypse, the divine urge to liquidate the sinners didn't abate. Soon after the Flood came God's announcement to Abraham that the sheer gravity of sin in the towns of Sodom and Gomorrah left Him with no choice but to wipe them out.

Unlike Noah, who declines to plead humanity's case, Abraham intercedes on behalf of Sodom and Gomorrah, winning God's concession that should fifty righteous men be found in them, He will spare the towns. Abraham then bargains God down in small increments to just ten. But the negotiations come to nothing: 'The Lord caused to rain upon Sodom and upon Gomorrah brimstone and fire from the Lord out of heaven.'

The Pentateuch doesn't let up in its record of God's punitive exterminations, reaching something of a peak in the Book of Numbers. When God sends twelve spies from the wilderness to spy out the land of Canaan, the future inheritance of the people of Israel, ten of them return and 'spread an evil report' of the territory, warning that it teems with the menace of enemy warrior tribes.

Furious at hearing His promised land thus spurned, God resolves to send a plague to destroy the people. This time it's Moses that intercedes on Israel's behalf, persuading God to refrain from total annihilation. But he cannot prevent God from visiting a deadly plague against the trash-talking spies and their followers, nor can his dire warnings help the Israelites who return to the top of the mountain in penance only to die by the Amalekite sword, unprotected by the God who, with grisly irony, abandons them to slaughter by the very enemies they had warned against.

The Book of Numbers goes on to tell of Korah's rebellion against Moses' God-given authority, which ends when Korah and his company, along with their wives and children, are swallowed by a 'mouth' that opened and sealed them in the earth.

The cumulative effect of these purgative visitations is to build a picture of God's anger as instantaneous justice, a kind of divine red mist that short-circuits any pause for reflection. Only the interventions of His chosen prophets can stay the scope and force of his unbound punitive rage, and even then, only within strict limits. Water, fire and earth, pestilence and the sword: the elements of nature, both non-human and human, become instruments of an educative divine terror, a fury so immediately realized in lethal consequences it can seem as though God's feelings are indistinguishable from His actions.

Is this not the ultimate model for the vengeful fantasies aroused by our own furies? I can vividly recall, several years before I'd read any Bible stories, the shoves and slaps of other kids in the kindergarten sandbox stirring me to visions of their instant mass combustion, triggered by the raised tip of my index finger.

To carry my anger within felt humiliating, a smarting body memory of injury and defeat. I wanted to consummate it in some magic act of aggression, one that would leave behind no trace of itself, as though my anger would be burnt out in perfect synchrony with the bodies of my enemies.

About thirty years later, walking down a busy street on a London winter night, I felt a hard slap on the back of my head, sending the peaked cap I was wearing to the pavement. Reeling from the shock, the words 'fuckin' wanker' resounding in my ears, I saw the fast-receding back of my assailant, his bald skull perched atop the folds of an obscenely thick neck.

Feeling the dull ache of shame as I picked up the hat, I shut my eyes and saw my fingers on the back of that neck, plunging his ruddy bowling ball of a head into a bowl of nitric acid. Rarely have I more vividly understood the annihilating wrath of God, not to mention the impotent rage of a wounded man.

What continues to trouble me about Abraham's bargaining with God is the suspicion that it's no more than a ritual dance, the two of them playing out the moves in the mutual knowledge that it makes no difference: that the incineration of Sodom, Gomorrah and its people, like all of the subsequent divine punishments of the Pentateuch, has already been decreed and is merely awaiting execution.

This only renders more intriguing the presentation of God's anger in the Book of Jonah, dated somewhere between two and four centuries after most scholars date the completion of the Pentateuch. The Book of Jonah begins with God appearing to the reluctant prophet, commanding him to go to Nineveh and proclaim against its spreading wickedness. Jonah's defiant response is to 'flee unto Tarshish from the presence of the Lord', triggering his protracted and strange pursuit by God – strange because Jonah is aware throughout that God's presence is looming over him for the entire chase. God sends the storms that threaten to wreck the ship on which he escapes and the whale in whose belly he resides three days and nights, until he is vomited onto shore.

Jonah doesn't resist God's second command to go to Nineveh, where he soon arrives and warns its people of its divine over-throw forty days hence. On hearing Jonah's prophecy, the King of Nineveh dons sackcloth and ashes and ordains a city-wide fast as penance. Seeing the people's repentance, God 'turns away His fierce anger'.

This is Jonah's cue to become 'exceedingly . . . angry', telling God that this is exactly why he fled from him in the first place, 'For I knew that thou art a gracious God, and compassionate, and long-suffering, and abundant in mercy, and repentest thee of evil.' In other words, he knew his prophecy of the city's destruction wouldn't be realized, which makes him look more like a ranting fool than a prophet. This is the wretched humiliation he was fleeing from, and that now leaves him feeling 'it is better for me to die than to live'.

'Art thou greatly angry?' God asks him, to which the book records no response. Jonah wanders to the east of the city to find rest in a booth. God has a gourd rise from the ground and cast sufficient shadow to protect Jonah from the heat. But as morning comes, He sends a worm to chew through the gourd, exposing Jonah to the full heat of the sun and causing him to repeat his earlier conviction: 'It is better for me to die than to live.'

'Are you greatly angry for the gourd?' God asks him, evok-ing a mother soothing her inconsolable toddler. 'I am greatly angry, even unto death,' Jonah replies. God's homily gives the diminutive Book its climactic, and wonderfully anticlimactic, words: 'Thou hast had pity on the gourd, for which thou hast not laboured, neither madest it grow, which came up in a night, and perished in a night; and should I not have pity on Nineveh, that great city, wherein are more than sixscore thousand persons that cannot discern between their right hand and their left hand, and also much cattle?'

What on earth (or in heaven) has happened to God across the centuries between Noah's Flood and Jonah's gourd? Contrast the way Abraham gingerly tiptoes around God's rage in appealing for mercy with Jonah's indignation at God's mercy, the complete destruction Abraham seeks hopelessly to prevent with the complete destruction Jonah seeks hopelessly to bring about.

It is hard to avoid the impression of a peculiar reversal in the interim, whereby Jonah has acquired something of God's annihilating fury and God has acquired something of Abraham's merciful empathy. Where Jonah has raised his mind to the great throne of divine judgement, God seems to have descended into the messy throng of humankind.

What so moves me about God's climactic words is that they ask the very questions I asked of my children's Bible: But are they really that bad? And what have the cows done, for God's sake? You do realise there are a lot of cows in this place?! I mean, did you even think about the cows, Jonah? Seen up close, the people of Nineveh appear to God as less evil than morally hapless, no less flailing and lost than the rest of us.

It's not that God's anger has abated, but that it seems to have lost its terrifying aura of finality. The fury of Noah's God exerted a pressure that could only find release in the watery extinction of humankind. It required an action fully commensurate with its absolute force. It is an anger of almost Platonic purity, free of any corrupting ambiguity or self-doubt.

It strikes me that the divine anger of the Flood might serve as a tacit model, or at least an inspiration, for Twitter anger, for the indignant summary judgements (so memorably documented by Jon Ronson in *So You've Been Publicly Shamed*) with which social media posters shame, belittle and damn the objects of their moral and political displeasure. Viewing the offenders from such a transcendent height ensures they are mere specks in the poster's field of vision, as easy to incinerate as an ant under a sun-struck magnifying glass.

God seems no less enraged with the Ninevites than with the denizens of the antediluvian world. But their repentance, assumed with the immediate, zealous remorse of the scolded child, induces in God a previously unsuspected empathy. In a sense, He becomes as confused as they are, shuttling abruptly from divine exterminator to exasperatedly loving Father, at a loss for what to do with these wayward, hapless souls he's created. Perhaps Jonah doesn't get it because he, unlike God, is childless. *You really expect me to kill all these poor chumps? C'mon Jonah, what kind of monster do you take me for? They're just dumb kids!*

Isn't this much closer to the anger vented on Nextdoor? Not the anger of summary judgement from on high, but the frustrated rage of human beings consigned to dwell in the world below, a world of infinite other human beings who get on your fucking nerves with their insistence on doing stuff you *really don't like.*

This second type of anger – the anger of frustrated rage – is the one we meet most frequently in our everyday life. But the first type – the summary judgement of God or the gods – cannot be consigned to the ancient past. It may be a mythic ideal, but mythic ideals can often be a real force in the world.

So much of the anger that circulates between individuals and groups is tacitly conditioned by the fantasy of a divine rage, in which the chaos of angry feelings would be redeemed in a single, perfectly cathartic action. In fact, it's this fantasy that can make anger feel so unpleasantly enervating. The desperate urge, so frequently heard in my consulting room, to liquidate the object of rage, tends only to exacerbate our feelings of injury and humiliation when it turns out to be impracticable.

This predicament is dramatized in the opening of the inaugural work of Western literature. The first word of *The Iliad*, Homer's epic poem of the dying phases of the Trojan War, is *menin*, variously translated as wrath, anger, rage, fury. Where *thymos*, the other word Homer uses to signify anger, is closer to passion or spiritedness, *menis* suggests a more explicitly destructive emotion.

The opening lines invite the Muse to sing the *menin* (the accusative form of *menis*), which the next line augments as *oulomenin*, the 'accursed anger', of Achilles, whose force 'hurled' the souls of so many Greek warriors down to Hades. It goes on to recount the quarrel of Achilles with Agamemnon, the implacably arrogant warrior-king who, in the tenth year of the Trojan War, brings calamity on his army.

Agamemnon has captured Chryseïs, daughter of the elderly Trojan priest Chryses, for a concubine. Chryses entreats Agamemnon to return her to him and is brutally refused. The distressed priest entreats the god Apollo to vengeance against the Greeks and is duly obliged. After Apollo fells columns of Greek soldiers with lethal arrows, their commanders gather for crisis talks.

Achilles leads a chorus of demands for Agamemnon to return Chryseïs. Impelled by narcissistic injury and envious spite, Agamemnon agrees on condition he is compensated by a prize of equal worth – Achilles' concubine Briseïs. The enraged Achilles reaches for a sword to slay the king, only to be held back by the goddess Athene.

Prevented from unleashing his fury, Achilles consents bitterly to the trade-off. Forced to bear the pressure of the *menis* he cannot act upon, he exacts the heaviest of prices from Agamemnon and the Greeks: Achilles, their 'great defence against the horror of war', will withdraw himself from fighting, exposing his fellow warriors to the worst peril.

Perhaps no work of literature since Homer's has chronicled more vividly this inexorable descent from indignation to accursed anger, *oulomenin*, anger that feeds off itself, becoming ever more impervious to appeasement or repair. All efforts to bring Achilles' rage under the rule of reason and proportion prove hopeless.

When the warrior Aias reproaches him, during the failed mission to persuade him to join the battle against the Trojans, for the 'savagery in his breast' and lack of 'thought for the love of his companions', Achilles doesn't deny the charge: 'All that you have said seems much after my own feeling.' 'But,' he goes on, 'my heart swells with anger whenever I think of that time, how the son of Atreus treated me with contempt in front of the Argives.'

In Achilles, we witness the annihilating wrath of the God of Abraham running up against the limits imposed by the human world. He can't deny that his grievance has come to be infected with all the vindictive spite he condemned in Agamemnon; but his self-awareness does nothing to salve the wound of being humiliated before his companion warriors. Stoked by the self-propelling force of the aggressive drive, his anger has taken on a life of its own, over which he himself seems to feel he has little command. Though he acknowledges its disproportion to Aias, it continues to swell his heart regardless.

The German philosopher Peter Sloterdijk argues that rage has both shaped and derailed the course of Western history precisely through its refusal of any logic of balance and proportion. With Achilles in mind, he observes that the West's cherished remedies for bringing to a halt the 'endless pendulum of hit and retaliation', from private spiritual exercises to public justice to foreign policy, are liable to run up against their own limits: 'Just as a festering wound can become both a chronic and general malady, psychic and moral wounds also may not heal, which creates its own corrupt temporality, the infinity of an unanswered complaint.'

Imagine a world in which our psychic and moral wounds could always find remedy in appropriate action, in which we knew just what was needed to relieve our dissatisfactions. In such a world, we'd never have to carry the burden of anger for long. Feeling angry would simply be the fleeting signal to do whatever the situation required, be it signing a petition or blowing up a building. Complaints would always be answered, wounds would always heal.

The problem is that action never exhausts feeling. Moreover, Sloterdijk suggests, this gap between the rage inside us and the aggression that externalizes it can very easily become a chasm. Aggression is a drive, and it is in the nature of the drive, Freud says, never to achieve full satisfaction. We may enjoy the passing sense that a given action has blown off enough steam or 'raged us out', but anger has a strange habit of regenerating itself. This is how a historical wound to an individual or group is always liable to shade into 'the infinity of an unanswered complaint'.

One of the key distinctions Sloterdijk makes in *Rage and Time* is between what he calls 'banked' and 'dispersed' rage. The popular revolutionary leaders of previous generations achieved power by harnessing and 'banking' the rage of the 'humiliated and offended' victims of political and economic injustice and oppression across generations. In doing so, they sought to gather the mass of anger into a 'rage bank' that could power a long-term transformation of society. A dispersed rage, in contrast, is one which is lacking a shared project in which to invest itself. This is the rage that has come to be so vulnerable to exploitation and manipulation by cynical or extremist forces from far-right populism to jihadism.

We can find an analogue for this distinction in individual psychology. A person's emotional life can be defined by a sense of integration and organization or, on the contrary, by a sense of dispersion and incoherence. In his 1949 paper, 'Mind and Its Relation to Psyche-Soma', Winnicott suggests that the way we experience our feelings has its roots in our developmental experience of our bodies.

Under conditions of what Winnicott calls 'good enough' care, a baby will be in perpetual contact with the ongoing life of her body: the rhythm of her breathing, the ever-renewed sensations at the surface of the skin, the undirected movement of the limbs, the curious emanations of the voice, the secretions and excretions flowing from every orifice.

This immersion in her own bodily life is the basis for the development of a psyche, which in the first instance, writes Winnicott, 'means the *imaginative elaboration of somatic parts, feelings and functions*, that is, of physical aliveness'. We are very close here to Damasio's understanding of feelings as the interior mapping of emotions.

It is this psychic dialogue with our own body that '*is felt by the individual* to form the core for the imagination'. The possibility of creative life begins in the fullness of bodily life. We might say, using Sloterdijk's terminology, that in healthy development, the psyche gathers or 'banks' bodily experience for its own nourishment and transformation.

This ordinary yet inestimable human achievement rests on '*continuity of being*', which allows a baby to grow and change undisturbed, at her own pace. Whereas when the baby's bodily

expression and freedom are constrained by a demand for compliance – for example, when she is put under pressure to sleep
or remain quiet or acquire cognitive skills very early – she is
at risk of forming a pathological 'mind-psyche' rather than a
healthy 'psyche-soma'. A mind-psyche experiences the body as
an alien entity, and so cannot feel fully alive. Instead of being
concentrated, emotional life feels fragmented and scattered. The
experience of the world feels eerily disembodied, the range and
freedom of the imagination acutely constrained.

In clinical work with patients of this kind, Winnicott suggests,
an awareness will likely emerge of a gap in the continuity of their
own selfhood. In one of his patients, the awareness that she has
been, as it were, trapped in her head all her life, leads to an enraged
assault on her own skull in which 'violent head-banging appeared
as an attempt to produce a blackout'. It is as though the head is
suddenly perceived as a kind of thief of life that must be destroyed
before it can be endowed with a new life *within* the body.

Without psychosomatic elaboration, emotional experience
is impoverished. The New Zealand-born French psychoanalyst
Joyce McDougall observed this impoverishment in the ways some
of her patients seemed unable to *feel* their emotional responses,
needing instead to be 'constantly engaged in immediately *dispersing in action*' whatever impacted them emotionally.

The predicament of such patients is that they cannot find a
path to their own psychosomatic life, and so cannot begin to find
the images or words to encompass what they're feeling. As with
Winnicott's head-banging patient, this is likely to have the effect
of inducing an irremediable state of rage and a permanent sense
of 'feeling empty, misunderstood or out of touch with others',
often expressing itself in 'the overpowering need for medication,
food, tobacco, alcohol, opiates and . . . frantic sexual exploits of a
perverse or compulsive nature'.

This description of dispersed inner life starts to get at the nature of our enervated and angry societies. We live under conditions of what we might call malign public care; governments that manipulate information, welfare budgets, democratic institutions and class differences to foment division, fear and mistrust – between 'native' citizens and migrants, leavers and remainers, red and blue states, workers and shirkers; internet and TV news media that distort, deny and invent facts in order to stoke the rage of their viewers and listeners; big tech corporations that place us under permanent surveillance and harness our private data to shape our private lives. Like Winnicott's overbearing parents, these modes of governance and communication at once demand our compliance and infuse our relationships to ourselves and others with anxiety and confusion. What the psychosomatic patient McDougall describes as 'feeling empty, misunderstood or out of touch with others' starts to sound eerily like any of us living in today's advanced societies. The pervasive use of antidepressant and anxiolytic medication may not be very surprising.

Addressing the permanent state of physical and psychic vulnerability experienced by so many, the political theorist and writer William Davies points to various forms of violence, from terrorism to computer hacking and trolling, that cast their shadow on our everyday lives. The effect of these latter, virtual forms of intrusion and attack may be 'primarily psychological,' writes Davies in *Nervous States*, but their effect can undoubtedly be called violent: 'What it damages are the feelings of security and trust that allow diverse societies to function, and it replaces them with nervousness.'

Once nervousness becomes the dominant mood of society, anger is given licence to spread and grow. The pathological insecurity and mistrust that tormented Winnicott's and McDougall's patients seem to have become dominant features of our everyday lives. Winnicott's head-banging patient, trapped in the alienated, fragmented 'mind-psyche' she seeks desperately to break open, is a powerful cipher of us citizens of the virtual world, trapped in informational bubbles that violently circumscribe our emotional and imaginative freedom, creating conditions in which disagreement and difference breed not curiosity and exchange but enmity and mutual cancellation from inside a self-confirming echo chamber. It's from this soil that the abstracted, grandiose anger of social media warriors grows; the anger of countless nervous 'mind-psyches' desperately trying to cancel out their own felt vulnerabilities and doubts, to brandish a clarity and certainty they crave but can never really achieve.

The epidemics of self-harm, eating disorders and opioid addictions blighting the lives of so many individuals and communities today are further symptoms of the spreading 'nervousness' tracked by Davies. In such malaises, the malign care internalized by Winnicott's and McDougall's patients seems to spread to the life of our disintegrated and agitated society.

Readers will notice that I seem to use the words anger and rage interchangeably. This is deliberate, in spite of my awareness that the two words signify quite different meanings. In discussions of anger with psychoanalytic colleagues, they have often appealed to this distinction, arguing that anger is a structured, integral feeling under the self's control, where rage is a kind of psychic and bodily dispossession, closer to madness.

While this distinction has pragmatic value, I think it is ultimately an artificial one that assumes anger can be brought under the command of the ego. Once we recognize that anger is never fully under our command, that at the moment we imagine we are in possession of it, it takes possession of us, rage becomes a possibility lurking inside anger rather than a feeling distinct from it.

In what follows, we'll explore the rage engendered by this collective agitation, which I divide into four broad types. We start with the split, paranoid politics engendered by the unshakeable conviction of one's own rightness, which I refer to as *righteous* rage. To be right, as Anthony Trollope shows us so vividly in his 1869 novel *He Knew He Was Right*, is to insulate oneself in advance from the risks and vulnerabilities of doubt and take refuge in the precarious comfort of one's own certainty. Lurking in this state of mind is a fantasy of anger that can be fulfilled and discharged in some ultimately purgative act of aggression.

The problem with such fantasies is that they fail, which leads us to the second form of anger. What I call *failed* rage is simply anger's failure to realize itself in action, and the consequent experience of being abandoned to an anger that has nowhere to go.

This often leads to a resolution, which might be embodied in a culture or a religious movement, to renounce anger altogether. The problem with this renunciation is that rather than expunging anger from individual and collective life, it tends to engender forms of rage which deny, disguise and displace themselves: the loudly proclaimed gospels of positive thinking, for example, or the much more subterranean strategies of passive aggression.

When anger is frustrated, it quickly becomes vulnerable to emotional and political manipulation and exploitation. This possibility gives rise to a third kind of anger, *cynical* rage. One place this can be stoked very damagingly is in the psychotherapeutic consulting room. The key instrument of psychoanalytic therapy is transference, the patient's necessary and unconscious misrecognitions of their analyst as iterations of formative figures of their past – parents or teachers, for example. If the analyst understands the mechanisms of transference, they can also manipulate the patient by exploiting the rawest and most vulnerable spots of their inner life.

What can this egregious form of intimate manipulation tell us about the forms of political manipulation that are driving and shaping so much of our present-day politics, particularly in the form of 'strongman' leaders and the cults that form around them? What makes the anger that drove Brexit and the election of Trump, or Russia's war on Ukraine, or the tragic exchanges of terror and asymmetrical warfare in Israel and Palestine, so dangerous, if not its dogged commitment never to question or examine itself? We assume we are right so as to evade the risks of others', or even our own, curiosity, questioning or doubt. So often debate about these essential issues becomes a kind of hostile informational warfare, the empty rehearsal of talking points from which the pain or value of the other has already been discounted.

If anger could be a means of fostering love and justice rather than closing it down, it would need to start from an embrace rather than a denial of one's own vulnerability and self-doubt, along with a real curiosity about the other, not excluding what might be making *them* angry. Only at this point, I suggest, will rage become *usable*. My hope is that this book can arouse that curiosity and open discussion around why this terrible and necessary force drives our world, and how we can learn to live with it.

Chapter One

Righteous Rage: Monsters, Revolutionaries, Jealous Husbands

We like to laugh at the intensity of childhood feelings from the superior heights of adult reason, as though to assure ourselves we have little to do with the child we once were.

I can see my ecstasy just after parting the gap in the wrapping paper on my sixth birthday and discovering the Six Million Dollar Man figurine I'd so fervently prayed for. I can catch an echo of the high pitch of my delighted squeal, a glimpse of my triumphantly outstretched arms. But I can't honestly say much about how any of this felt.

I am a little closer to the terrible mortification, age eight, of watching a ball pass through the gap between my feet and into the goal I was supposed to be keeping, and even more so to the crushing boredom and resentment, age nine, of placing decimal points in endless columns of sums as the sun shone tauntingly into my bedroom.

I remember these moments of joy, shame and boredom with the fondness of a relative visiting from abroad, reminded for a short while that, after all, the place and family in which he grew up are still part of his life, of who he is. They evoke gentle amusement, wistful nostalgia, a wonder that any of this once really mattered.

1

But when I close my eyes and recall moments of childhood rage, the effect is much closer to a possession, a takeover of the senses, an invasion of the skin and breath, a violent scrambling of my inner vision. My entire self is gathered in my locked teeth and tight facial muscles. The distance between then and now collapses, as though time has been swallowed up in a black hole, as though perception, reflection and judgement have been crushed in a compactor of fury.

The last figure to appear before this red curtain of rage descends, blocking out everything but itself, is my brother, older by three years, unquantifiably bigger in size and guile. For example, I am five. I enter the kitchen and as he drains the last of a can of lemonade, he fixes me with a demonic smile. I ask him if the can is his, a trap I can see I've fallen into the moment he shakes his head.

The awareness that I must play out this scene in the certain knowledge of where it's going compounds my rage with humiliation. So . . . whose is it? I ask, lip trembling, already sure of the answer as he wordlessly raises his arm, still drinking, and points his finger at me, eyes wide in triumph.

Curtain.

Through the mist of my shouts and tears and flailing punches, his laughter and mocking apologies stoke my rage to a level that overwhelms my small body and mind. I am filled with enough fury to destroy the world but am unable to make the smallest impact on his person or his mood; the bile I seek to unleash is instead backing up and filling my lungs. I am drowning in my own anger.

'Once you have a reason to be angry,' writes the philosopher Agnes Callard in her essay 'On Anger', 'you have a reason to be angry forever.' Callard suggests that anger is as permanent as the offences that provoke it; steal from me, and you will have stolen from me forever. Whatever restitutive efforts you can make subsequently, the original theft can never be undone.

Why should an offence against me possess such indelible force? Is Callard simply conferring philosophical respectability on the nursing of grudges? An injury will indeed live on in my mind, but surely this afterlife is fluid, contingent both on the changing ways I come to remember it and on my changing relationship to the person who inflicted it.

Reasoned out in this way, the claim that a reason to be angry lasts forever sounds rigid and inhumane. In my current relationship with my brother, the story of the stolen lemonade is pure banter, one item on a long list of overblown accusations and resentments passed back and forth with comic zeal.

So why do I feel so unsettled by Callard's formulation? What makes it feel so painfully *true*? 'Once you have a reason to be angry, you have a reason to be angry forever.' In nearly five decades since that incident in the kitchen, I've had further occasion to feel angry and exasperated with my brother, much as he has with me.

In almost all these instances, I've found that I can't dwell for more than a few seconds on the current source of anger without being involuntarily transported to the lemonade scene and that uncontrolled, impotent rage, as though some essential truth of our relationship was crystallized in the moment his eyes found mine in the kitchen, as though the reason I once had to be angry with him is a reason to be angry with him forever.

My compulsive return to that scene whenever I've been even slightly at odds with my brother speaks to some deep-going unconscious anxiety that I'm about to be abandoned once again to an anger I can do nothing with. It takes me back to a place in which I am forever too small, too inferior in physical and mental resources, to protect myself.

When the aggressive drive fails, when we're denied the means of redress or retaliation against an injury done to us, we are left with our anger. Life is constantly serving up rude reminders of our powerlessness and inadequacy in the face of larger forces – parents, teachers, older brothers. Anger is the guise that this experience, so endemic to human life, most often comes to assume.

Because this experience induces such bitter dissatisfaction, it provokes in us a fantasy of perfect satisfaction, scenarios in which our antagonists can be effortlessly vanquished with a casual put-down or judo throw. This, I think, is more than a mere revenge fantasy (though it certainly is that). It is a fantasy in which we are liberated from the feeling of suffocating constriction anger so often induces.

This constriction is also a particular experience of time. To be angry without a ready outlet for my anger is to be stuck in a hellish immediacy, a present from which it's impossible to break out. This is what we mean when we say of our rage that we can't get past it. Rage stops the flow of time, consigning us to the claustrophobic cell of the same moment, to the throb of the same wound.

No wonder, then, that we try to compensate for this feeling of enervated paralysis with the fantasy of absolute freedom to use our anger as we wish. Our mouths, no longer stopped up in airless inarticulacy, are suddenly vehicles for seamlessly delivered take-downs as brutal as they are elegant. We throw enemies around like so much wastepaper, startling them into submission with the sheer magnitude of our strength and power.

The appeal of these fantasies is that they invert an unbearable reality. In her 2023 book *On Marriage*, the writer Devorah Baum notes that love is a state into which we're famously said to *fall*; a fall, of course, being an accident, an unforeseeable event that comes upon us from outside, over which we have no control. The fact of falling is surely what brings the ecstasy of love into such tantalizing proximity to agony.

The observation applies equally well to anger. When I walked into the kitchen, I hadn't remotely anticipated this sadistic demonstration of my own helplessness, of the bigger person's licence to do what he likes to me with total impunity. Like the lightning strike of love, the combustion of rage is a kind of trauma in the strict sense of an experience whose sheer force is too much for us to master or even to bear.

Both feelings return us to an early infantile state in which we are inchoately aware of being at the mercy of other beings, dependent for our survival on their willingness to care about us. But what if the person I love cares nothing for me? What if the person I'm angry with laughs at my rage?

It's at this moment of contact with the most vulnerable core of our self that fantasies of omnipotence will exert their seductive grip. We might say we are forever revisiting the strategy of Winnicott's newborn infant, who turns her intuition of absolute helplessness before the world into a conviction of absolute command over it.

If my rage in the real world only amplifies my feelings of inadequacy and weakness, why not retreat to an alternative world in which it affirms my perfect efficacy and power? What if, instead of feeling like a helpless prisoner of my rage, I could wield it as an awesome superpower?

I was already heavily investing in such fantasies of omnipotence when, at the age of seven, a new series aired on British TV gave them unexpected force. Rounding off the school week on a Friday afternoon, *The Incredible Hulk* quickly stole its way into my inner life.

The show's accessibility was assured by the familiarity of the basic conceit: the coexistence of two beings in one body. At school, I'd been told the story of Jekyll and Hyde, while at Sunday Hebrew classes, I learned of the division of my soul between righteous and evil inclinations.

But the fascination of the Hulk was that the basis for this internal division wasn't a moral one, unlike those in Stevenson and Judaism. David Bruce Banner may be a soft-spoken and highly educated weakling where the Hulk is an inarticulate mass of muscle and rage, but they aren't defined in opposition to one another.

The Hulk expresses instead Banner's total identification with his own anger. 'Don't make me angry. You wouldn't like me when I'm angry,' runs Banner's famous cautionary refrain. What makes the warning so memorable is that it turns out to be true in a sense more literal than its recipient could ever have imagined; the 'angry' of Banner's 'when I'm angry' isn't a qualifier, an indication of a mood, but an exact existential equation. In the Hulk, Banner has become one with his anger.

The Hulk does not feel angry, he is anger itself: Banner's anger as an objective and separate worldly entity. Aged seven, I may not have had words for this distinction, but I understood it nonetheless, and it thrilled me to my core. It wasn't just that I felt the reverberation of my own imaginative life in the sudden, violent pullulation of that green colossus from Banner's tightly bounded human body. It was the possibility of *becoming the anger I felt.*

Since Marvel introduced the character in 1962, the Hulk's origin story has been through many different iterations, each offering some variation both on Banner's role in his creation and on the monster's level of intelligence. The TV series portrays Banner as a physician and scientist who has unwittingly bombarded himself with an overdose of gamma rays, which cause him to transform into the Hulk whenever he becomes angry.

Each episode finds Banner in a new location, assuming a new name and identity. Presumed dead after a fire in his laboratory, he moves around the country pursued at every turn by Jack McGee, a tabloid journalist who suspects some link between Banner and the Hulk.

In each new place, Banner is faced with some new set of villains – drug dealers, corrupt scientists, truck hijackers, abusive fathers – ready to show him the grave consequences of his interference. This leads inexorably to the profound satisfactions of the episode's pay-off: the tough guys, rolling up their sleeves to beat Banner to a pulp, discover that where their victim was, a roaring green monster now is.

The giddy joy I felt as the camera closed in on the thug's face as the Hulk came into his field of vision is palpable to me even today; the sudden shift from sadistic sneer to primitive terror, from the self-assurance of the casually violent man to the helplessness of the abandoned infant.

Like any version of the Hulk, the series had to walk a tightrope; on the one hand, Banner's anger was righteous, directed towards the worst excesses of cruelty and corruption. On the other, the Hulk's rampages always teetered at the edge of indiscriminate violence. How could they not? He was pure rage made flesh, endowed with only a primitive intelligence, apparently undiluted by the smallest measure of reason.

In later blockbuster movie versions, the Hulk, now a towering immensity hovering over the cityscape rather than the mere seven-foot beast of the TV series, would tear up the roads, causing cars to collide and fly in an ever more baroque tableaux of chaos and destruction. This Hulk, even when susceptible to the emotions felt by his alter ego (notably love), has much more of the cosmic indifference of the mythic gods than any recognisably human rage.

In fact, during the decades following his first appearance, Marvel Comics would produce a dizzying proliferation of alternative origin stories, variations and spin-offs of the Hulk narrative, each remaking the relationship between Banner and Hulk. In most versions, Banner's powers are the consequence of his father David's scientific experiments, a trauma overlain and amplified by the same man's physical and emotional abuse of his child. In some versions, the Hulk is under Banner's moral command, in others he has slipped loose from it. There is a Hulk of primitive intelligence and a Hulk of pure violence, a Banner of cold reason and a Banner of criminal insanity. In fact, all attempts to separate Banner and Hulk only succeed in rendering the intellect of the one and the brute power of the other more dangerous and uncontained.

Taken as a whole, the elaborate patchwork of Hulk folklore might read as a dizzyingly intricate enquiry into the relationship between angry feeling and aggressive action. Is it possible for the one to realise itself in the other, for the itch of anger to be relieved in full by being discharged appropriately?

The decades-long archive of the Hulk universe seems to respond with a multi-part chorus of anxious and vacillating uncertainty. It can seem as though the abuses and injuries and griefs that have befallen Banner are so numerous, so thickly layered, as to engender a rage to which no expression, not even the marauding rampages of the green monster himself, could ever be adequate. But it can equally seem as though the trail of destruction wrought by the Hulk radically exceeds any feelings Banner could have.

The predicament underlying these perpetual imbalances is nicely formulated by the American writer Joel Achenbach: 'The key element to Hulkness is the rage-to-strength feedback loop. The madder he gets, the stronger he gets – ad infinitum.' If we were looking for an encapsulation of the logic of the drive, we could do worse. The aggressive drive is never satisfied because it feeds off itself, as though recharged by the energy it discharges. It is always too little, and always too much.

Perhaps what I found so satisfying about the TV series was the sense of a sweet spot, a delicate adequation between Banner's anger and the Hulk's aggression. How gratifying it would be for my actions to express what I felt, to visit on my antagonists no more and no less than they deserved.

In his TV series incarnation, the Hulk punished evil without effecting collateral damage. Somehow, the rages always stayed this side of arbitrary. The unbound rage of the monster remained within the bounds of right and justice, as though still operating under the direction of Banner's moral sense. By the end of each episode, Banner and the Hulk would have seen off some nefarious criminal enterprise before Banner, sensing his cover was about to be broken, left with a new surname for a new town, where the wheel of justice would turn again the following week.

The series managed to circumvent the question that bedevils the rest of the Hulk universe, namely how can anger be both unlimited and just? If anger feeds off itself, gathering force faster than it can expend it, how can it avoid punishing the bystander to evil along with the perpetrator, the innocent along with the guilty? The question is framed with nice concision by the American philosopher Judith Butler: 'What if violence is precisely the kind of phenomenon that is constantly "getting out of hand"?'

As a child (and as an adult too), my dread of the burden of anger, the itchy insistence of a private fury for which there seemed to be neither effective nor legitimate expression, sealed my infatuation with the Hulk. But hovering at the edge of that infatuation was something like a rudimentary version of Butler's troubling question.

I would pace my bedroom after an episode, flinging my imaginary enemies across the room as the Hulk just had his real ones, daring them to tease me again. But these reveries weren't really cathartic. They didn't slow the pumping of my blood or calm my restless nerves. I would leave my room with hands flapping, an obscure excitement coursing through my veins.

Violence is a phenomenon that is constantly getting out of hand: I knew this from the inside, from the annihilating lust with which I fought imaginary and, where my brother was concerned, real fights, feeling his own unbound murderousness answering mine, wondering even as we strived with fingernails and teeth and feet and fists how I could get out of this alive. The thought wasn't altogether idle; one particularly brutal kick in the balls had already landed me in the emergency room.

All of which cast an oblique shadow of suspicion on the gratifying tidiness with which those *Incredible Hulk* episodes resolved themselves. It seemed odd that the Hulk's fury would start to subside at just the moment it might have escalated, that Banner's weakly human body would be restored to him before his green avatar could wreak some properly violent chaos and destruction. Odd and secretly a little disappointing.

Yes, it was good that things somehow never got too far out of hand, in the way that the restoration of order and equilibrium was always good. But after a while also a little dishonest and predictable. For the very embodiment of uncontrolled rage, this Hulk was peculiarly controlled, his rampages reliably ending just at the point they might have got really incredible.

Moments after I met him for the first time, before I'd had the chance to ask him any questions about himself or his life, Victor informed me he doesn't do small talk. At least not when he's engaged in anything serious, which he understood this process to be. He didn't *banter* or exchange pleasantries. If he was going to pay for these sessions, he wanted results, so please, could we not waste time?

Taken aback, I remarked that he'd only just arrived and was already anxious about wasting time. I wondered what that was about.

He wasn't sure it was *about* anything, he said, more testily still, other than what he'd said it was about. He had an aversion to aimless chatter and preferred to stick to the matter at hand.

Steeling myself a little, I asked what he thought might happen if we didn't stick to the matter at hand.

He let out an exasperated sigh and said that frankly, my question was a perfect example of what he was talking about. He was here to address major issues in his life, and I had just confirmed every suspicion he had of psychotherapy as little more than a pointless parlour game.

I said nothing. After a moment of thick tension, he broke the silence. In a tone of resentful surrender, he repeated my question. 'What happens when we don't stick to the matter at hand? We get off the point, surely. We lose clarity and focus and wander all over the place. If I wanted to do that, I could have stayed home and talked to my children.'

I told him I thought he was already telling me quite a lot about himself. But if he felt we were getting off track, I was happy to be redirected.

He looked at me cautiously for a moment, then: 'Well, the problem as I see it is very straightforward. People don't like me, and I can't say I especially like them.'

When I asked if this upset him, he snapped 'Nope' reflexively. He would be entirely indifferent to the matter if it didn't cause unwanted difficulties. 'At work and at home,' he added.

Victor worked for a civil engineering firm, consulting for government and local authorities on safety in public infrastructure. His main brief was the inspection of bridges, a subject about which few people knew more. In performance reviews, the same complaints from colleagues would come to the surface: he was offhand, arrogant, contemptuous.

I asked if they were right, wondering if he might explode. But he seemed relieved by the question, as though we were finally getting to the matter at hand.

He looked down, hard reflection creasing his forehead. 'It's hard for me to say. I'm dealing with life and death matters. Whether it's a major suspension bridge or a little pontoon, the wrong call can mean serious injury or fatality. I'm not tolerant of laxity, in myself or anyone else.'

Recently he had exploded at a junior employee under his supervision, who'd gone to inspect an old stone beam bridge and missed a significant crack. He'd lost it with her, yelling at her in the middle of the open-plan office, demanding to know if she was genuinely stupid or just lazy, or did she want people to break their spines or drown? 'DO YOUR FUCKING JOB!' he recalled shouting at her, reproducing the moment so vividly I was left to wonder if it was her he was addressing, or me.

'So while you're fixing bridges, you burn them too . . .' I said.

He rolled his eyes. 'Very clever,' he muttered.

'But you must have noticed the paradox. You dedicate your life to structures that connect people and places and make them accessible to one another and then make a virtue of refusing connection and making yourself inaccessible.' I swallowed and added, 'That's rather how it's felt talking to you today.'

He fixed me for a moment with a murderous stare, as though about to let rip. Then he cast his eyes down dejectedly and said he saw my point, but I was imposing my therapist's notion of what bridges meant, all that sloppy symbolism about connection. He had long ago given up on connecting to anyone else or making them happy, God knows, his wife would tell me in no uncertain terms that he wasn't up to that.

'I can't make anyone's life better, but I can make lives safe. Because that isn't a matter of being good, but of being right. I have given up on being good, frankly I don't think anyone knows what it means. But I can be right. What I was trying to tell that young woman, admittedly not in a helpful way, was that it was her job to be right, that being wrong is unforgivable.'

Being right was a matter of life and death, not just for the innumerable people that walked and drove over bridges, but for Victor himself. As I'd discover over the coming months and years, Victor had a great deal to be angry about, so much that he felt the only way he could survive would be to restrict the scope of his anger, to keep it within the tightest possible bounds.

'Look at Trump,' he said, months after that first meeting. 'Most people hate him because he's cruel or bigoted or misogynistic. Well, no doubt, but all that's old as time. I don't hate him because he's bad. I hate him because he's wrong, *demonstrably* wrong, because he lies compulsively and mangles truth and drags half the world into the same black hole of wrongness.'

Surely Victor was right about the spreading poison of wrongness? Haven't all the catastrophic political phenomena of our time – the election of Trump and other figureheads of the populist right, the victory of the Brexit campaign, the global movement against Covid precautions and vaccinations, the war in Ukraine – been founded on brazen lies? Most seriously of all, the imminent collapse of the systems that support life on earth is being accelerated by corporate lobbyists and politicians who diminish or even deny outright the reality of the climate crisis.

Yes, as I write this I can feel my blood rising and teeth grinding, my fingertips itching to launch a cathartic rant against the growing power and influence of liars and manipulators. The preceding paragraph expresses what I think accurately enough, but it's also infused with the zeal of one who knows he's right and therefore is licensed to decide who is and is not telling the truth. There is something exhilarating about this state of mind, a freedom from the burdens of doubt and reflection that arouses a giddy feeling of invincibility.

I'm writing this book not to ride the wave of this feeling, but to question it. It's surely at the moment anger feels most right that it becomes most dangerous, because it is most liable to seal itself tightly into its own self-certainty. In the mode of absolute rightness, anger doesn't need to be carried over into overt aggression to become violent. Who among the anti-Trump progressives or the remainers hasn't annihilated the enemy in their own mind, dismissed their thoughts and feelings and perceptions of the world as so much trash to be tossed down the darkest chute?

This was Victor's stance, and I could find it all too easy, pleasurable even, to lose myself in his eloquent polemics against the flood tide of lies sweeping the world. Here was the engineer of the soundest structures lamenting the collapsing foundations of global public life. There were times, in the midst of one or other surgical dissection of the latest outrage against truth of a Brexiter or the Trump administration, when I wanted simply to cheer him on. Instead, putting a brake on my enthusiasm, I took a breath and wondered aloud whether he'd noticed that in his unbound rage and contempt, he was at risk of mirroring the attitudes he railed against.

'Well of course,' he said with breezy hauteur, 'having googled you I'm aware that you're one of those postmodern literary types who thinks truth is all a matter of perspective. You're wrong about that I'm afraid. If my profession has taught me anything, it's the supremacy of facts. And yes, I get angry with anyone who threatens that supremacy and I make no apology for it. The difference between me and the liars, which is all the difference in the world, is that I speak for facts.'

Victor readily acknowledged his own rage was no less florid than his enemies' but saw no irony here, nor in the fact that the same claim to speak for truth against lies was made, with many of the same rhetorical flourishes, by the conspiracy theorists he decried.

'Of course liars made grand claims to truth,' he argued. 'Of course they sought to paint anyone who spoke for the facts as a fake news peddler or a dupe of the lamestream media. That's what makes them liars. If you take the line that we're the same, you're doing their work for them.'

This wasn't the line I was taking, but I didn't argue; a psychoanalytic consulting room isn't a debating chamber. Instead, I tried to point him to the powerful undertow of personal history lurking inside his passion for facts.

Victor was sceptical if not contemptuous of the idea that his childhood had any bearing on the adult man he was now. But even he couldn't deny the resonance of his response when I asked him about his parents: 'I was born to a pair of liars.' His father was a compulsive philanderer whose minor aristocratic family had provided him only a modest private income. He made little secret of having married Victor's mother for her much vaster fortune or of his disdain for her middle-class origins and taste.

'He wouldn't give my mother even the minimal dignity of a plausible excuse for not having come home the night before,' Victor told me. 'He would claim there'd been a train strike or motorway closure when she knew as well as he did there'd been no such thing. I think I was around eight or nine when I cottoned on to the truth. I would ask my mother, "Daddy's staying at an-other lady's house, isn't he?" and she would force this supercilious little laugh and say, "Why no, Vic, whatever gave you that idea?!" I once asked in front of my little sister. She burst into tears and whined, "Daddy was out working all night! Daddy is a good man, Mummy says so!"'

Having grown up in an atmosphere thick with fear of the truth, Victor had resolved by the time he was an adolescent never to lie himself, nor to let lies go unchallenged, a resolution that was only becoming more urgent as the claw-grip of lies on the world tightened daily.

Knowing he had no truck with sentimentality or false af-firmation, his wife had long ceased asking his view on her journalism or anything else; 'I'll tell her straight if the piece she's written is boring or her skirt makes her look fat. So she no longer asks.' His young daughters had likewise learned not to show him their pictures or read him their stories or play him their piano pieces.

Hearing this, I remarked that his family seemed not to want to show him anything of their lives or of themselves.

'Apparently not,' he agreed. 'They're afraid of honesty, sad to say.'

'Rather like the family you grew up in and have been so angry with for so long.'

He lay on the couch, silent for a moment, then got up and walked to the door. The end of the session was ten minutes off. He turned, fixed me with a gaze of cold, dead contempt and said, 'You're nothing but a bloody con artist, a cheap variety act,' slamming the door as he walked out.

But he returned for his next session as though nothing had happened.

*

Unsurprisingly, sessions frequently evoke and reflect what is happening in the news. More unsettlingly, reading the news can occasionally evoke and reflect what's happened in a session. I'd started seeing Victor in early 2016, when the Brexit campaign was stoking so much popular bitterness and resentment towards 'experts' and 'elites'.

From the first, Victor had been offering a running polemic against what he saw as a reactionary upswell of aggressive and wilful ignorance. As we've seen, my observation that he seemed possessed by the same boundless and compulsive anger as those he so bitterly decried didn't land well.

My point wasn't, as he'd quickly assumed, an instance of 'both-sides' relativism. It was that whether he was talking about his colleagues, his family or Dominic Cummings, he seemed never to recognize how thoroughly his words and thoughts were shaped and driven by his rage. In Victor's mind, the failure of a mass of people to recognize their own irrationality and vulnerability to delusion was bound to provoke rage in anyone remotely reasonable.

But how reasonable is it to think of other people's rage as rabid delusionality and one's own as entirely consistent and justified? As I perused the latest chapters in the Brexit and Trump sagas during my lunchtime, I felt as though Victor was unwittingly instructing me in every way the progressive defenders of facts and reason were going wrong, in thought and deed.

As arbiter and spokesman for reality, Victor could never countenance the possibility that the facts as he relayed them were in any way coloured by emotion or politics. 'The fact that I get angry about people who lie about the facts has no bearing on the facts,' he would say. 'The facts are simply what they are.'

But can facts ever be 'simply what they are'? How could anyone possibly tell the unvarnished truth without omission, selection, heightening, emphasis, without freighting the facts with the teller's conscious and unconscious interests and beliefs? As the philosopher Hannah Arendt observes in her seminal essay 'Truth and Politics', this is never more the case than in a community in which 'everybody lies about everything of importance', for under such conditions, 'The truth-teller, whether he knows it or not, has begun to act; he, too, has engaged in political business.'

As the political writer William Davies has shown, in the so-called post-truth era, rather too many public voices advocating for purity and primacy of the facts failed to see how politically and emotionally charged their advocacy had become. Davies points to the March for Science staged across several cities simultaneously three months after the 2017 Trump inauguration, in protest against the new administration's relentless assaults on truth in regard to a broad range of issues including vaccinations (even prior to Covid-19), school curricula and climate.

The risk of mobilizing politically for facts, writes Davies, is of 'turning "facts" into precisely the type of hot political issues that religious conservatives, climate sceptics and conspiracy theorists already deem them to be'. In the process, scientists and the broad community of 'experts' make themselves vulnerable to the lethal charge of hypocrisy. Across the bubble of right-wing social media, scientists were pilloried for wanting both the cake of a dispassionate commitment to facts and the eating it of using the facts politically.

The populist animus against knowledge elites has its heart in this apparent hypocrisy, the perceived sneaky pincer movement whereby the expert at once asserts the objective indisputability of a given fact and uses it as political ammunition. With this double advantage of knowing better and shouting louder, the expert is always bound to win the argument. The undeniable ingenuity of populist rhetoric has been to turn this guaranteed win on its head, to render its trump card a losing hand.

You see, say the scourges of the knowledge elite, the so-called 'experts' are no less opinionated loudmouths than you or me. The only difference is they pretend to be objective and fact-driven so as to ensure they're always right. Precisely insofar as they are always right, experts are now always wrong. The more experts protest in the name of facts and truth, the more they discredit themselves in the eyes of the people they want to persuade. In psychoanalytic terms, this is politics as splitting.

In a late fragment of writing in 1938, Freud put forth the thesis that the ego, the agency of the mind charged with mental and bodily control, responds to the apprehension of danger by splitting itself. One side of the mind reluctantly acknowledges the reality of the danger, while the other denies it.

Elaborated politically, splitting conjures a dividing line, the near side of which is occupied by a mass of fellow citizens, includ-ing me, united in their moral righteousness, integrity and truth. On the far side of the split is the enemy, a vicious rabble bonded by their shared corruption, stupidity and cowardice.

The intoxicating appeal of a politics of splitting is that it abol-ishes doubt and ambiguity at a stroke. It doesn't need to enquire or explore, as it comes to the public square forearmed with its impregnable certainties. It requires no questioning of its own motives and aims because it already knows itself to be on the side of right. It is the appeal of a perfect harmony of affect and drive, feeling and action. Rightness and anger are an ideal couple, each urging the other towards the shared aim of expelling the bad and dangerous from the world.

This is the collective psychic atmosphere required for the flowering and proliferation of conspiracy theories, stories of the nefarious powers secretly pulling the strings of global government and economy. QAnon, the most baroque and politically influential conspiracy theory of our (if not all) time, reveals the satanic paedophile cult holding the deep state in its concealed claw-grip, and the always imminent but never realized arrival of 'the Storm', the cabal's final exposure and defeat by heroic keepers of the Trumpian flame.

We will return to the political function of this permanently suspended conflagration in Chapter Three. For now, its interest lies in the fantasy at its heart of a united mass of citizens bound together in divinely righteous anger working to realize itself in an ultimate and total triumph over evil.

But how does anger become so self-certain, so brazenly confident in pushing for action on its own behalf?

It's difficult to answer this question without returning to the psychology of the individual. Righteous certainty of this kind is made not of impersonal words or ideas but of feelings that flow in the most personal recesses of the body. For as long as it remains unsatisfied, the conviction of rightness presses on the musculature and nervous system, constricting movement and breath, redirecting every perception and thought to the same wrong.

As any of us can attest, there are few torments crueller than the world's failure to recognize that we're right. When our mother eventually found me furiously and ineffectually pummelling my brother, the initial injury was exacerbated exponentially by her lack of concern to see justice done. 'Never mind!' she said, smiling at me with uncomprehending benignity as she stroked the top of my skull, 'It's just a can of lemonade!'

This had the effect of turning my sobbing into high-pitched wailing, the only remedy for which she could think of was to assure me that she'd buy me another one, she'd buy me a million cans of lemonade! How could she fail to understand how much worse she was making everything, how no new cans could ever restore to me the loss of *that* can, the one I'd so looked forward to drinking, now gone forever, its pleasures egregiously stolen from me? Why did she not see that the only just resolution to the affair was for him to be *beatenhardwithacricketbattillhewasbleedingeverywherethen-toldhewouldneverdrinkANYTHINGeveragainexceptmaybewarmwater-andthenhewouldcryandsaysorrybutnoonewouldlistenandhewouldDIIIE!*

'Sorry Mum,' said my brother, 'I didn't realise it was his. But why are you so upset anyway?!' he asked me, flashing me a poisonously forked smile he knew would send me off the edge. I screamed, stamped my feet and pulled at my hair, willing the ceiling, if not the sky itself, to collapse and fall on our heads. 'Poor Joshy,' my mother said softly.

I'm aware that the ironic distance I'm placing between my child and present-day selves in telling this story is blatantly defensive. While sugary carbonated drinks may mean rather less to me today, rageful madness is not something I can safely consign to the past as a cute emotional relic of childhood.

Adult life, both intimate and public, overflows with the wounds of unacknowledged rightness and the indignation that comes with their continued denial. Individual acts of jihadi and far-right terror, of incel violence against women, of irate citizens against climate activists, the physical assaults on democratic institutions by mass movements for Trump and other populists; all the ways that rage is discharging itself in aggressive action across the world involve the same psychic state: resentment at an unanswered injury or injustice.

It's equally true that the same sense of unanswered injury fuels the movements for racial, gender-based, economic and climate justice. Anger, we might say, feels more or less the same regardless of the cause in which it's enlisted. That the burning injustice felt by the #MeToo activist is felt equally by the trolling incel is an uncomfortable truth to which we'll return in Chapter Four. The distinction between a destructive and an affirmative anger is an essential one but, for that very reason, it needs to be grounded in criteria more robust than a subjective preference for the cause in question, which is liable to descend into the dangerous insistence that anger is good in the name of my cause but bad in the name of yours.

For now, let us stay for a little longer with the feeling rather than the content of anger, with what it does to our psychic and bodily experience. Anger puts the self under siege, blocking access to everything other than the source of its own provocation. In this regard, it behaves rather like pain, which not coincidentally so often colours and amplifies the angry state.

Freud's observation regarding pain, that it sends the psyche into a state of narcissistic contraction, applies equally to anger. What he calls 'the familiar egoism of the sick person' in his paper 'On Narcissism' (1914) is the tendency to withdraw all the energies the sick person has invested in the world outside 'back into his own ego', so that the entirety of his interest is concentrated in his own pain.

Anyone who's ever been consumed with anger will recognize this scenario. When anger takes over, it wipes out the world beyond itself, so that its contours shrink to the dimensions of whatever has caused it. Interest in external reality is abrogated unless it pertains to my sense of offended rightness, while the space in my internal life for any other feelings – love, pleasure, joy, peace, sadness – contracts to nothing.

Literature, from the Bible, Homer and the Mahabharata to the present day, provides some of the richest sources of illumination of this state of emotional and physical suffocation by rightness. We find one apogee of such illumination in Shakespeare's *Othello*, whose tragic hero is cynically and maliciously manipulated into this state of impenetrable rightness by his pretend ally and secret enemy Iago. So it makes sense that *Othello* should inspire one of the most powerful portrayals of the predicament of rightness in the history of the novel, Anthony Trollope's *He Knew He Was Right* (1869).

Trollope's central character Louis Trevelyan joins Othello and Melville's Ahab in a gallery of men possessed to the exclusion of all else by the agonizing condition of knowing themselves to be right, exacerbated yet further by finding their claim to rightness disputed, thwarted by the failure of those around them to see with the clarity and certainty afforded by a split psyche.

He Knew He Was Right is a classic Victorian novel, sprawling and panoramic, its array of decorously comic subplots diluting the psychological force and intensity of Trevelyan's story. Himself the embodiment of moderate, cautiously reformist English liberalism, with its steady faith in reason and incremental progress, Trollope seems at once fascinated and horrified by his central character's inexorable fall into a black hole of madness and self-destruction.

Rage, the novel seems to say, has a capacity to lay waste to the ordinarily good life. Shuttling uneasily between observational comedies of courtship and Trevelyan's inexorable descent into paranoid malevolence, its overall literary significance is fatally compromised by its unevenness of tone. But the Trevelyan strand remains a brilliant anatomy of the compulsive, overwhelming logic of being right, throwing us into its central drama from the very beginning. Having married Emily Rowley, the beautiful daughter of a minor colonial governor, and returned her to a new home in Mayfair and a brief marital idyll, Trevelyan is quickly unbalanced by the visits his young wife receives from Colonel Osborne, an old bachelor friend of her father's with a distinctly rakish social reputation.

'With a flashing eye and an angry tone' he tells his wife that she should cease receiving Osborne so frequently, setting in train a marital dynamic of mutual entrenchment. Feeling that her husband's imputations insult her virtue, she defends herself by continuing to receive the visits he's sought to prohibit.

From the first, Trevelyan is conscious of the precariousness of his conviction, how dangerously close it sails to an impugnment of his wife's honesty. Aware from the moment of his first outburst that Emily has heard his demand as an egregious insult, his impulse is to go to her and apologize. 'But,' writes Trollope, 'he was one to whose nature the giving of any apology was repulsive.'

An apology, of course, is a gesture that requires an internal distance between myself and my certainty, a capacity to escape the straitjacket of my immediate feelings and see them through the eyes of another. This is precisely what Trevelyan's knowledge of his own rightness disallows.

Knowing I'm right will often confer a quasi-metaphysical status on my rightness. Instead of a merely personal conviction, being right is underwritten by the highest truth. In *Moby-Dick*, appearing in print some eighteen years before Trevelyan and subtly anticipating him, Melville's Captain Ahab transforms his personal vendetta against the white whale into a grand and irresistible cosmic destiny.

When Starbuck, his first mate and the *Pequod*'s redoubtable voice of sanity, begs his captain to call off his doomed chase, Ahab tells him that when it comes to the whale, Starbuck's appeals simply cannot reach him. Your face, Ahab says, might as well be the palm of your hand: 'a lipless, unfeatured blank'. Starbuck's error is to think of the hunt for Moby Dick as Ahab's personal quest, but no: 'This whole act's immutably decreed. 'Twas rehearsed by thee and me a billion years before this ocean rolled. Fool! I am the Fates' lieutenant; I act under orders.'

To surrender the fight, Ahab implies, would be to defy the cosmic order itself. Starbuck's arguments are puny because they are restricted to the narrow confines of the present. From such a perspective, you *might* turn out to be right but you'll never *know* you're right. This is what makes a fool of Starbuck to Ahab's all-seeing eye.

In *He Knew He Was Right*, Trevelyan withdraws himself from his wife while in the same house and sends imperious notes to her dressing-room iterating his demands and declining to apologize: 'As I have done, and doing what I think to be right,' he writes, 'I cannot stultify myself by saying that I think I have been wrong.' Like a domestic Ahab, Trevelyan is the man who knows, and cannot stoop to playing the man who doesn't.

Trevelyan's version of Ahab's cosmic grandiosity is his insistence on the immutable, a priori truth of a husband's power over his wife. Throughout their marital war of attrition, he invokes the law of wifely obedience that trumps in advance any protest or counter-argument Emily can make. His growing vindictive rage and eventual descent into madness and isolation is provoked not by belief in his wife's infidelity but by her refusal to concede that he's right.

We've seen that a drive is a force in us that never stops seeking its own satisfaction. Separating from Emily, sending her to live in obscurity, depriving her of their child, fleeing abroad: with each escalation of his aggression, Trevelyan seems to want to fulfil his quest for a definitive action, one forceful enough to relieve his enervated rage and return him to a state of equilibrium. But in each case, he succeeds only in aggravating his rage and entrenching his sense of isolation in the face of an uncomprehending world.

As aggressive action fails, in other words, angry feelings grow. The problem with knowing one is right is that it requires precisely what does not happen: that the parties in the wrong realize this and to say so. In the absence of such real-world satisfaction, Trevelyan has to fall back on increasingly vivid fantasies of an act that will finally consummate his anger:

> He had almost come to have but one desire – namely, that he should find her out, that the evidence should be conclusive, that it should be proved and so brought to an end. Then he would destroy her, and destroy that man – and afterwards destroy himself, so bitter to him would be his ignominy. He almost revelled in the idea of the tragedy he would make.

Trevelyan here imagines himself as Othello, so consumed by his illusory cuckoldry that he craves the indisputable proof that would free him to perpetrate the ruinous violence that would discharge and redeem his rage. For Trevelyan and Othello alike, appeals to calm and reflection only accelerate the urgency of rage. Iago well knows this when he counsels Othello, 'Patience . . . your mind perhaps may change.' 'Never, Iago,' Othello replies, falling into the precise psychic and rhetorical trap his ensign has sprung for him:

> Like to the Pontic sea
> Whose icy current and compulsive course
> Ne'er feels retiring ebb, but keeps due on
> To the Propontic and the Hellespont;
> Even so my bloody thoughts, with violent pace,
> Shall ne'er look back, ne'er ebb to humble love,
> Till that a capable and wide revenge
> Swallow them up.

As he describes it, Othello's rage mimics the movement of the drive, his 'bloody thoughts' powering through every possible break or hesitation, hurtling towards their own combustion, or 'swallowing up' in the act of murderous revenge. Othello and Trevelyan alike can only ride the destructive tidal wave of their anger; stemming it has long ceased to be an option. The difference between them is that no one dares to get in Othello's way, to try to interpose themselves between his angry feelings and his murderous action. Trevelyan, on the other hand, finds the passage from anger to action perpetually blocked by the friends and family, who rally to the side of his estranged wife. This leaves him effectively stranded with his own rage, deprived of any outlet for it but the perpetual rehearsal of his grievance to anyone who will listen. His anger soon becomes 'rather a bore to his friends'; with nowhere to go, it turns compulsively around itself, repeating the same story of the same wrong, the same insult, the same humiliation, like an exhibit in a rolling display of his own unassailable rightness.

To be possessed by rightness is to live in a split world, one side of which holds a monopoly on truth and justice, which the other side can only traduce. This other side is occupied by his wife and her co-conspirators, whom he perceives to have 'behaved with such indiscretion as almost to have compromised his honour; and in return for that he was to beg her pardon, confess himself to have done wrong, and allow her to return in triumph!'

Splitting is an unhelpful misnomer; yes, it creates an irreconcilable division within the mind, but it also holds it together. In insisting on the absolute opposition of his own rightness to the wrong perpetrated by his wife and her allies, Trevelyan seals the tight cohesion of his worldview, keeping out the smallest intimations of doubt or questioning. He cannot beg Emily's pardon without causing a catastrophic crack in the foundations of his mental home.

This mode of thinking might feel strikingly familiar to us from our own culture's saturation in conspiracy thinking. Like every good devotee of conspiracy cults, Trevelyan invests his otherwise corroded trust in a single figure, misidentified as an unimpeachably truth-telling guru, his hired private detective Bozzle, 'whose business it is', as the narrator has it, 'to detect hidden and secret things', and who is 'very apt to detect things which have never been done'.

It is the conspiracist's task to nurture and sustain a split reality. Trevelyan is continually confronted by his own doubts and others' refutations regarding his wife's suspected infidelity. Unable to turn up any positive proof of this infidelity, Bozzle, keeper of his client's paranoid flame, resorts to the favoured ruse of every good conspiracist. Just as the engineers of QAnon turn the failure of every Q prophecy into proof of its higher truth, Bozzle renders Emily's irreproachability the ultimate demonstration of her dangerous sexual duplicity.

But as Bozzle slowly withdraws his services, Trevelyan finds himself abandoned to the intolerable disparity between his own rightness and the objections and criticisms of the world outside, amplifying his sense of persecution and injury. The precarious supports of his split world begin to buckle underneath him, plunging him into madness and eventual death.

In his growing delirium, his obsessive anxiety is that Emily will recover the child he snatched from her, and the world will judge him, not her, to have been at fault. This is the outcome he cannot contemplate: 'Let it once be conceded from all sides that he had been right, and then she might do with him almost as she willed.' Paranoid thinking requires nothing less than this total concession. If the split between his irreproachability and her sin is other than absolute and unassailable, the edifice of his rightness crashes down at a stroke.

Trevelyan expends the last drops of his vital energy in a vain effort to hold up this edifice. When his friend Stanbury tells him of his engagement to Emily's sister, Trevelyan's bitterly facetious counsel now reads like the ramblings of a modern men's rights activist: 'Don't be too particular. Let her choose her own friends, and go her own gait, and have her own way, and do you be blind and deaf and dumb and properly submissive; and it may be that she'll give you your breakfast and dinner in your own house – so long as your hours don't interfere with her pleasures.'

When Trevelyan finally dies from the effects of his self-neglect, as though dramatizing in his own body his abandonment and persecution by the world, the doctor tells Emily that the hallucinations of his last days arose not from 'belief in her infidelity' but from 'an obstinate determination to yield nothing'.

If there is a flaw to the Trevelyan narrative, it's that it narrates his descent into madness and slow suicide from the vantage point of this doctor and the other reasonable men and women around him, as though he were an exhibit in a vivid psychology lecture. It is when we hear his madness speak directly out of his letters and conversations that we are brought up against the grain of his rage and are made for a moment to breathe its strange air.

Rage always looks and sounds absurd from the safe distance of the uninvolved. The chasm of age has the same effect, rendering the infant's tantrum comical to the adult and the adult's fury terrifying and incomprehensible to the child.

As long as this distance governs our perception, we can't hope to understand rage. Only in physical and emotional proximity do we start to intuit rage less as an agitated expression of a belief than as a state of possession, a conviction in our rightness that is felt first of all in the organs and musculature of the body, weighing on these with such force that, as Freud says of pain, it blocks access to anything else in our range.

When Emily's father Sir Marmaduke Rowley, a fine portrait of the archetypally apoplectic English patriarch, confronts his son-in-law towards the end of the novel, he begins in a tone of outraged demand, only to find himself disarmed by Trevelyan's profound physical deterioration:

> He was as wretched a being to look at as it might have been possible to find. His contracted cheeks, and lips always open, and eyes glowing in their sunken caverns, told a tale which even Sir Marmaduke, who was not of nature quick in deciphering such stories, could not fail to read. And then the twitching motion of the man's hands, and the restless shuffling of his feet, produced a nervous feeling that if some remedy were not applied quickly, some alleviation given to the misery of the suffering wretch, human power would be strained too far, and the man would break to pieces – or else the mind of the man.

A man tormented by anxiety over how he appears to the world, Trevelyan is too bound by conscience and convention to discharge his paranoid aggression in murder. He is very much an Othello of the nineteenth century, his violent rage withdrawn from its external object and turned on himself. For Sir Marmaduke, 'not quick in deciphering such stories', nor in anything else, the signs of Trevelyan's bodily and mental breakdown are so palpable and urgent that he cannot fail to read them.

Trevelyan's imminent unravelling is really a slow suicide, an excess of aggressive energies reversing direction and mounting a kind of autoimmune attack, its ravages evident in the cadaverous face. His twitching hands and shuffling feet display the pantomimic enervation of a classic hysteric, hinting at murderous impulses that are no sooner expressed than they are withdrawn.

We cannot look on Trevelyan without seeing a starving man, an organism no longer in contact with the laws of necessity and the basic demands of self-preservation.

Rather more frivolously, his image also triggers my association to the portmanteau word 'hangry'*, popularized by advertising and social media, which fuses the states of hunger and anger. Neurological research has shown that hunger causes a disruption of homeostasis, the state of equilibrium, in the limbic system, causing a temporary flood of hormonally induced panic. The signal of dissatisfaction will eventually give rise to the irritability we've all experienced when we've gone too long without food, an unmistakable echo of the hungry baby's cry and similarly charged with emotional as much as physical agitation.

Under normal conditions, both the baby's cry and our own bad temper are relieved by the arrival of food, thus licensing us to popularize a jocular coinage like hangry. But we need not travel far historically or geographically before we come across conditions far from normal, where countless populations are afflicted by food scarcity, malnourishment and famine.

Trevelyan disturbs the high-living society around him by intruding a kink into its façade of well-fed contentment. His deep 'hanger', the loss of body mass to the destructive rage coursing through him, is felt by all around him as a freakish madness, an exception to the good bourgeois imperative of indulgent self-care.

There is an implicit understanding here that if hunger were to be a structural feature of everyday life, it would afflict the life of the social and political body, as much as the individual

---

* The word first appeared in the 1956 article 'Psychopathology and Problems of Oral Libido in the Use of Language' by the Hungarian psychoanalyst Nandor Fodor. Fodor invokes it as an example of the fusion of two words in one.

physical body. This is the argument made by Hannah Arendt in *On Revolution.*

Arendt is concerned with the explosive entrance of the poor into the political life of Revolutionary France. Poverty, and its attendant state of unsatisfied biological need, she argues, is a 'pre-political' force. The essential condition for political community is human solidarity, the creation of a common space for demo-cratic contestation. We can enter into such a community only if we have secured for ourselves, at very least, the basic means of biological survival.

In public arguments over the distribution of liberty and power, a near-empty stomach will put anyone at a serious disadvantage. This is the sense in which poverty is inimical to politics. Where politics is concerned with the exercise of freedom, poverty places a person under the compulsion of necessity, the very opposite of freedom. Hunger and cold belong to the realm of needs rather than of politics.

'The direction of the French Revolution,' writes Arendt, 'was deflected almost from its beginning through the immediacy of suffering; it was determined by the exigencies of liberation not from tyranny but from necessity.' Needs can give voice to themselves only in the wordless language of force, so that their insinuation into the revolutionary project could culminate 'in the unleashing of a stream of boundless violence'.

For all its triviality, our experience of hanger and its capacity to temporarily disorganize our practical and emotional function-ing gives us the smallest intimation of what hunger might do to political functioning. The hungrier I am, the more restricted the scope and range of my interest, until my mind has contracted almost entirely into the tight confines of my stomach's shrill, helpless emptiness.

The slide of the French Revolution into the Terror finds its roots here, in the increasing compulsion of its leaders to let the misery of the hungry masses drive its course. Hunger is an essentially antipolitical force; it cannot argue, and one cannot argue with it. Politics proper can begin only once the vital needs of its participants have been secured.

The rise of the *sans-culottes*, or class-conscious working masses, as a political force over the first years after the Revolution, was rooted in the growing realization that the new order, while it may have instituted liberty and equality in the political realm, had done little to change the economic conditions of the poor. From the soil of this discontent emerged leaders who vocalized workers' anger – anger at the continued dominance of 'speculators and monopolists' over the economy, 'bloodsuckers of the people' who set the prices of vital commodities like grain crops at levels 'which three quarters of all citizens cannot afford without shedding tears'.

These words come from radical Catholic priest Jacques Roux's 'Manifesto of the Enragés' (1793), a fiery polemic against price-gouging profiteers and the willingness of bourgeois Revolutionary leaders to tolerate them. It demands of the representatives of the National Convention that they implement price controls to ensure the affordability of necessary commodities to all and 'decree the general principle that commerce doesn't consist in ruining, rendering hopeless, or starving citizens'.

He addresses the 'Deputies of the Mountain', the representatives of Robespierre's Jacobin faction, telling them

if you would climb from the third to the ninth floor of the houses of this revolutionary city you would be touched by the tears and the sobs of an immense people, without bread or clothing, reduced to a state of distress and misfortune by speculation and monopoly because laws have been cruel to the poor, because they were only made by and for the rich.

Roux's appeal is brazenly emotional, a vivid portrayal of the daily misery of the *malheureux*, of people lacking the basic means to survive. The sentimentalism of his rhetoric is inextricable from the violence of his threats against 'the rich, that is, the evil'. His florid pity for those afflicted by desperate need is the motor of his rage against the speculators.

Arendt's point is that once this kind of pity took over the political realm, it could only culminate in vengeful rage: 'The *malheureux* changed into the *enragés*, for rage is the only form in which misfortune can become active.' The fury of Roux and the other *enragés* leaders was bound to express itself in violent action because politics has no other means of translating it.

Roux was announcing that the *sans-culottes*' capacity to endure further suffering had reached its limit. Arendt implies that this announcement is the effective prelude to the Terror: 'Suffering,' she writes, 'whose strength and virtue lie in endurance, explodes into rage when it can no longer endure; this rage, to be sure, is powerless to achieve, but it carries with it the momentum of true suffering, whose devastating force is superior and, as it were, more enduring than the raging frenzy of mere frustration.'

When we're possessed by the 'frenzy of mere frustration', we are unable to discharge our anger in aggressive action and are consigned instead to an impotent rage that can only eat away at us from within. But when 'true suffering' drives our rage, its force bursts into the world outside, laying vengeful waste to its real and imagined causes.

This course of events was inevitable, argues Arendt, because the Revolution occurred under conditions of mass poverty. Once 'necessity invaded the political realm', it could realize itself only in unbound violence. In the language of psychoanalysis, extreme hunger and cold are the points at which the drive reaches its highest pitch, when its dissatisfaction is liable to express itself in the most brutal and extreme forms.

Put yet another way, necessity is the ultimate seal of rightness. In his vituperation of the rich in the name of the cold and hungry poor, Roux employs a righteous rhetoric that brooks no contest or dissent. His agitation for price controls, which would be enacted in the Law of the General Maximum a few months after he delivered the 'Manifesto', presents the policy not as a political proposal to be argued for, and which might thus be argued against, but as an act whose justice is given and beyond dispute. To resist price controls, he proclaims, is wilfully to deprive the suffering masses, to take the last crust out of the mouth of the starving baby.

When the Law of the General Maximum was passed three months later, Roux's demand to kill the profiteers was realized: those deemed to be violating it (by setting commodity prices too high) became victims of the Terror in large numbers. For Arendt, this is the necessary consequence of the intrusion of biological needs into politics; necessity imposes solutions which turn all dissenters into criminals punishable only by death.

The problem with treating any questioning of price controls as an outrage against the starving poor is that it effectively abolishes the assessment of whether they work. As it turns out, the Law of the General Maximum did not. Farmers and traders forced to reduce prices below the costs of production responded by lowering output and causing food shortages. Breaches of the law frequently ended at the guillotine, ensuring the General Maximum became one of the major drivers of the Terror.

The Terror, anticipating the revolutionary purges and repressions that would spread across the world over the next two centuries, emerged from the tight fusion of rage and rightness. Political rage puts paid to anger as a feeling that can inform and shape action; anger instead becomes the cheerleading instigator of action too blind to question or reflect on itself. It is feeling become intoxicated with itself, with the fantasy of its consummation in an ultimate, radically purgative action.

Roux's 'Manifesto' portrays a world in which the most vulnerable are living in the shadow of a permanent threat to their survival, which can only be dispelled by eliminating it. In a rhetorical move that splits society in two, the rich are explicitly identified with evil, the poor with justice and the good. Once this split was sealed in the minds of the Revolutionary leadership, a short and clear path to the Terror was assured.

As rage, anger is enlisted to oil the wheels of violence against the other, who is identified as a danger to the survival of the good. This violent logic, so central to the operation of mass revolutionary terror, also tacitly underwrites acts of individual terror; in its zeal to justify itself, anger proves skilled at adjusting its reasoning to any context. The published 'manifestos' of mass shooters and bombers of recent decades all share an insistence on the part of the writer-perpetrators to present themselves as the vulnerable and injured person taking a stand against the mortal danger presented by their victims.

In her grimly exhaustive study of contemporary misogyny, Laura Bates cites numerous cases in which incel killers are portrayed online by themselves and their defenders as having suffered unendurable humiliation, for which mass murder could be the only meaningful relief. In April 2014, Elliot Rodger drove into and shot students at UC Santa Barbara, killing six and injuring fifteen in avowed revenge on the many young women who failed to show any sexual interest in him.

Eighteen months later, Chris Harper-Mercer committed a similar atrocity, shooting dead seven victims and himself in a community college classroom in Umpqua, Oregon. Citing

Rodger as an 'elite' inspiration, Harper-Mercer used the manifesto he left behind to call out to other young men who had felt like 'a loser, rejected by society'. 'When the girls would rather go with alpha thug black men,' he continued, 'we can all agree that something's wrong with the world.'

A further three years later, once again before turning the gun fatally on himself, Scott Beierle shot six women, killing two, in a hot yoga studio in Tallahassee, Florida. His posthumously reported YouTube channel decried the 'collective treachery' of 'sluts' and 'whores' and lamented the predicament of incel icon Rodger, who had so long suffered 'not getting any, no love, no nothing', languishing in an 'endless wasteland that breeds this longing and this frustration'.

In each case, shuttling between sentimental self-pity and unbound psychopathy repeats itself in the same narrative pattern. Each begins with a story of acute dissatisfaction of the erotic drive, in which romantic overtures are ignored or spurned, a yearning for love is sent out but never received or acknowledged. This abandonment to lovelessness can be redeemed only by means of an act which transforms his helplessness into absolute power.

Rightness is a kind of knowledge whose substance is rage rather than truth. It is knowledge that resides not in the external world but in the self. The brilliance of Trollope's title is that it conveys a knowledge that is irremediably lonely, felt with complete certainty in the deepest cells of the body and mind, and yet impossible to prove to the world. Trevelyan, Ahab, Othello – all men consumed by a knowledge they are condemned to hold in the solitude of their souls, impelling them to suicide, murder or both.

Roux would end his own life in the Bicêtre prison, where he was held after being arrested on Robespierre's orders. Like the other leaders of the *enragés* movement, the final months of his life were mired in the violence to which he too eventually became victim, just one of the thousands of children (to invoke the famous formulation of the Royalist anti-Revolutionary Jacques Mallet du Pan) devoured by the Revolution that gave birth to them.

His knowledge of his own rightness was importantly different from the likes of Trevelyan, insofar as he was acting for a shared public cause rather than a hermetic private one. And we would certainly wish to separate his radical advocacy of the immiserated poor from the misogynistic rantings of the incel mass shooters. But this is only to note how readily good as well as evil causes can get swallowed up in the frenzies of rightness. As Arendt points out, by giving voice to the subjective rage of suffering rather than the objective imperatives of political justice, Roux was impelled willy-nilly towards explosive violence.

The perpetrators of the Terror and the incel shooters could not be more different in their motives and morality. But the murder of their victims is impelled in both cases, and perhaps in all cases of rageful violence, by the same overwhelming internal conviction: there is nothing else I can do.

It won't have escaped your attention that the individuals discussed in this chapter, real and fictional, are all men. Women, of course, are hardly immune from the compulsion to know they're right. But men, long conditioned by patriarchal imperatives and pressures to assert their power and invulnerability, have proved much more liable to push that compulsion to its furthest edge.

Trollope has Trevelyan doubting himself from the very beginning of his campaign to force his wife's submission. He doesn't believe that Emily has committed adultery, nor does he at any point ascribe to her the desire or intention to do so. There is no hint of any febrile fantasies, even in decorously coded Victorian form, of his wife's illicit couplings. Her offence is rather her failure to recognize the nature of her husband's grievance against her: not her desire for another, but her refusal of his demand for total compliance.

It transpires, in other words, that what Trevelyan knows he's right about isn't the sanctity of the marriage bond so much as his permanent and unquestioned right to be right. His psyche is too fragile to survive the absence of this guarantee. What he keeps iterating with increasingly hysterical force is that he must be right because to be wrong would cause mortal injury to his soul; and ironically enough, he turns out to be entirely right on this point.

In his very late essay, 'Analysis Terminable and Interminable' (1938), Freud identifies the 'bedrock' of all psychological illness as 'the repudiation of femininity', which he sees not as a contingent feature of some minds but 'a biological fact' of all minds. Freud doesn't attach masculinity or femininity to the male and female sexes, but sees them instead as fundamental psycho-biological tendencies that flow through both sexes and, we might add, those who identify with neither sex. 'Femininity' here has nothing to do with conventional female behaviour or comportment; it is a tendency, common to the female and male psyche alike, towards passivity and receptivity.

Femininity in Freud's understanding is a permeability to the full range of emotional and bodily experience. The French psychoanalyst André Green coined the term 'passivation' to describe the conditions for becoming a patient in psychoanalysis: placing one's mind in the analyst's care requires a readiness to make oneself fully vulnerable to another. In reality, no one can do this without resistance. There will always be places in me I don't want to go to myself, let alone expose to someone else. Analysis involves both patient and analyst perpetually running up against barriers to the true self.

There is no more impassable barrier to receptivity than

knowing oneself right, an insight beautifully encapsulated in a celebrated short poem by the Israeli poet and peace activist Yehuda Amichai, 'The Place Where We Are Right'. The first two of its three stanzas read thus:

> From the place where we are right
> Flowers will never grow
> In the spring.
>
> The place where we are right
> Is hard and trampled
> Like a yard.

The hardened ground of this place is impermeable to the water that would nourish the flowers' growth. Rightness coats a place in a masculine armour into which neither air nor liquid can penetrate, sealing it off from encounter or change.

For the men explored in this chapter, the integrity of this armour, however illusory, is a matter of literal survival, a fight to the death. The incel shooters above all lay bare the destructive potential of the repudiation of the feminine. Their unsatisfied drive for love and recognition compels them towards indiscriminate murder, as though there were no other remedy for the insufferable wound of their own feelings of inadequacy and self-doubt.

But the repudiation of femininity need not always lead so inexorably to suicide and murder. After all, we see it at work clearly in Victor who, for all his undoubted difficulties, never comes close to either. Victor also knew he was right. He too baulked at having to acknowledge fallibility and fell into a rage when he sensed his vulnerabilities might be exposed. And yet Victor's defensive grandiosity manifested not in murder or suicide but in an almost messianic zeal to save lives and protect truth.

Having slammed the door on his session, he returned to the room two days later, his face bearing the same haughtily neutral mien, as though expressivity were a trap he'd never be stupid enough to fall into. I could normally rely on him to begin talking within seconds of lying on the couch, but today he remained silent for a minute, two, seven. He seemed deadly still; I could swear in all that time I hadn't seen him blink. He began finally to speak in his familiar lulling baritone.

'I suppose you feel I was very harsh when I left on Monday.' He seemed to wait for a confirmation, but I said nothing. He continued, 'What you said about my having been angry for so long, well, my whole life you were implying. It caught me off guard.'

'Difficult for someone who's always on guard,' I said.

'Hmm. So I decided to tell you a few ugly truths. But walking down the street straight after, I had the peculiar sensation, which felt quite new and deeply unpleasant, of not quite believing myself, as though trying to tell you the truth had turned me into something of a liar.' In his mind, Victor continued, the truth wasn't a weapon but a value, a matter of honour not of anger. He tried to tell himself that this was the spirit in which he spoke to those around him.

But thinking of how he spoke to his wife and daughters, he felt instead sad and rather shabby. It came to him like a blow to the stomach that there was nothing terribly truthful in belittling them. 'You see, I ended up walking out of the session instead of telling you that the night before I'd heard Pru, my older daughter, tell my wife how much she hated me, how nasty I was. And Barbara tried to tell her what a good and important man I am, which only made Pru angrier and more tearful, repeating to her mother, 'He's not good, he's not important, he's horrid,' over and over.

'They sound a little like you and your mother.'

He was silent, and an ambient sadness filled the room.

The difference between him and Pru, he said, was that his daughter was full of feeling when she shouted at her mother. 'Even as a young boy, I never cried or yelled. When I told my mother and sister that father was a liar and a cheat, I was stone-faced and matter-of-fact. At least, that's how I remember it.'

What Victor came to realize over the weeks that followed was that this apparent lack of feeling had been the confused effort of a small boy trying to protect his mother. He had perceived as young as four or five that strong feelings acutely distressed her, that she seemed to unravel helplessly in the face of her children's tears and anger, shaking and telling them to stop with a tormented urgency that made her seem more like their sibling than their mother.

He found himself simply speaking the unvarnished truth about his father less like an angry child and more like an official messenger bringing bad news. A young child's confused understanding morphed, as he got older, into a fixed formula in his mind: I mustn't upset mother with my feelings. It would be much better to just tell her the facts.

As adolescence took over, the news coverage got wider and worse: he dismissed his sister as a whiny sap, dropped friends when they became boring and childish, and eventually looked hard into his mother's eyes one day and asked her, really, what was the fucking point of her? He remembered turning away, walking upstairs, closing his bedroom door on her sobs and impassively completing his maths homework.

Impassive: impervious to feeling or passion, the state of letting nothing in. 'I told myself I wasn't going to be like a girl,' Victor said. It wasn't that he was without passion or anger, but he wasn't going to waste it on sentimental causes like the poor or fighting sexism or racism; all of that was just banging your head against a brick wall. Few men I had met had more comprehensively repudiated their femininity.

Graduating from university at the top of his year in mechanical engineering, he was inundated with offers to work on the most glamorous projects in construction and design, all of which he turned down with the same undivided self-certainty. His only interest was in public safety. 'There is no bigger killer than factual error,' he told me. 'Look at the droughts and floods and fires we're all going to die from sooner or later, simply because people don't want to look at the facts.'

All his feelings and energies were channelled into correcting errors that could endanger lives. These alone became the object of his indignation and rage. In his unconscious, his feelings would be realized in actions that would save the world. But Victor had risked listening to his unsettling, half-conscious intuition that he might not be entirely right after all, or perhaps that his being entirely right wasn't helping himself or anyone else. It was insulating him in the cell of his own rightness, where he could rely on the hardness and impermeability of the ground beneath his feet.

Perhaps this ground, afflicted by sterility and drought and lovelessness, wasn't as secure as he thought. Perhaps he was doing at least as much harm as he was trying to prevent. More than three decades ago, he had simply shut the door on his mother's sobbing, ensuring it couldn't penetrate his coldly engineered world. But somehow, he was unable to do the same when he heard his daughter sobbing. He was beginning to sense there were dangers and wounds that couldn't be remedied, that might even be made worse, by exclusive attention to facts.

The third stanza of Amichai's poem:

But doubts and loves
Dig up the world

Like a mole, a plow.
And a whisper will be heard in the place
Where the ruined
House once stood.

Pru's tears had tentatively opened Victor's ears to his own doubts and loves, digging up a space in him to receive a truth other than the hard verity of fact, a truth darker and more ambiguous, that manifests not in the confident clarity of speech but in barely audible whispers.

Chapter Two

Failed Rage: Positive Thinkers, Anger Managers, Protestors

When anger is captured wholesale by aggression, the two are liable to become confused, as though anger were merely the accompanying mood music to acts of violence and destruction. As Chapter One showed us, angry feelings are often experienced as the cheerleaders for aggressive action, a rowdy internal crowd rallying the team to attack the opponent.

But anger is only rarely so tightly in league with aggression. More often we try to keep them apart. Who isn't familiar with that smart of offended justice, pride or fairness which, in the absence of a ready outlet, simply churns in the gut? Most of us are liable to swallow anger more often than we act on it to prevent aggression from having its way.

I'm recalling myself at fifteen, bespectacled and slight, being greeted by the same daily insult from a massive gurning bully as I entered the classroom for maths: 'Ah, it's Cohen!' Except it was pronounced as 'Cho*een*' on the understanding, shared by his gormlessly chortling sidekicks, that this sounded 'Jewish', especially when accompanied by the sliding of his index finger down the bridge of his nose and beyond, miming the grotesque elongation of mine (which, for what it's worth, was and remains exaggeratedly small), usually to the tune of 'If I Were a Rich Man'.

I remained silent each time, trying to convey contempt rather than fear. I'd stare past the chalky equations and triangles for the next forty-five minutes, teeth grinding and blood rising as I composed endless comebacks, each more venomous than the next: 'Do you even have a nose, Pete?' I'd imagine asking him nonchalantly. 'It's hard to tell under those layers of pustular disease.' On occasion I enhanced the scene with a pretty girl glancing at him and giggling on cue, perhaps absently touching her slender fingers to the tip of my shoulder.

At other times my comeback was eloquently wordless, a punch so devastating it would drive his nose back into his skull, opening a vacuum in the middle of his face. 'Anyone else?' I would calmly ask his stunned, cowering friends. 'Thought not,' I'd conclude, languidly shaking out my right hand.

Nasty? Vicious? Vindictive? Indeed. Anger is never so ugly as when it's denied an outlet. I felt the force of my murderous aggression in these moments. But no one else did. My sadistic impulses were diverted from my coiled fist to my brooding mind, from the realm of action to the realm of fantasy, where they simmered impotently at the highest temperature.

These episodes come to mind when I return to Freud and Breuer's brief account of the beaten employee, the man who consulted Freud about hysterical attacks which, under hypnosis, were revealed as performances of the frenzied rage he felt as his boss publicly beat him with a stick. Anger here is an unbearable accretion of tension denied an outlet in the external world, forced to remain bottlenecked inside the tight spaces of the mind and body.

I feel like I know something of this man's predicament, of how it feels to be provoked into a response that is immediately blocked. When the aggressive drive is aroused, it presses for action in the external world. But when the path to action is obstructed, the drive is subjected to all manner of displacements, reversals and detours. Diverted from its aim of intervening in reality (say, retaliating against a sadistic boss or bully), it has to find somewhere else to go, some new form to assume.

So an impulse that begins life as an intention to act morphs into a heightened feeling state. We might recall here Darwin's idea that emotional expression is a vestige of action, such as when we clench our teeth and turn red or white in the face in the act of fighting an enemy. Feelings may seem like a prelude and guide to action, as when we say we acted on our feelings, but in this account we feel because we act and not the other way around. We start with the preparatory gestures of action, only evolution has repressed the impulse to bite, socializing us into a more pacific stance. The bite stays inside, morphing from an action into a feeling.

I never punched Pete, but my nostrils flared, my blood ran hot and my fists and teeth clenched as though in suspended readiness to strike. Then my impulse to aggression met the obstacle of my anxiety of self-preservation, rendering me all feeling, no action. Like the employee, I could enjoy neither the immediate pleasure of retaliation, nor the delayed satisfaction of justice. Instead, I carried my load of rage like the Mariner his albatross.

What other feeling works in this way? It makes little sense to think of either joy or sadness as being frustrated. Frustration or dissatisfaction is what occurs when a wish or desire is left unfulfilled. But neither joy nor sadness desires or aims towards anything. Joy, of course, is its own end by definition – if it involved a wish or demand for something more, it would cease to be joy.

Sadness is more complicated in that the sad person does wish for something, namely whatever would bring their sadness to an end – a permanent summer holiday, say, or the return of a lost love. But if we had the power to prolong summer indefinitely or bring back those we have lost, we couldn't be said to have satisfied our sadness, only to have brought it to an end.

Of all the emotions, it is only anger and love that are defined by their perpetual liability to dissatisfaction. In anger and love we are forever wanting things and failing to get them. It's no coincidence that these emotions correlate with aggression and sexuality. Aggressive action and sexual union are the respective means by which anger and love seek fulfilment in the external world. Human beings, moreover, are able to send these protean forces down innumerable different paths, enlisting them as much for self-destruction as for self-preservation, for death as for life, for stasis as for growth.

But as more or less every human being knows, such attempts at fulfilment often fail. Neither aggressive action nor sexual union is guaranteed to satiate our rage or desire. Both can be disappointing, deflating, anticlimactic, as though failing to provide what they seemed to promise.

Freud suggests that there is something in the nature of the sexual drive that doesn't permit full satisfaction. The object of the drive is forever elusive, slipping out of our fingers the moment we think we possess it. The same is strangely true of the aggressive drive.

In his harrowing memoir of his years imprisoned in Dachau concentration camp, the French writer Robert Antelme portrays the SS as possessed by a rage to eliminate the humanity of the victims they beat and killed. But in so doing, they ran up against the limits of their own power to destroy. 'It's because we're men like them that the SS will finally prove powerless before us,' he writes. You can kill a person, in other words, but you cannot banish them from the human race. Even at its furthest edge, the drive to dominate and destroy can never fulfil itself completely.

*

In its early history, psychoanalysis tended to be far more interested in the drives than in feelings, in sexuality rather than love, in aggression rather than anger. But between the 1930s and 1980s, the tide turned and psychoanalysis developed the new theory of 'object relations' in the work of key figures such as Ronald Fairbairn, D. W. Winnicott, Marion Milner and, later on, Christopher Bollas. It became more interested in emotional relationships, and abandoned the theory of drives on the grounds that it was too mechanistic and insufficiently attuned to human feeling.

But this is to assume, mistakenly, that feelings and drives are opposed to one another; on the contrary, they are intimate companions. I would go so far as to say that drives are central to understanding why we *have* feelings.

One key reason for this misunderstanding of the concept of the drive is that James Strachey, Freud's English translator, rendered the original German word *Trieb* as instinct rather than drive. Strachey saw this as a pragmatic solution to the absence of an adjectival form of 'drive', which created all kinds of translational problems. After all, he argued, doesn't instinct mean more or less the same thing?

In fact, it doesn't; and while this might seem like a pedantic theoretical objection, the distinction between drive and instinct has significant implications for how we understand who and what we are as human beings.

As we saw in the Introduction, an instinct is a piece of inbuilt biological knowledge that ensures the attainment of our vital needs, as when a bee gravitates towards nectar. A drive contains this instinctual component, but it also complicates it. A baby may by instinct seek the nutritive satisfaction of her mother's milk when she feeds off the breast; but she is also seeking the more sensually and emotionally charged pleasures of the milk's warmth, the breast's yielding softness against her cheek, the nipple's reassuringly tensile resistance against her tongue.

If we were reducible to biological instincts – if our sexuality, for example, was nothing more than a wish to discharge libidinal energy, or even to reproduce the species, what we call love could be conveniently satisfied by the odd bout of efficient rutting. But because drives rather than instincts are what animate us, we are destined always to want something more, to feel some nagging sense of lacking what we most desire, and to yearn for that ultimate fulfilment we never achieve. This is why sexual life can be so fraught and unpredictable and strange and joyous, or alternatively, this is why we call it love.

The failure of drives to fulfil themselves, we could say, is how and why feelings come into being. We may activate our aggressive drive only to fail to get the justice or revenge that we want. Or we may get what we want and discover it wasn't really what we wanted. In such instances, our aggressive impulses might be spent or smothered, but our anger remains, eating away at us from the inside.

It's worth recalling at this point Antonio Damasio's distinction between emotions and feelings. Following Darwin, Damasio defines emotion as the way an organism instinctively and unconsciously seeks to ensure its own preservation. On this definition, emotions are those reflexive reactions that occur without our having to think about them – the disgust we feel on walking past a bin full of rotting food waste, our delight as we scan the display cases of our favourite patisserie.

But feelings involve mapping these reactions, producing images of and ideas about them. Feelings process creatively what emotions react to automatically, facilitating 'the possibility of creating novel, nonstereotypical responses'. Anger, from this perspective, is of a higher order than aggression, a transformation of reactive behaviour into a kind of self-reflection.

The psychoanalyst Hans Loewald developed a similar insight

along more clinical lines, arguing in 1971 that psychoanalytic work involves transforming inchoate instincts into experienced feelings, so that what might first present in a patient as an inchoate unconscious aggression would become, in the course of a treatment, felt anger.

Darwin saw anger as a kind of expressive husk of aggression, all gestures and no action. For Loewald and Damasio, in contrast, angry feelings are less a diminished version of aggression than a move to a higher form of psychic life. Anger is a way of doing something with our aggression, of transferring it from the realm of action to the realm of feeling.

Both Loewald and Damasio see this movement from impulse to feeling as a wholly positive one. For Damasio, it is the expression of the organism's teleological design, which always operates for its own maximal self-preservation. Loewald too has a conception of the mind as aspiring to ever higher levels of emotional self-understanding.

But in our daily lives, is this transition from action to feeling always experienced as an unambiguous good? Hardly. Having to carry painful feelings without knowing what do with them is more often a torment than an education, as the victim of bullying, lumbered with an anger he cannot convert into 'specific action', well knows.

When Freud's beaten employee's aggressive impulses were forcibly suppressed and made to take up lodging in his mind and body, he felt only an overwhelming pressure on the nervous system, just as when my own retaliatory urges towards Pete were denied any active response, they accrued in me as a tight knot in my stomach and a scream of protest in my mind's ear.

When our anger is tightly coupled with aggression, it gives us a bodily sensation and mental conviction of knowing what we're doing. Anger sharpens our sense of clarity and righteousness in taking action, whether that means a physical attack, a street protest or a marital row. But the uncoupling of anger from aggression has the opposite effect. It deprives us of an immediate outlet for aggressive action, leaving us with an enervating pressure on our nervous system. I'm so angry, we might say to ourselves or someone else, I don't know what to do with myself.

At this point, our anger can take us down many different paths, all of which feel in one way or another like diversions. It can lead us to the raw frustration of undischarged rage, or to presenting our anger in the guise of some other attitude (exaggerated politeness, overfriendliness, moroseness). It can also induce a state of repression, in which we may be quite unaware of the anger we're feeling. In such a state, anger is liable to be turned unconsciously on the self in the form of depression, self-harm, addiction, psychosomatic disorders or even suicide. Or it can persist in the depths of the psyche until it erupts in some explosive act of violence.

All these diversions and displacements of anger can take both individual and collective forms, shaping private and public life alike. What does it mean for an individual person's life to be shaped by an anger it cannot make real contact with?

'Hmm. I'm not *aware* of feeling that way.'

This was Olive's soft-spoken refrain, frequently intoned during the first year of her three times weekly therapy with me. For years, it was how she responded any time I ventured she was experiencing a 'difficult' feeling – despair, resentment, irritability, contempt, envy, and anger above all.

Three weeks after beginning therapy, Olive arrived about ten minutes late to the session. Despite her efforts to retain her usual immaculate composure, I caught an intimation of distraught embarrassment somewhere around the pinched corners of her downturned mouth.

'I'm so *very* sorry!' she began, as soon as she walked in. 'I was at work, trying to clear the inbox, when I suddenly saw the time and rushed here. I'm afraid I still feel a little flustered. I really *am* sorry.'

I noted she seemed quite upset, to which she agreed before gently qualifying her agreement, a one-two move that had already become familiar to me: 'Yes. Well, I mean, I'm a *little* upset, because I hate to waste anyone's time. It strikes me as discourteous. I'm sure you have better things to be doing than waiting for me. It's very unlike me to lose sight of the time so carelessly.'

'Hmm . . . well, maybe you didn't much feel like coming here,' I said.

There was what felt like a stunned silence before she repeated, '. . . didn't feel much like coming here?!' In a tone of hushed surprise, she assured me that she was very happy to come here, that she had after all started therapy of her own accord. The more I implied that her lateness might have been a signal of reluctance or resentment, the more desperate her appeal to me to believe her unalloyed willingness to be here.

The exchange revealed just how distressing it was for Olive to have the faintest hint of bad feeling ascribed to her, a distress exacerbated by the barrier she'd interposed between herself and her irritation at me for suggesting it. My insinuation that she might want to scream at me or worse made her, I suspected, want to scream at me or worse, the more so because she couldn't possibly do anything of the kind.

Olive was under perpetual siege from her own anger, forever beating back its movement towards the front of her consciousness. Just pointing to this predicament caused me increasingly to feel like a gleeful sadist, as though coercing her into looking head on at something whose very existence she couldn't bear to acknowledge.

But why was someone so phobic towards her own feelings seeing a psychoanalyst three times a week? Olive's avowed reason was her ever more debilitating migraines, which she ascribed at our first meeting to the intense 'stress' of her job.

Work-related stress is undoubtedly real, but it is also a conveniently fuzzy way of depersonalizing anxiety and unhappiness, ensuring they are imputed to purely external causes. As deputy head of a charity raising awareness of child poverty, Olive's claim on job stress was certainly credible. But it also left her own life and self entirely out of the account.

As it turned out, the aim she assiduously pursued during the entire first year of our sessions was to defend this self-exclusion, to insist there was nothing in her history or her present life that contributed to her malaise, that her headaches, insomnia and loss of appetite were all symptoms of the job's demands. Of course, she was continually exposed in her job to stories of she called 'real suffering' – child labour, hunger, disease – with what felt like the gentlest swipe of disdain at herself and me, and this was bound to get to her sometimes; she was only human after all.

A year of work passed in this way, at the end of which Olive told me in an unmistakably apologetic tone that her migraines were getting worse. 'That can't have been easy to tell me,' I said, 'given the amount of time and money you've invested in this work.'

'Oh no, not at all!' she replied, 'I don't think of it like that. I don't expect you to magic my headaches away – how could you?'

When I asked if that wasn't why she'd come to me, she became audibly upset. 'Really, I'm not upset or disappointed or anything like that! If anything, it's my fault, imagining I could get rid of migraines I've had nearly all my life by just . . . talking.' Realizing immediately that she'd somewhat diminished the therapy, she continued in a panicky tone, 'I think you do a great job, really!'

And then she burst into tears.

*

Negative feelings like anger arise not because we are aggressive, but because we must live at a distance from our aggression. If we always knew what we wanted and faced no obstacles in obtaining it, we would have nothing to feel angry about. Seamlessly acquiring whatever we desire, we would be aggressive – acquisitive, entitled, self-assertive – but never angry.

'All who desire something and cannot obtain it,' writes Aristotle in his *Rhetoric*, 'are prone to anger and easily excited.' Anger stirs in us only when we're confronted with the limits of our power to get what we want. The first such confrontation, unfortunately, occurs more or less at birth; as the American psychoanalyst Michael Eigen puts it, 'Rage seems built into an infant's scream.'

When an infant first comes into the world, he is thrown into an environment full of dissatisfactions he'd never known during his gestation. The space around him is open on all sides instead of snugly bound; his feeding can be delayed, alerting him to the physical and emotional pain of hunger.

Recall Winnicott's idea that the baby manages these un-expected shocks by forging an illusion of his omnipotent control – his cries cause the breast, and all the tender attentions that accompany it, to magically appear. However, the baby can only develop by gradually recognizing a world outside himself, what Winnicott calls a 'not-me' world. But this means reckoning with dissatisfaction, with the non-fulfilment of all his desires for love, pleasure and power.

At first and for a long time, all this can make us very angry. Tantrums visit on our carers our imperious outrage at the temerity with which they defy our demands. Something of this infantile fury stubbornly persists in us for the remainder of our days, finding a new lease of life in adolescence, continuing to lurk at the edges through the various stages of midlife before its last-ditch return in our senescent rage against the dying of the light.

From the moment of birth, life can seem like a rolling bad news channel, its chyrons flashing word of our helplessness, our dependency and our separateness across the bottom of the screen. All these bulletins remind us that the world isn't our exclusive preserve, that it must be shared with numerous other beings, each with their own needs, desires, interests, antipathies and hopes.

Tantrums stop, or at least reduce in frequency and number, once a child realizes the limits on the power of his own aggression to effect what he wants. If he grabs a toy that isn't his, it might be wrested from his hands; if he screams for its return, it will be withheld. And if he is docile and cooperative, it may be granted.

The process of accommodating to this reality, of not getting everything we want on our own terms, takes its toll. When the drive we call aggression is thwarted in the external world, it doesn't disappear. It makes for itself a different kind of existence in the interior life of the mind and body, an existence we call anger.

Anger is so commonly twinned with aggression, so readily seen as the horse to aggression's carriage, that we lose sight of how precarious and opportunistic their coupling really is. As often as not, anger swills in our stomach and snakes through our bloodstream, searching for a pathway to discharge that it fails to find. This was the insight Freud had already arrived at in 1893 with the case of the beaten employee. Deprived of any external outlet for his anger, first by his boss and then by the courts, the employee must instead bear its insupportable burden in his own mind and body.

Freud generalized this insight in *Civilization and Its Discontents*, where he argued that the maintenance of an ordered and equitable society demands that we renounce the largest portion of our aggressive energy. In one way or another, we are all the beaten employee, denied a channel for aggressive action and so abandoned to an anger we must keep to ourselves, occasionally discharging it in empty bursts of sound and fury, more often letting it quietly corrode our physical and psychic insides.

Alternatively, anger conceals itself, sometimes undetectable even to ourselves, in the guise of some other mood. This was a practice Olive had perfected over many years, to the degree that she had no idea that this was what she was doing.

The flood of tears that came unbidden that day was accompanied by a low and prolonged howl, shockingly strange yet perfectly apt, like an unexpected visitor whose arrival you'd been anticipating without realizing it. In the sessions that followed, Olive gave voice almost without interruption to a litany of resentments, from the ruined state of the earth to the broken state of her marriage, from the emotional injuries of her childhood to her own vanishing chances of bearing a child, all of which seemed to converge in the diffuse, radiating soreness of her head, neck and back.

She laid out these experiences less in a straight narrative line than a kind of rageful collage, in which all the layers of pain and loss overlapped and bled into one another. As I listened, I felt a sensation of blissful deflation, as though a mass of bottlenecked tension was being granted release. Only now was I aware of how my joints and muscles had been tightening in unconscious solidarity with Olive's as soon as she entered the room.

Her entire life felt like it had been lived under a cloud of prohibition on all bad feelings. While she knew that therapy was meant to lift that cloud, the prospect had seemed unimaginable to her. 'Don't say you're angry or upset or disgusted,' she had told herself silently in sessions, 'He'll only hate you.' But the moment she'd broken down in the session, it came to her in a flash that she could howl and cry and that I wasn't going to scold or reject her for it.

She had given a rather sketchy picture of her childhood when we'd first met. What had inhibited her from giving a more detailed account, she now told me, wasn't the bad memory she'd apologized for at the time, but the deep shame at the hate that she, her parents' only child, felt towards them. In association to this admission, she recalled walking to the park with them one summer afternoon at the age of twelve, when they'd stopped at the ice cream van.

'I was short for my age. My hair was very long and straight; I wore an Alice band. Round, tortoiseshell glasses. I love ice cream, but when my father urged me to tell the man what I wanted I panicked. I think I'd wanted a sundae with all the trimmings but was worried I'd be told off for being greedy. So after dithering, I said I wanted a lemonade ice lolly. The man handed it over and said, "A pretty girl is even prettier when she smiles!"'

'My mother laughed out loud and said to him, "I wouldn't hold your breath! Not for our little Miss Misery-guts!" I don't remember the guy's reaction, only Dad joining in the laughter, adding "Lemon for the sourpuss!" Then, seeing me upset, he eyerolled and said, "Oh dear, sensitive soul again! Take a joke, Olive, take a joke!"'

Perhaps it was the cheap humiliation in front of a stranger which had burnt that episode into the epicentre of her memory. But the story was soon revealed as but one stitch in an intricate weave of gratuitous emotional injuries.

'Waaaaah! The big boy *kicked* meeee!' Her mother's grating falsetto squeal, mimicking Olive's tearful report at the end of a Year 2 school day.

'Are you competing to put off as many lads as possible?' Her father's quip one Friday evening as he passed Olive, sixteen, clad head to toe in regulation black, black eyeliner circled thickly round her eyes, ready to go out.

'D'you always talk to him like that? My god, what a nightmare. What *does* he see in you?' Her father again, having overheard her and her then boyfriend, now husband, in her old bedroom, squabbling in hissing undertones.

'Are you sure you want to wear that frock? It needs very slim arms to pull it off.' Her mother on the morning of her wedding day.

Olive had come to perceive herself through the lens of casual hostility and derision her parents had been training on her for as long as she could remember. But the curious thing about this hostility was that as soon as she tried to raise a mirror to it, it abruptly dissolved. The moment either parent saw their aggression reflected in their daughter's tears or distress or withdrawal, they would ask her in a tone of bewildered incredulity what on earth she was talking about, what did we *do*? Could they not say *anything* without it causing a major incident?

It isn't quite accurate to call Olive her parents' only child. There had also been a boy, stillborn, two years before her birth. Born into families who dismissed or derided strong feelings, her parents had no language for the depth and force of their rage and grief, no means of attuning themselves to it. The boy was never talked about. If he had a name, Olive had never heard it.

They resolved instead to 'get on with it', put the pain behind them, try again. But the pain carried over surreptitiously into their lives as parents, forever seeking some covert avenue of expression. Derision was a rage they could express as though behind their own backs, a form of abuse they could plausibly and perhaps even sincerely deny: not the waterworks again, why must you be so precious, why can't you take a joke, why must you be such a wet blanket?

Steamrolling Olive's sadness and anger was an act of desperation, a displaced violence against their own feelings, desperate

because the alternative was to bear those feelings, to let themselves surrender to them, and somewhere within themselves they
had intuited that this would mean unravelling irrevocably. As
long as painful feelings could be laughed at, they didn't have to
be felt; this was a matter not of preference but of survival.

Unable to mourn the unlived life of their son, the storm of
pain went underground, rising to the surface in their casual,
disavowed attacks on their daughter, the daughter who wasn't a
son, who had somehow taken up the place in their hearts meant
for him.

'The thing that always hurt and shocked me most,' Olive remarked four years into her analysis, 'was the way they mocked
and denigrated me for being a girl. When I discovered feminism,
I thought their behaviour was misogyny, and I don't think I was
exactly wrong. But perhaps if having a girl hadn't been such a
constant reminder of what and who I wasn't, they wouldn't have
needed to be so misogynistic.'

Anger is where aggression becomes a psychic rather than an
external force, to be felt rather than acted out. And sometimes,
when anger so exceeds what we can bear to feel, it is preferable
to act out, to take refuge in disowned aggression. To ridicule a
child's feelings rather than suffer one's own.

'Thinking negative won't get you anywhere, you know!' This
caution, frequently directed at Olive by her father, strikes me as
a choice instance of the ways prevailing ideologies seep imperceptibly into our private relationships.

An effective prohibition on the expression of anger and other
negative emotions has long been in place in many different regions of our daily social life. In 1983, the sociologist Arlie Russell
Hochschild published *The Mortgaged Heart*, a now classic study of
new forms of service-oriented work (Hochschild's key case study

was of flight attendants) done mainly by women, which mar-shalled, alongside physical and cognitive labour, the burgeoning discipline of emotional labour, most commonly the demand that the customer should perceive the worker's palpable pleasure in serving them while being shielded from any intimation of her strain or discomfort.

Emotional labour is no longer the preserve of customer service professionals. Online culture has made emotional labourers of us all. It isn't enough to let the world know what we do, to pro-mote our competencies in carpentry or nursing or folk singing; we must display our ideal selves, disseminate a personal brand radiating effortless success and contentment while editing out any hints of failure or unhappiness.

One effect of the culture of compulsory happiness Hochschild uncovered is to drive 'bad' feelings underground, where they languish in a cloud of shame, unspeakable and unwanted. The gurus and preachers of positive thinking encourage us to see emotional negativity as a drain on dedication, productiv-ity and cooperation and a fatal obstacle on our path towards self-optimization.

As Barbara Ehrenreich memorably showed in her 2009 book *Smile or Die*, the gospel of positivity spread by a proliferation of self-help books and motivational speakers doesn't counsel mere disapproval or avoidance of bad feelings and the people who have them. It enjoins us to cast them out of our lives. 'GET RID OF NEGATIVE PEOPLE IN YOUR LIFE,' commands one business coach quoted by Ehrenreich; 'Negative People SUCK!' proclaims another: 'They suck the energy out of positive people like you and me ... Avoid them at all cost ... Trust me, you're better off without them.'

Others' bad feelings arouse the annihilating rage of the positive thinker, perhaps because they remind them that such feelings exist, along with the world which gives rise to them, which includes themselves. The result is a burst of unbound negativity, unencumbered by irony or self-awareness.

We might imagine the positive thinker would encourage followers to pity or pep-talk negative types rather than ruthlessly expel them. But the predicament is spelt out in the words of the gurus and coaches: a negative person's bad feelings will 'suck the energy out of positive people like you and me'. The negative person is both parasitic and infectious, such that in trying to make them more positive, you may find instead that they make you more negative.

The positivity guru's zero-tolerance response to anger makes for an interesting contrast with the more moderate 'managerial' stance of modern psychology, which implies that anger can be controlled and kept within bounds. Unlike the advocate for total positivity, for whom all internal and external pathways to anger should be blocked off, most mainstream anger management therapies and books begin by acknowledging the universality and inevitability of angry feelings.

Their emphasis is instead on how to ensure that those feelings are kept under control by employing a range of practical techniques. These might include breathing, relaxation, exercise, creative activity, 'cognitive restructuring' (moderating the language we use in talking to both ourselves and others), defusing a situation with humour ('silly' rather than harsh) and avoiding known triggers.

All these techniques are directed towards bringing anger under the command of a sovereign and reasonable self. A mainstream psychologist today is likely to allow that daily life is bound to stir up occasional angry feelings, sometimes justifiably so. Our task at the onset of such feelings is to call up the resources of logic and moderation to overcome them.

'Logic defeats anger, because anger, even when it's justified, can quickly become irrational,' states an article on the American Psychological Association (APA) website. Anger management is premised on anger's liability to distort reality, to turn minor slights, inconveniences and irritations into wounds and catastrophes. To manage our anger is to reassert the hierarchy of the rational cognitive mode over its irrational emotional counterpart, to recover our perception of things as they 'really' are.

The difference between the sober moderacy of the anger management therapist and the stridency of the positive thinking coach is essentially quantitative; the former acknowledges that we all experience some measure of anger and should seek to minimize it, while the latter outlaws anger altogether as a toxic force. Of the two, surely the anger management approach, allowing for anger as an inevitable feature of everyday life, is both the more accurate and more humane? And in encouraging us to marshal our powers of cognition against the overbearing force of emotion, it places us on the side of reason and common sense, an impression amplified by the eminently clear and measured tone and language used by the APA.

In contrast, Ehrenreich's coaches and gurus, with their injunctions to get rid of 'negative people', would seem severely lacking in both realism and empathy, snake-oil merchants peddling the fantasy of a world expunged of all bad feelings.

So why do I find myself feeling that the anger managers miss an essential, if not *the* essential, point about anger to which the positive thinkers, in spite or even because of the brutality and clumsiness of their thinking, are more attuned? In the irrationality of their repudiation of anger, the preachers of positivity show us what anger does to us.

In fact, the anger management approach is just as self-contradictory as the positive thinking one – less glaringly so perhaps, but more profoundly. It counsels a shift into cognitive clarity at the very moment we're possessed by the strength of our feelings; how can we assume this stance of reason if anger is, according to the very same theory, the force that corrodes and undoes reason?

'Logic defeats anger, because anger ... can quickly become irrational,' say the anger managers. But is it not oddly – irrationally – presumptuous to assume that logic ensures the defeat of irrationality? We might amplify the point by recalling that we live in a world in which millions of ordinary citizens ally themselves to a movement organized around the belief that the US government is being run by a secret cabal of satanic paedophiles, while the largest proportion of global political and industrial leaders are ignoring, if not actively accelerating, the collapse of the planet's basic biological and social ecologies. In this context, it is hard not to hear the appeal to logic as itself a kind of madness.

The positive thinkers are themselves tethered to a different denial, of the reality of grief, anxiety, anger and their underlying causes. But their insistence on anger as dangerously infectious, corrosive and self-perpetuating gets much closer to the experiential marrow of angry feelings, especially as they manifest in our own moment.

Take a particularly charged tableau of this present-day anger. A small band of Just Stop Oil protestors form a line directly in front of a dense three-lane flow of road traffic, bringing it to a sudden halt. The weather is hot. Boxed into their near-stationary cars, scorched by the sun, the skin and tempers of the motorists start to overheat. The protestors walk at a provokingly stately pace, as though leading a funeral march. The motorists react with their own spontaneous coordinated action, leaning on their horns in unison, producing a screaming, atonal dirge that perfectly soundtracks the scene. Until one motorist in an orange vest exits his van and starts shoving protestors hard, grabbing their banners, throwing one young man to the ground and kicking him before being ushered back to his vehicle by a woman with no obvious affiliation to either party.

YouTube is replete with videos of such scenes, as though eruptions of public rage are a new kind of pornography. And watching them induces something of the same enervated compulsion, a fascination for the sheer strangeness of the conflict. We are witnessing a confrontation of two bodies of rage occupying two different regions of time. The protestors come as though from the future, grieving the demise of life on earth as though it has already occurred, turning the urgent flow of traffic into a zombie crawl, evoking those post-apocalyptic movies in which shell-shocked survivors stumble across the scorched plains of a dead planet. The expression of their rage is muted not only for tactical reasons but because it is aroused by what the philosopher Timothy Morton calls a 'hyperobject', an entity scattered everywhere and nowhere, encompassing all earthly life – both what life is and what it does.

How are we to get angry at a hyperobject? No one can locate it in space or time because it cannot be apprehended in a single place or event. As Morton has it, every turn of a key in the ignition is statistically meaningless, and yet 'billions of things such as key turnings in ignitions are exactly what is causing global warming and mass extinction'.

If the protestors are thinking and acting in a time and space beyond the present, the motorists are entirely in the grip of the now – the heat, the forced immobility, the abrupt incursion into the flow of their daily lives all press on their nerves. The sheer immediacy of this pressure concentrates their attention entirely in this moment. They do not see the far distant fossil fuel and governmental and financial interests blocking their way, the billions of key turnings. They see only a ragged line of random men and women, walking at a speed calculated to infuriate them.

But perhaps this inference of the motorists' feelings is too simplistic. It's hard to imagine that some, a few at least, even as they press furiously on their horns, don't somewhere intuit the deep irony of their predicament: the pounding heat, the system breakdown, the helplessness in the face of some intrusive force about which they can do nothing. Are they enraged at the protestors giving them the smallest taste of the future awaiting them?

There are few acts more human than shooting the messenger. Unable to address the real object of our anger, we lash out at whatever or whoever evokes it for us, in this case the bearers of bad news, blocking the sightline to prosperity and success.

Can the anger managers help with the provoking anger of the protestors and the answering rage of the motorists? There may be a social and political chasm dividing them, but in some peculiar way they are united, as we all are, by living (as Greta Thunberg puts it) in a house that's on fire. Given which, perhaps the two sides can agree on one thing: there could be no madder response to this scene than an appeal to logic and moderation.

There may be another point on which they converge: neither will enjoy the satisfaction of an aggressive action that realizes and thus dissolves their rage. The protestors know that as long as the horns are blaring and the drivers are ranting, blocking their ears to the one alarm they need to hear, they will need to continue to trudge slowly along the road, drawing hatred along the way. The motorists know that their righteous cries of 'How dare you?!' and 'What gives you the right?', like their flailing shoves and punches, will do nothing to ease the congestion or assuage the inexorably rising temperatures within and without.

*

Positive thinking can seem like a distinctly modern confection, a way of spreading the demands of emotional labour across the whole of society, ensuring that the forced smiles of Hochschild's flight attendants are eventually worn by us all. One of the most striking symptoms of this spreading demand is the popular revival of the ancient Roman philosophical tradition of Stoicism. A quick Google search will turn up dozens of books, podcasts and online courses promoting Stoic wisdom as the ideal remedy for the stress and chaos of modern life.

Daily life in our time stirs up insupportable levels of emotional stress and enervation, emanating from multiple sources – the cost of living, overwork, global unrest, the perpetual distractions of consumerism, social media's constant stoking of anxiety, envy and outrage, the insinuation of violence and division into mainstream politics and, underlying all of these, the increasingly audible murmur of ecological breakdown.

As our feelings are impelled ever more towards the furthest extremes, it is easy to see the appeal of a way of life based around management and moderation of strong emotion. In this regard, Stoicism is especially censorious towards anger, which it routinely castigates as at once the most destructive and the most futile of all feelings.

The primary text for this repudiation of anger is *De Ira* (*On Anger*) by the Roman philosopher Seneca, written around 45 CE. Extracts from Seneca's essay were recently retranslated and republished as one in a series of books adapting ancient wisdom to the practical problems of modern life, under the title *How To Keep Your Cool: An Ancient Guide to Anger Management*.

De Ira is a kind of manifesto for maximal emotional labour. Its key practical counsel is that we should always, under all circumstances, suppress our anger. This is a matter not only of how we feel inside but of how we appear to the world. Seneca's startlingly

vivid portraits of states of rage anticipate Darwin's view of emotional expression as a palimpsest of action. 'Their eyes blaze and
sparkle,' Seneca writes in the book's opening aphorism of men
(and only men) possessed by anger:

> their whole face is a deep red with the blood which boils up
> from the bottom of their heart, their lips quiver, their teeth
> are set ... their breath is laboured and hissing ... they groan,
> bellow, and burst into scarcely intelligible talk ... their whole
> body is highly-strung and plays those tricks which mark a
> distraught mind, so as to furnish an ugly and shocking picture
> of self-perversion and excitement.

This is a body in the throes of what we would today call fight
mode, dangerously excited and pressing urgently to discharge
its tightly coiled aggressive energies. Seneca put weight on the
appearance of anger because he places it in dangerous proximity
to its conversion to violent aggression. Under Seneca's gaze, an
angry comportment is already a kind of violence. In it can be seen
and heard the 'ugly and shocking' act it will become.

It's for this reason that as his essay ends, Seneca implores us not
merely to avoid acting on our anger but to eliminate all signs of
it, to give away no hint of our irate mood. His point is that once
our face betrays us, we have betrayed ourselves, handing over to
anger the mastery of our inner self. 'Let it rather be locked in the
innermost recesses of our breast,' he counsels, 'and be borne by
us, not bear us.' Indeed, given that 'our inward thoughts gradually
become influenced by our outward demeanour', we should use
the occasion of our anger to present the mildest and most composed possible version of ourselves.

Reading this passage, I'm reminded of the first year of my
work with Olive, who seemed intuitively to share Seneca's view

of the perilous closeness of feelings of anger to acts of violence. Whenever her husband seemed to catch some hint of displeasure or irritation in her expression, he would say something like 'What's up with you?' and she would freeze, breathless with panic, before calling up every last vestige of her will to smile brightly and say 'Nothing!'

After telling me of one such instance on a Monday morning, I wondered if she had any sense of why he'd asked the question. Knitting her brow, she said that he'd told her he'd invited friends for dinner for the following evening without consulting her.

'So he'd seen how unhappy you were about this?'

'But I wasn't, I wasn't unhappy! It's fine, it's Jeff's home, he can invite people. It's just he often does it at short notice without telling me, and I happened to have a report to finish on Sunday night, so it was bad timing, and he tends to expect me to cook and to say something like "I would do it, but you know how terrible I am in the kitchen", and then he'll go on to say, "Just make some spaghetti or something!", but if he was really happy to serve spaghetti he really could do it himself, so when he says that, I tend to think he's saying the opposite.' Then, after a deep sigh: 'But it's fine.'

I asked her why, if it was all so fine, she had been so panicked when he asked what was up.

'Because obviously I hate the idea that he'd think I'd be angry with him. He even apologized to me later, because he should have asked me first, and I said to him no, no, not at all, it was, it was . . .'

'Fine?'

She looked at me with a rictus smile that clearly concealed a grimace. 'You're teasing me.'

I paused. 'You're right, I suppose I was. I wonder how that makes you feel?'

She looked away from me, then laughed nervously: 'Well, I'd better not say fine.'

I said it must be exhausting, always pressing down the lid on her anger.

She asked me what the alternative was: 'Punch him? Scream in his face, smash up all the crockery, hurl myself to the floor and beat it with my fists? Should I tell you to eff off for laughing at me and slam the door on my way out?'

Perhaps, muses Seneca, we should paint anger as a woman, 'most frightful to behold':

> her eyes glowing with fire, her voice hissing, roaring, grating, and making worse sounds if worse there be, while she brandishes weapons in both hands, for she cares not to protect herself, gloomy, stained with blood, covered with scars and livid with her own blows, reeling like a maniac, wrapped in a thick cloud, dashing hither and thither, spreading desolation and panic, loathed by everyone and by herself above all, willing, if otherwise she cannot hurt her foe, to overthrow alike earth, sea, and heaven, harmful and hateful at the same time.

In this view, merely to feel angry is to launch oneself on the path towards the most extravagantly excessive violence. The figure of Anger is stained with the blood she spills, as though an angry look, a furious shout is not the prelude to a blow of the sword but the very blow itself. It was a version of this woman, less lurid in appearance but no less harmful or hateful, whom Olive seemed to see reflected in the face or voice of the other the moment she felt herself betraying the smallest stirring of anger.

Perhaps in no thinker other than Seneca is anger so tightly coupled with aggression. But in his view, anger is very much the worse of the pair, the emotional fuel that infuses aggression with gratuitous cruelty, sadistic pleasure and florid rage. This is the inverse of a contemporary perspective like Antonio Damasio's, for whom anger is an evolutionary and developmental achievement, a movement from behavioural reflex to feeling experience.

Senecan anger is a fall into unbound violence, extinguishing all measure and every boundary, and ultimately reason itself. And yet very near the beginning of *De Ira*, he concedes that anger is an emotion that can be ascribed to human beings alone, 'for, while anger is the foe of reason, it nevertheless does not arise in any place where reason cannot dwell'.

The problem is that Seneca fails to extract the proper insight from this concession, namely that anger is less the other of reason than a possibility within it. Anger, as we've seen, can certainly be marshalled by individuals and groups as a support for violence and aggression. But it is also distinct from them; as a psychic rather than an external entity, it represents the possibility of feeling rather than acting. If it can impel the movement of aggression, it can also slow, halt, reverse or divert it.

Olive, it seemed to me, had come to psychotherapy in part because she was struggling with the Senecan relationship she had long ago forged with her anger. She had learned to see her anger as sign and seal of her own hatefulness, to fear it as the incubator of a destructiveness that would damage others and undo herself if she released it into the world. As she spoke aloud those violent scenes of punching her husband and slamming the door on me, she entered into a feeling of intimacy with her anger that was very different from acting on it, an imaginative rather than action-oriented way of working through it. This is the possibility Seneca must deny if he's to sustain his view of anger as a kind of psychopathic handmaiden to excessive cruelty.

One of the paradoxes of *De Ira* is that while it treats feeling as near identical with action, its rendition of anger is so emotionally vivid, conveying a profound immersion in its psychic and bodily reality. It reads not merely as a treatise on anger but as a report from the inside of it, its descriptive rhetoric brimming with the violence it wants to impugn. Seneca arrives at the imperative to suppress our anger by taking us through its most thrilling and dangerous hinterlands.

The anger Seneca enjoins his readers to suppress is explicitly the privilege of Rome's ruling classes. It is exclusively to the rage of the slave owners, judges and governors that he addresses himself, as though the fury of slaves, women and ordinary citizens was too insignificant to warrant recognition or acknowledgement. It is precisely because the high-born man's anger is endowed with objective weight and force that he must renounce it – not to place himself on an equal footing with his inferiors, but to remain worthy of the dignity endowed by his birth.

Reading Hochschild's study of (mostly female) flight attendants alongside Seneca, we see just how firmly this hierarchy of entitlement remains in place, even as the division of emotional labour is reversed. 'The lower the status,' she writes, 'the less acceptable is the expression of open anger.' The attendants are required to receive the rudeness and aggression of passengers with a smiling equanimity that belies the frustration and outrage stirring invisibly within.

Answers to the question of what they want to do when they get angry include 'Cuss. Want to hit a passenger. Yell in a bucket. Cry. Eat.' The sequence of actions turns the attendants' aggression increasingly from the offender to themselves. 'If you think about the *other* person,' their instructor tells them, 'and why they're so upset, you've taken attention off yourself and your own frustration. And you won't feel so angry.'

The ultimate aim of emotional labour is the effacement of the feeling self, such that anger is not only unexpressed but imperceptible to its object, in a collective implementation of the Senecan trick: 'Let us replace all its [anger's] symptoms by their opposites.'

Corporate customer service is founded on this demanding work of emotional disguise, in which feeling is exchanged for wages.

The exhibition of the wrong feelings is liable today to get you deprived of welfare benefits as well as fired from your job. In 2014, notes William Davies, the UK government made attendance at cognitive behavioural therapy (CBT) sessions mandatory for some claimants of disability benefits, part of a broader push to instil a positive attitude among the non-working, especially those debilitated by depression.

As popular anger over corruption, incompetence and unfairness grows, the political and business classes have a vested interest in uncoupling that anger from aggression, ensuring it doesn't mutate into social unrest or labour militancy. But the importation of positive thinking into corporate and governmental culture is about more than preventing disruption; it seeks increasingly to cut us off from any live contact with our anger, to render it an internal enemy, an unwanted trespasser on our emotional turf. The injunction to 'GET RID OF NEGATIVE PEOPLE IN YOUR LIFE' includes you above all. If you repeatedly fail to observe it, your employer and your state are liable to get very angry with you indeed.

As a solution to the problem of anger, forced positivity does little to address an obvious difficulty: what are we to do with our anger if not express it directly? If we are under perpetual pressure to conceal ill feelings, is there some way they could sneak out under the radar?

We are fortunate that human ingenuity has devised a surprisingly effective means for at once concealing and communicating anger, popularly known as passive aggression. Like chronic overwork or narcissistic display, passive aggression seems at some unspecified point to have become a defining symptom of our time.

Passive aggression is the surreptitious, indirect and often insidious mode in which we express antagonism or noncompliance while ensuring the plausible deniability of any such intentions. It is a key currency of both domestic life and the workplace. If it is especially effective at work, it is because passive aggression, as the code of workplace communication, has become a kind of protected behaviour. More often than not, relationships between work colleagues are suspended in a peculiar grey zone between familiarity and strangeness that breeds anxious uncertainty around the boundaries of communication. Odd remarks, too friendly, too abrupt or too coded, break through a baseline tone of cagey, withheld politeness. In an atmosphere that tacitly discourages straightforwardness, passive aggression thrives, ever present yet unremarked. To call out passive aggression directly would be a violation of the passive–aggressive code.

Our intimate relationships tend not to enjoy such protection. Over the years, couples and families and close friends accrue a rich store of unconscious knowledge of one another's coded languages and stratagems, which makes them harder to get away with. A silence or pause, a forced smile or a stiff 'thank you', words and gestures that to an outsider might seem entirely innocuous or devoid of any meaning, are loaded with significance for those in physical and emotional proximity.

Living under an effective prohibition on the explicit expression of anger, Olive inevitably found herself having regular if unconscious recourse to passive aggression. Recall her abrupt freeze when her husband told her about the following evening's dinner guests. Jeff reflexively asked what was up with her because he caught sight of the fleeting, involuntary grimace that had preceded the freeze.

Olive's panic was in response to the sensation of being seen and found out. Jeff knew she was angry, and she knew he knew it, and it was this mutual knowledge that must now be urgently denied. Teeth gritted and lips stiffened, the tight smile she had given him, sealing the denial, was likely the same smile she had given me when I'd 'teased' her.

The smile recalls the insights, developed across the 1930s and 1940s, of the famous (and eventually notorious) Berlin psycho-analyst Wilhelm Reich, who saw such gestures as an expression of what he called 'character armour', a kind of marshalling of the body's musculature in the service of a defensive blockade against feeling.

Olive had recoiled in fright at the prospect of her anger being seen and felt. The function of character armour is to shield what Reich calls 'the affective personality' or feeling self. 'The ego,' writes Reich, 'the exposed part of the personality, under the continued influence of the conflict between libidinal need and threatening outer world, acquires a certain rigidity, a chronic, automatically functioning mode of reaction, that which is called "character".'

Character armour is a resonant concept for our age of enforced positivity. It is a kind of systematic restriction of our internal freedom, setting impassable barriers at the entrances to all difficult feelings. In a single moment, Olive caught her anger and confined it behind the bars of her tight smile, from where it wouldn't be allowed to escape; before it could become active, she ensured her aggression was rendered passive.

As a feature of modern everyday interaction at work, in cafes and shops, on the roads, passive aggression has become the stuff of comedy, of arch lifestyle articles and social media memes. But in more intimate settings, its effect is corrosive. When Olive sensed me teasing her, she revealed many months after the event, it put her right back in her parental home, where her distress was always the occasion for a joke or a sigh of exasperation.

Unable to take responsibility for the resentment they felt towards their daughter for not being their son, Olive's parents concealed their rage in the guise of teasing. The effect on Olive was what we would today call gaslighting in particularly virulent and insidious form, her parents perpetually hinting that what she felt unmistakably as hatred was just affectionate fun, if only she could bring herself to join in.

The reason intimate forms of passive aggression are so damaging is that they are so frequently unconscious. Olive's parents were very far away from conscious awareness of the contempt they showed their daughter, just as she in turn knew almost nothing of the unsettling power of those smiling denials.

As her phobia of her own anger gradually decreased, Olive began to observe the ways in which her parents' style of relating had seeped into her own marriage. While Jeff never mocked her, he would repeat the same pattern of pleading innocence the moment he upset her, insisting always that he'd not *intended* to upset her. The last-minute dinner guests were a prime instance, an unwanted surprise infused with an aggression Jeff immediately disavowed.

Olive, of course, had been all too willing to join this dance, freezing in the face of his pleas of innocence, remaining quiet, fixing her smile and repeating that it was absolutely *fine*, the more insistently the more evidently it really wasn't.

The back and forth of denials and disavowals in such stand-offs are self-perpetuating. The two were equally invested in *not* being the one who'd provoked the other, nor the one who'd reacted angrily. And so it went on: You're angry! Me?! As far as I can see, you're the one getting angry!

The twisted logic of passive aggression is that it confers power not on the expression but on the concealment of anger. It is one of the most effective forms of character armour, of shielding the vulnerability of the 'affective personality'. If you know I'm angry, it implies, I'm left dangerously undefended.

The obvious value of passive-aggressive communication is that it enables the expression of anger and aggression without the attendant risk. This may be why it is so congenial to the workplace, whose accepted codes of interaction allow passive aggression to flourish. We must assume not only an attitude of politeness and cooperation, but of good faith.

We cannot accuse our colleagues of nefarious or insidious motives, however much we might suspect them. Hence the colleague reliably generous with such 'compliments' as 'your presentation was surprisingly good'; the boss who wonders at 5.30 if their employee 'might like to stay a little late this evening' for the call with Australia.

This is provoking or obstructive behaviour at once performed *and* disavowed, so that the offender can assure you that whatever you may now feel, that certainly wasn't what they meant. Whatever they have said or done to upset you, they did so with no conscious awareness or intent, leaving you to feel that you're the one with the problem.

This strategy provides the perfect cover for myriad behaviours: procrastination or forgetfulness, often with knowingly sabotaging effect, accompanied by excuses that border on accusation ('You didn't say it was *really* urgent'); antipathy that is skilfully projected onto its object by way of doublespeak ('I'm sorry if you took exception to what I said'); as well as a constant yet barely perceptible attitude of sullen resentment, easily recast as 'just how I am'. A workplace often sounds like the dissonant metallic clash of competing character armours.

The issue of workplace aggression was thrust vividly into relief in April 2023, when Dominic Raab, the UK's former Deputy Prime Minister resigned after the publication of an independent report upholding two of the complaints of former civil servants that he had behaved intimidatingly and aggressively towards them.

But his resignation statement, conventionally an expression of contrition and regret, was itself aggressive. No sooner had he resigned than he launched a media offensive in which he attacked putative flaws in the inquiry and conjured up a sinister backstory to his departure: 'What you've got,' he told the BBC, 'is the risk here of a very small minority of very activist civil servants, with a passive-aggressive culture of the civil service, who don't like some of the reforms, whether it's Brexit, whether it's parole reform, whether it's human rights reform, effectively trying to block government.'

The invocation of passive aggression is notable, firstly in the way Raab links it to a conspiratorial narrative of secret, unaccountable state operatives sabotaging the popular will, a theme by now very familiar from Trumpian broadsides against the so-called deep state. But it is notable also for its explicit politicization of the codes of workplace culture. Raab implies that he's been caught up in a game he can only lose, between his own frank, 'robust' and direct leadership style and the passive aggression of a cabal who retaliate quietly and invisibly, evading all accountability (and so, by implication, exacerbating his justified and considerable anger).

The problem with Raab's defence is that it relies on the conspiracist mode of thinking it claims to be repudiating. The manifest case he makes is for himself as a tireless and unapologetic warrior for the popular will. He might have stopped there, arguing that his electoral mandate trumps the sensitivities of civil servants. This, we might say, would be the argument for honest active aggression against sneaky passive aggression. But in a move unmistakably redolent of the Trump playbook, Raab's key message was that he's the victim here. He'd done nothing wrong, after all; on the contrary, he's the one wronged by the 'activist civil servants' intent on obstructing his agenda, an 'activism' the more insidious for its passivity. To add irony to paradox, in taking this line of defence, Raab falls into the classic 'Who, me?!' pose, the startled 'I didn't do anything' protest so characteristic of the passive aggressor.

Passive aggression is an exemplary illustration of the aggressive drive's essential flexibility and wiliness. If it can't find satisfaction through the direct route, it will find an indirect one through which it can assert itself more surreptitiously and so evade detection. Olive couldn't bring herself to tell Jeff she was angry, or even to acknowledge the fact to herself. But her unconscious devised a way of bypassing her conscious intent and giving disguised expression to her irritation.

André Green's 'passivation', describing the psychic and bodily state clinical psychoanalysis presses on the patient, is the capacity to give oneself over to the analytic situation, in which the patient typically lies on a couch under the gaze of the analyst sitting behind her. The patient enters a session without the support of an agenda, ready to follow and give voice to the unpredictable flows and diversions of her mind.

Having spent many years in analysis as part of my training, I know this experience from the inside. I see myself walking across the room to the analytic couch for the first time, staring at the ceiling and registering the atmosphere of silent expectation, feeling a sudden contraction of the muscles as though my body were seeking to withhold the openness I was now supposed to yield, to protect me from a total and painful self-exposure. In that moment, speaking felt like a risky surrender, as though I was under compulsion to give up my right to silence, to entrust the contents of my mind to a man I had no particular reason to trust.

I was surprised to feel a twinge of anger lurking under the surface of my anxiety, a kind of protest against the feeling of powerlessness aroused by my recumbent position, by the demand to speak, by the wish to shout at the analyst, 'What do you want from me?'

It's hard for me to imagine a more vivid experience of the uncoupling of anger from aggression. The analytic situation removes both patient and analyst from the external world in which they act and intervene, asking them to inhabit a purely psychic reality for the hour. It requires the patient to bear bad feelings instead of discharging them in action. Passive aggression is one way we can quietly refuse that requirement, a route to power over the other in the guise of saying or doing very little to them.

The capacity to bear our own feelings is an always incomplete achievement, forever being wrested from our resistance to it, from the impulse to deny and hold back one's own vulnerability. Psychoanalysis is just one of the many kinds of love relationship in which we might find ourselves at once surrendering to and refusing the care of another.

Anger, as we've seen, is perpetually frustrated or diverted from achieving its aims. Nowhere do we see this tendency more painfully borne out than in regard to the climate emergency. Why does the prospect of impending ecological collapse seem to engender so much frustrated impotence and relatively little effective anger?

Few writers in recent years have raised this question with more urgency and force than Andreas Malm in his 2021 book, *How to Blow Up a Pipeline*. Indeed, he pushes the question further, asking why it is that the climate justice movement remains so determinedly pacific in the face of ecological collapse. Confronted by the brazen daily violence of fossil capital, why are we squeamish of anything even resembling a commensurate response, like the various acts of ecotage he enjoins against SUVs, pipelines or any of the property and infrastructure accelerating planetary breakdown?

The problem this raises seems to me to have less to do with the ethical and strategic knots of violent against non-violent protest and more with the complex relationship between the feelings elicited by climate change and the action, and indeed inaction, it fuels. What, for so many of us and certainly for me, obstructs or obscures the passage from anger to effective action? Why is the anger we feel in the face of the climate emergency so often coloured by a sense of impotence or melancholy?

At the climax of his book, Malm describes what it feels like to have successfully traversed this passage from feeling to action. He had been a participant in an action by the German civil disobedience movement *Ende Gelände* against the *Schwarze Pumpe*, an enormous power station in the east running on lignite, or brown coal. Having blockaded the plant, the activists spontaneously resolved to break in. They pulled down the surrounding fences and roamed the area before being beaten back by the police.

The following morning, the energy corporation Vattenfall announced the suspension of electricity production to the fury not only of the CEO but of the climate-denying far-right party Alternative für Deutschland. Malm's climactic paragraph describing the feeling of this local victory is worth quoting in full:

But if destroying fences was an act of violence, it was violence of the sweetest kind. I was high for weeks afterwards. All the despair that climate breakdown generates on a daily basis was out of my system, if only temporarily; I had had an injection of collective empowerment. There is a famous line in *The Wretched of the Earth* where Frantz Fanon writes of violence as a 'cleansing force'. It frees the native 'from his despair and inaction; it makes him fearless and restores his self-respect.' Few processes produce as much despair as global heating. Imagine that, someday, the reservoirs of that emotion built up around the world – in the global South in particular – find their outlets. There has been a time for a Gandhian climate movement; perhaps there might come a time for a Fanonian one. The breaking of fences may one day be seen as a very minor misdemeanour indeed.

We are witness here to the transformation of anger from the iner-tial rage of despair into the effective rage of direct action. There is a distinctive utopian undertow to this passage, which derives from the sense of an ideal convergence of feeling and action, a disappearance without remainder of the one into the other, which he calls, after Fanon, 'a cleansing force'.

The passage is a telling crystallization of Malm's case for a vio-lent flank of the mainstream climate justice movement. Violence, on his account, raises lumpen, shapeless rage to a higher-level emotional state in which the self is purified of fear and self-doubt. The invocation of the Algerian psychiatrist and political theorist Fanon, of course, places us in a particular psychoanalytic territory, a kind of psychopathology of everyday rage and despair.

From Malm's Fanonian perspective, despair is an unbearable accretion of tension denied an outlet in the external world, and so forced to remain bottlenecked inside the tight confines of the mind and body. This tension is a sign, from a psychoanalytic perspective, that the aggressive drive has been aroused – that is, the drive that seeks sovereignty over its external environment.

Malm celebrates an ecstatic release of those aggressive drive energies from the claustrophobic cell of despair. But enraged despair won't always be redeemed in this way, as Freud saw very early on. Let us recall once more the failed rage of the beaten employee and those spontaneous hysterical attacks in which he falls into frenzies of silent fury.

Under hypnosis, he reveals that he's been 'living through the scene in which his employer had abused him in the street and hit him with a stick' and then, a few days later, he tells of a second attack, during which he mimes the event that had triggered his illness: 'the scene in the law-court when he failed to obtain satisfaction for his maltreatment'.

The case strikes me as at once anachronistic (hysterical attacks, bosses taking sticks to their employees in public) and replete with contemporary resonance. It captures something of the strangulated fury and voicelessness so many of us feel in the face of the continued and brazen corporate and state destruction of the earth.

It is also a kind of mirror image to Malm's self-portrait in a state of triumphal release. Instead of the bent posture of despair flowering into the upright alertness of effective action, the beaten employee is as though sunk in the mire of his humiliation, a feeling which only redoubles when he tries to find redress for it.

To use a well-known phrase from Freud's theory of the drives, Malm describes a *soldering* of rage to violence, which induces a bodily sensation and emotional conviction of knowing just what he's doing, a sharpened sense of clarity and righteousness. The hysterical pantomime of Freud's failed seeker after justice, on the other hand, depicts the radical uncoupling of anger from aggression. This uncoupling deprives us of an immediate outlet for aggressive action, leaving us with an enervating pressure on our nervous system, an anger stranded with no place to go.

How do we understand this pressure in the context of the climate emergency? The question sends us back once more to Malm's book, more specifically to his account of the historical lineage of the climate justice movement: the struggles against slavery, colonialism and apartheid and for women's suffrage and Black civil rights.

Each of these struggles has undoubtedly aroused profound anger and despair towards overwhelmingly oppressive avatars of power, whether imperialist nations, legal and economic systems, terrorizing mobs or the police and judiciary. And each has at some point had recourse to methods of violent resistance, to those figurative or literal explosions of 'cleansing' violence that redeem the despair of the oppressed.

Malm sees climate justice as fully continuous with these earlier movements, and underplays, even disparages, any arguments for a basic discontinuity with them. Fossil fuel capital, in his view, is a purveyor of structural injustice on much the same lines as a colonial occupation or a racist legal system. The despair and anger it provokes need to be harnessed and discharged in aggressive action against its physical locations in much the same way that, say, Nelson Mandela (as head of the ANC's armed wing MK, or Spear of the Nation) coordinated attacks on apartheid South Africa's military, energy, communications and transport infrastructure.

So why should we argue that the climate emergency is any different? Perhaps, on the contrary, the universality and critical urgency of the threat it presents only amplify the call for a commensurate anger to be realized in appropriately forceful action. Why should climate action be deprived of the tools of resistance previously employed against race- or gender-based oppression?

The question returns us to Sloterdijk's *Rage and Time*, and his case for the *thymos* or rage of Greek philosophy and poetry as a kind of primary energy, 'undeducible, like the storm and the sunlight'. Rage, he posits, has been an elemental force in the unfolding and shaping of human experience.

Viewed through the lens of *thymos*, the history of modernity is the history of the ongoing struggle to produce and preserve rage as a motor of revolution and resistance. More than any other collective mood, rage is cultivated by political movements as 'an ongoing project', 'a treasure trove for its possessor'. To harness and direct popular rage is to subject it to a transformation in form and shape: 'Rage undergoes a metamorphosis from a blind form of expenditure in the here and now to a far-sighted, world-historical project of revolution for those who have been humiliated and offended.'

There is more than a hint of Malm's Fanonian transition from the bent humiliation of despair to the upright empowerment of self-respect here. 'All history,' writes Sloterdijk, in his signature tone of playful provocateur, 'is the history of rage applications', or what we might more commonly know as wars and revolutions.

Revolutionary action is that optimal moment when affect and drive, or feeling and action, unfold in perfect harmony, such that feeling fuels action in the exact degree that action realizes feeling. For this to occur, dispersed local currents of anger must be 'banked', deposited in a single 'bank of rage' that 'draws its force from an excess of energy that longs for release'.

The bank of rage holds the accounts of a mass of beaten employees, concentrating in one place all the injuries and humiliations of generations of the oppressed, which are thereby transformed into 'an active mass of value and energy'. Is this not the mass of value and energy being channelled by Malm in his climactic self-description? Does he not evoke the same liberation of stored rage in a single, cathartic instance?

Sloterdijk contrasts this concerted gathering and release, in which rage and action are seamlessly coupled, with a contemporary condition in which rage is instead chronically dispersed, 'a state of organized weakness' lacking any unifying idea. Referring to the Parisian *banlieue* riots of 2005, he observes that 'none of the political parties could, nor wanted, to offer itself as gatherer or transformer of the emergent dirty energies'.

Sloterdijk here casts into relief the anomalous quality of Malm's moment of redemptive exhilaration, in which he presents himself as a kind of 'gatherer', concentrating the energies of a collective actor in his own person by means of action against a discrete target, the *Schwarze Pumpe*, which becomes the synecdoche of fossil capital, which itself is a synecdoche of ecological destruction.

I'm aware that I'm placing what may seem an unfair burden of significance on this paragraph of Malm's. I'm doing so because it crystallizes for me the crucial question of what style of protest the climate emergency calls for. Malm's subjectivity of protest employs a distinctly Romantic language of inspiration and self-affirmation, of the collective breathing through every individual. This kind of subjectivity implies a perfect harmony of affect and aim, of rageful feeling and aggressive action. But I'm doubtful this attitude accords with the experience of most of us confronting the climate emergency. Currents of anger and despair no doubt course through us all, but there is no single party or 'bank' in which to deposit them.

For many of us, our protests and actions, like our efforts to change daily behaviours, are scattered, confused, anxious, inconsistent. The gnawing awareness that we're not doing enough is conditioned by our sense of the sheer magnitude of what must be done. Anger is best placed to realize itself in effective action when it can drive itself in a purpose-built vehicle towards its object.

The historical struggles against slavery, colonialism and apartheid, for women's suffrage and civil rights, for all the unimaginable scale of the oppressive forces confronting them, were each bounded by localized historical situations, geographical territories and determinate aims: for slavery to end, for women to obtain the vote, and so on.

The aim of the climate justice movement, to keep global

heating to the lowest level possible, requires the intricate coordination of multiple aims, implicating the global population in action both with and against nation states; international scientific and political organisations; agricultural, transport and energy corporations; and financial institutions. Once again, we are describing not so much an object as what Timothy Morton calls a hyperobject, an entity on such a colossal and intricate scale it resists all mapping or apprehension.

If climate anger has an object, in other words, it is sublimely diffuse, scattered everywhere and nowhere. Even if we reduce that object to the single component of fossil capital, we are still talking about a fiendishly complex network of forces traversing physical, financial and political modes of despoliation, exploitation and corruption, forces which implicate all of us, especially in the global North, even as we protest against them.

And as George Monbiot and many others have noted, fossil capital is far from being the sole driver of planetary systems collapse. Food production alone, Monbiot has pointed out, would on current models 'bust the entire carbon budget two or three times over, if we want to avoid more than 1.5°C of global heating'. This is to say nothing of the 'soil degradation, freshwater depletion, ocean dysbiosis, habitat destruction, pesticides and other synthetic chemicals'.

The labyrinthine complexity and hydra-headed persistence of the forces driving the climate emergency are liable to arouse a mirroring form of rage – a rage many of us feel as insupportable – that struggles to find adequate representation in any given protest or action. Under such conditions, anger can become melancholic, mired in its own impotent despair.

What can psychoanalysis tell us about this melancholic despair?

The concept of the drive casts us as creatures destined to

dissatisfaction. The drive sets in train a quest for a fulfilment that is never fully achieved. 'Something in the nature of the sexual drive itself,' writes Freud, 'is unfavourable to the realization of complete satisfaction', and no doubt the same is true of its counterpart, the aggressive drive.

As we've seen, anger is what we feel at the moment satisfaction fails us. Winnicott, we recall, suggests that in the first months of life, a mother nurtures her baby's illusion of omnipotent control over the world. Ill equipped to receive and process the news of her helplessness, dependency and separateness, the baby cooks up a scheme to deny it and tell herself an entirely different story composed of alternative facts. And because this baby's aversion to reality persists in us, as adults we continue to find ways to remake the reality around us.

We may not do this in the gross form of active denialism, conspiracy theorizing and wilfully excessive levels of carbon consumption. But many of us do so in more surreptitious ways: postponing both the individual modifications necessary to reduce carbon consumption and active involvement in the collective movement for climate justice.

Because carbon consumption is woven so intricately into the fabric of our daily lives, in the ways we eat and heat and move and enjoy ourselves, we – like Winnicott's baby – excise and overwrite the bad news of our interdependency with the systems whose breakdown we're helping to accelerate.

It could be said that in the historical struggles that preceded climate change there were unambiguously just victories over unambiguously unjust ruling powers. In the struggle for climate justice, it is difficult to set two sides apart so cleanly. We can distinguish the state and corporate drivers of global heating from the rest of us, but as soon as we look closely at the issue, we become aware that those entities draw the rest of us into the same destructive political, economic and cultural circuits. Our rage at the inertia, cynicism and venality of politics and business is at once intensified and deadened by the ways the political and business classes implicate us in crimes against ourselves as well as everyone and everything else.

Another, simpler way of putting this is that no one, not even the corporate leaders of Shell, BP, Aramco and the rest, will benefit from the heating of the planet. None of us is shielded from responsibility for the emergency, nor from its calamitous effects. This strikes me as another way Malm simplifies the subjectivity of climate protest and action. At one point in *How to Blow Up a Pipeline*, he disparages an XR banner from a London street protest reading 'Police, we love you – it's for your children too' as an expression of misplaced obsequiousness ignoring the role of the police in the brutal suppression of climate activism. The point of the banner, at least as I read it, is not to greenwash the police but to remind the police that they will die with the rest of us, that the climate emergency, unlike apartheid or sexism, benefits no one. As global heating hits two and then four degrees and beyond, even the oil companies and their executives, having inexorably killed off their customer base, will die off soon enough.

None of this is to ignore the profound inequities between North and South, or between rich and poor, everywhere in the distribution of the malign effects of climate change. But as temperatures rise, the wealthy will be consigned to what we might call worldless lives, artificial bubbles of precarious survival at best. There is no meaningful incentive, even of the most callously self-interested kind, to keep heating the world.

'Cui bono, who benefits?' Ernst Toller, the pastor at the centre of Paul Schrader's 2017 film *First Reformed*, puts the question to his diary following his exchanges with anguished climate activist

Michael Mensana (this surname, 'healthy mind', of a broken melancholic readying himself for suicidal violence, is one of the film's many deliberate ambiguities).

Toller meets with Mensana at the request of the latter's wife Mary, who is twenty weeks pregnant. Michael is an anti-natalist who's urged her to terminate, telling Toller he can't justify bringing a new life into an unliveable world. Toller ends up a little like the pastor in Freud's famous joke, who is called on by the village atheist, an insurance broker, for a deathbed visit. At the end of a long night, the broker remains an atheist, but the pastor is fully insured.

In Schrader's mirthless rewriting of this joke, it isn't insurance that's bequeathed by the man on the verge of death, because the coming crisis invalidates all policies. Instead, Mensana passes on to Toller an interminable legacy of despair, the same despair he's sought to fend off for many years through drink and an increasingly threadbare theological conviction. The physical manifestation of this despair is Mensana's suicide vest, which Mary finds in his shed and hands over to Toller to dispose of.

In Malm's vision, the subjectivity of resistance converts a lumpen mass of internal despair into a live and conscious anger that fuels a fearlessly targeted violence against fossil infrastructure. Mensana's despair, on the other hand, is not transformed into a different emotion but instead intensifies to the point where it shades imperceptibly into impotent rage. When that rage is discharged as anger, it has none of the carefully calibrated harmony Malm envisions between emotion and action. Rage dispossesses him to the point where it authorizes a kind of unbound violence whose first target is the self, in which the join between righteousness and nihilism has dissolved.

Toller meets Mensana in a state of aggravated melancholia arising from the loss of his son, an army chaplain, in Iraq. A former

chaplain himself, like his father before him, Toller bears the terrible guilt of having encouraged his son to join up, overriding the
explicit objections of his wife, and so, in his own mind, sending
him to his death in a meaningless war.

So when Toller, having received a text from Mensana to meet
him in a local park, arrives there to find him dead in the snow,
his head blown through by his own rifle, he is all too ready to
receive the younger man's legacy of violent despair. Even before
her pregnancy, Mary tells Toller after Mensana's suicide, 'He was
just so full of anger', unaware as she says this that she's speaking
to a man similarly ravaged by his own rage.

As the new recipient of Mensana's suicidally rageful legacy,
Toller, writing to his diary in the dead of night, asks the question,
'Cui bono, who benefits?' The phrase belongs to Lucius Cassius, a
Roman politician of the second century, praised by Cicero as the
most honest and wisest of judges, who would never fail to ask the
question when adjudicating lawsuits. The question places crime
in an ideally rational perspective, assuming not only an unbro-
ken line from motive to action, but a proportionate fit between
them. If I can obtain a benefit by killing one person, there is no
need to kill ten.

Toller's question concerns the various natural sites in the region
turned into toxic waste dumps courtesy of Edward Balq, a local
tycoon and stationery manufacturer, whose factory was the likely
target of Michael's suicide mission. The desperate exchange between Toller and Michael and the discovery of the suicide vest
drive the film into the generic territory of the race against time
thriller. But the pace and composition belie this urgency, as the
film unfolds in cold, static long shots, as though infected by the
same melancholy as its characters. Every face, every room, every
landscape is rendered with a kind of irremediable, elegiac sorrow.

When Schrader's camera (the film is beautifully photographed by Alexander Dynan) lingers in eerie stillness on Handstown Kills, the lake site poisoned and ravaged by Balq's industries, where rusting metal, plastic and chemical waste bleed into the waters, the image conveys depths of irreparable natural and psychic damage that seem to make a mockery of any response.

A strange sequence towards the end pulls the film abruptly into hallucinatory anti-naturalism. Mary visits Toller and asks him to re-enact an intimate ritual she would perform with her dead husband: she would lie on top of him, both fully clothed, pressing into each other for maximal bodily contact and facial proximity.

In doing the same with Toller, Mary completes the unsettling identification of the two men. The pair levitate and are suddenly launched into the cosmos, which resolves into a series of kitschily beautiful tropical landscapes, which themselves morph into tableaux of ecological horror, most memorably an unending field of scorched rubber tyres. As he floats over these ruins, Toller's face is contorted with an anguish that completes his full absorption into Michael's legacy of violent despair.

It's following this scene that Toller hatches his scheme to detonate Michael's suicide vest at the 250th anniversary celebration of the First Reformed church, financed by Balq, when it will overflow with local people. Ordinary citizens will die alongside Balq, as though the climate crisis has fatally eroded the distinction between the innocent and the guilty, so that action too cannot differentiate between divine justice and a crime against humanity. Along with the church and its occupants, the vest explodes Toller's 'cui bono?', the question that seeks to cut an exact pathway to the guilty as though with an Ockham's razor of justice. The bomb answers the razor's precise justice with the chaotic rage that lays waste to justice.

Before she moves away from Snowbridge, Mary promises to return for the anniversary. Toller implores her to stay away, but just after he's buttoned up the vest and concealed it under his cassock, and before entering the church, he spots her arriving. In horrified panic, he removes the vest and replaces it with a long string of barbed wire, which he wraps tightly around his torso, an act of self-mortification excruciating to watch. Placing his cassock over his bleeding trunk, he pours a glass of Drano drain cleaner, which he's lifting to his lips when Mary enters the room. The glass falls out his hand and they run to each other and kiss hungrily, ecstatically, the camera circling around them vertiginously before very abruptly cutting to black.

One could almost overdose on the allegorical significance: Toller runs to Mary, the divine mother and carnal lover. Their wild embrace redirects all the energies of rageful despair into an omnivorous love, as earthly as it is spiritual. Instead of being entirely discharged in violent aggression, rage realizes itself in erotic surrender.

Among the easily missed quiet exchanges in *First Reformed* is a moment soon after Michael's suicide, in which Toller asks Mary how she felt about her husband's activism. 'I share his views,' she says, with an almost offhanded nod. But those 'views' aren't identical with the ways he or she might choose to act on them in the world.

Michael renounces love in the name of a formless and infinite rage he transmits to Toller with his suicide. Only at the moment Toller's rage is about to realize itself in an act of indiscriminate violence does Mary enter the scene to offer it an alternative itinerary, an immediate and miraculous redirection into boundless love. I'm not sure this climactic delirium is anything as straightforward or sentimental as a conversion from rage to love. It seems to me something more like a strange combustion of rage in love, which keeps both feelings fully alive.

Perhaps this ending affects me so powerfully because it brings to the surface what I know without knowing it. If I'm not as angry as I 'should' be about the climate emergency, it's because somewhere I've intuited how insupportable my anger and grief might be if I gave myself over to it fully, if I really let myself *know* about the precariousness of our own and our children's future.

Thus far, I've done more or less nothing about this, a poor state of affairs that I'm resolved to change, partly as a consequence of writing this book. But I have needed first to try to understand why I've done nothing, why when I try to give anything like imaginative shape to my rage it just doesn't feel like the apt, cleansing action that restores self-respect, but more like the dispossessing chaos and disorganization the infant feels when she intuits the existence of a world beyond her control.

Chapter Three

Cynical Rage: Demagogues, Charlatans, Emotional Predators

Gerard, the day's first patient, is readying himself on the couch. I look over, notice the knotting of his brow, the squeeze of his lowered eyelids, and feel the air between us thicken.

Gerard is beset by physical and emotional afflictions that stick to each other like a co-dependent couple. Crippling headaches and insomnia merge inexorably with his fear of being consigned to permanent, irremediable loneliness. He frequently discharges this double malaise in breathless monologues, fraught with panic and rage.

Gerard begins today by telling me it's just not working with Amanda, the woman he's been seeing for the last couple of months. He's tried to tell her what it's like, carrying these pounding headaches through the working day, practically hallucinating after another sleepless night, but she doesn't really get it. Barely two months and she's fed up, and who can blame her? He goes on to rail against the dating apps he's forced to use, and their steady drip-feed of misinformation – out-of-date pictures, misleading self-descriptions, sometimes outright lies. Whom does any of it benefit beyond the platforms themselves, venal parasites on human vulnerability?

I can feel his breath quicken as he inveighs against people's preference to present themselves as generic fictions online rather than as fleshly human beings in the real world, which leads him in turn to me, no doubt possessed of a lovely wife and adorable children, feeling sorry for him. Well, he doesn't need my pity, he won't be patronized; oh, and speaking of which, did I see Boris fucking Johnson's puffed-up speech in Parliament yesterday? How do the people of this country tolerate that hideous tone of entitled condescension? He wants to grab a tuft of that mussy blond hair and bang his forehead on the desk till his skull cracks.

Gerard rants with a force that seems to exceed the causes he names. As I listen, I have the thought that something is out of sequence. It's not that he thinks of the dating app or Johnson and is made furious, more that he's grabbing at irritants to make sense of a fury that's there from the moment he wakes up.

Freud observes a similar confusion about the sexual drive. When we fall in love, the powerful rush of tender and erotic feelings we experience fosters the belief in an intimate and direct relationship between the *drive* (that strange impulsion to love) and the *object* (the person we love). Hence the myth of the 'one true love'.

But this is an illusion. The variety, unpredictability and volatility of our loving feelings tell us that, on the contrary, 'the sexual drive and the sexual object are merely soldered together'. The drive is a desire desperately seeking the thing that will satisfy it. Occasionally it finds an object that makes it think, 'OK, perhaps this is what I'm looking for.'

This seems to me very much how Gerard's anger was behaving, a free-floating, diffuse force that powered through the world searching for the cause that would explain it, bring him the relief of saying *this* is why I'm so angry! But like a restless and fickle lover, no sooner would he identify one object of his rage than another came into view, then another, and another. Gerard's anger was wildly promiscuous.

If rage is so insatiable, how do any of us manage to keep it within bounds? How is it possible to live with a force that agitates us so powerfully so much of the time?

I've been arguing throughout this book that aggression is more primary than anger, that anger comes about only when we allow ourselves to feel our response to a provoking object rather than discharge those feelings in reflexive action.

But it doesn't always feel this way in real time. It can often seem as though anger, as it gathers momentum in us, impels us towards action, or what we commonly call aggression. In fact, in such cases we've tried to confine our anger to the psychic realm, to feel and think it rather than act it out, only for it to reach a pitch so overwhelming that we feel we can keep it in no longer; we simply *must* yell, punch, smash . . .

The capacity to stay with anger as a purely internal state is what prevents the rush into blind action. We lash out in hot verbal or physical aggression when we can no longer represent our anger to ourselves, when we can no longer bear the pressure it is exerting on our minds.

If, on the other hand, we can gain sufficient mental distance from our anger to be curious about it, to ask what it's about and how it might be relieved, then rather than being the midwife to aggression, anger can promote self-reflection and stay the automatic impulse to aggression. This isn't to say, of course, that anger can't or shouldn't lead to decisive action, perhaps even to aggression. But in self-reflective anger, action collaborates with the mind instead of overriding it.

A boy shouts at the best friend who, he suddenly realizes, has just swiped the chocolate bar from his lunchbox as his back was turned; the friend, still chewing the last of the bar, smiles mischievously, sheepishly apologizes and promises to buy him another. Because the source of the anger is immediately clear, and relief quickly follows, the loss inflicted is felt as minor and temporary.

But what if instead the entire lunchbox is grabbed from him daily by a bigger boy who menaces him with the prospect of untold tortures if he tells? Feeling bound to comply, the boy's anger is overridden by his fear. This is the bullied child's predicament: in his own mind at least, *he is forbidden to tell*, to voice his experience in the form of a story. Denied representation, his anger gradually becomes a mute, formless mass spreading through his interior, casting its shadow over his daily life. If this experience goes unaddressed for too long, the man the boy becomes is likely to struggle to bear his anger, to find a language which lends it shape and form.

When it can be spoken and heard, D. W. Winnicott suggests, anger contributes to our developmental health. A hungry baby's cry is a kind of primary anger, an assertion of a fundamental need. This, Winnicott says, is a positive, if very rudimentary statement of the infant's determination to live his way, to be led by his own needs rather than adapt to another's.

When a cry achieves its aim − for example, when the mother feeds her baby in response − it helps him learn what his anger is for. But a cry that is met by indefinite delay and neglect, that has no discernible effect on the adults hearing it, has the opposite effect. 'The individual,' says Winnicott with characteristic understatement, 'is left with some confusion about anger and its expression.'

This 'confusion' is akin to what is later experienced by the bullied child, an injury that has no means of being told or heard. The more unintelligible his experience, the more his anger diffuses and intensifies. Like the hungry baby, he is seeking ever more desperately for a satisfying response that doesn't arrive.

When I think of Gerard, I can't help seeing an eerie continuity with these two figures. His rants about his physical ailments or women or the horrors of digital life or the political class are arrows in search of a target. It's as though he's seeking the one antagonizing object that will finally satiate his rage and bring it to an end.

But none of them do, which might explain why sessions with him can feel like a punishing eternity, but also (and somehow at the same time) swallowed up in an instant. I often find myself wondering what he wants from me. Simply to provide a space into which he and his anger can expand? Perhaps that would explain the mental image that has at times assailed me during sessions: the room suddenly occupied by a monstrous grey inflatable, expanding so quickly that it raises me aloft and threatens to push me face up into the ceiling, the torrents of air squashing my nose against the plaster.

Faced with this feeling of inexorable suffocation, it's tempting to let myself be drawn into whatever personal or political or moral controversy he might be trying to provoke; to disagree perhaps, and so force him to recognize me as a separate person rather than an empty vessel for his ire. Or agree, and enjoy the solidarity of shared rage and frustration, affirming his conviction that the world is indeed cruel and stupid and infuriating. Yes, let's take turns banging Boris Johnson's head on the desk!

Why do neither of these approaches work? The most basic premise of clinical psychoanalysis, known as transference, is that the patient's responses to the analyst are repeating a much older pattern of relating. If the analyst isn't aware of this tendency, they are likely to perpetuate this repetition instead of resolving it.

For Gerard, the possibilities of agreement and disagreement

would immediately conjure up the spectre of his late father, a celebrated QC whose withering style of argument carried over reliably from court to home. Gerard's mother, herself regularly put down by her husband for the alleged crudity and illogic of her thinking, would laughingly recall to the older Gerard his father's exasperated correction of his grammar and syntax from the age of two. 'I tried to tell him that it was natural for a toddler to speak as you did, but he'd always insist you were never too young to learn!'

As Gerard got older, each new stage in the development of his speech and writing and thinking would be shadowed by his father's unsparing correction. Gerard's every idea or opinion would be mercilessly dissected for errors of expression and consistency, for inadequate evidence or political immaturity or lack of independence of mind. Gerard was alive to the irony of the last criticism. 'For GOD's sake,' his father would hiss at him, as the adolescent Gerard dejectedly argued his case against Thatcherite economics or for electoral reform, 'why not try to use your own MIND for once, instead of lifting some poorly digested phrases from the latest *Guardian* leader?'

But how could any son of such a father be expected to have a mind of his own? Gerard had dragged himself through school, university and a range of careers under a cloud of self-doubt and inhibition, intellectual, creative and social. Always anticipating the disdain of teachers, peers and colleagues, he would revert to a resentful silence. If he gave himself freedom to speak, his mind would only let him down; better to keep quiet.

Gerard came to identify with his father, taking over from him the unending task of putting himself down. But alongside this attitude of impatient contempt towards himself, he nursed a rage towards the world whose pleasures and ambitions he could never enjoy. He would scorn the world that scorned him. He couldn't trust himself to play or dream or love. He trusted only the weary hopelessness that powered his endless rants.

And his rage ensured that I was merely the latest in a series of characters who would confirm and amplify his father's dim view of him. My silence didn't fool him, he told me, he knew just what I was thinking, so why not say it? That he was a grown man having his pathetic daily toddler tantrum, unable to control himself or exercise the smallest power of reason.

Over the course of an analysis, the analyst will come to be experienced by the patient, sometimes consciously, more often not, as an avatar of key figures from earlier stages of their life: a parent at one moment, a teacher at another, a sibling, a friend, a lover, a colleague or a composite of two or more of these, the aforementioned transference.

Transference often arouses unruly intensities of feeling in the patient. The analyst is liable to become an object of love, hate, trust, mistrust, fear, comfort, reverence or contempt, often within a single session. But underlying all of these feelings is a profound sense of dependency, derived from the earliest period of life, when our very survival depended on the ministrations of our carers.

When Gerard lies down on the couch, he experiences me as possessed with a power to make him or break him with a few words. This awareness of his vulnerability to my judgement magnifies both his anxiety and his anger. How has he landed back in a room with his father?

And this alerts me in turn to the power with which the role of analyst endows me. Both characters in the analytic drama are alive to the patient's impulse to please and mollify the analyst, as well as the wish to sabotage and reject what they offer. I can feel in my bones both the deep relief that can be aroused in Gerard by my smallest affirmative hum, and the intense dismay felt when he hears me question or doubt him.

The basic scenario of psychoanalysis is fraught with power and all its attendant anxieties; a person brings the most vulnerable and hidden region of their psyche and places it in the care of the analyst, in the hope that this gesture of trust will not be abused or exploited.

But the anxiety implied in this hope can never be fully dispelled. How can I know the analyst is my ally? What if their show of benign curiosity and availability are subtly disguised forms of control and manipulation?

Framed in this way, the risks of the psychoanalytic relation bear a striking resemblance to the risks of the political relation. Machiavelli's core teaching in *The Prince*, that every ruler must be at peace with his people, reminds us that governance by autocrat and democrat alike is sustainable only on the basis of at least a minimal bond of trust. The autocrat must assure his subjects that their interests are best served by submitting to his absolute sovereignty. The democrat must persuade her citizens that their interests are best served by voting her into office.

In short, a citizen needs to see herself, her own aspirations and wishes, represented in her leader. The spreading crisis of social division today stems from the betrayal of this need. In liberal democracies across the world, it seems that close to half of the citizenry look at their political class and see in it no recognition of the reality of their own lives and hopes, a phenomenon that has oiled the wheels of the authoritarian demagogue's rise.

The longer and more completely rulers are perceived by the populace to be failing them, the greater the eventual risk of civil unrest. At such moments, the rulers can unleash the machinery of state power – the police, the courts, the secret services – against its angry citizens. But as Hannah Arendt reminds us, a ruling class's reliance on this threat of violence signifies weakness rather than strength, a breakdown of the basic contract that grounds political consent and an implicit admission that their governance is failing.

It's no accident that the metaphor of parenthood abounds in the discussion of analytic and political trust alike. There are many good reasons to find the metaphor objectionable in both contexts. Neither analytic patients nor political citizens want to be thought of as frustrated or angry children making demands of their harassed parents; both are more often mature individuals struggling with the social and personal responsibilities of adult life.

And yet the metaphor isn't entirely without value. When we petition or protest against the state, or approach an analyst for help, we are speaking out of our child as much as our adult selves. The adult, after all, has been primed by successive institutions, from family to school to workplace, to keep a lid on their frustrations in the name of compliance and self-preservation. The child is the force in us that refuses to do this, to sacrifice its own needs and wishes for those of the adults.

Perhaps this accounts for the global resonance of Greta Thunberg as an exemplary protestor of our time. Thunberg's anger disarms us because of its childlike directness and clarity, which she has ascribed to the autism she calls her 'superpower'. Youth and autism together ensure that her message is unadulterated by the hedges of a jaded 'realism'.

Thunberg's uncompromising impatience with the global political class alerts us to the uncomfortable truth that in the face of lethal planetary emergency, the adult stance of caution and 'reason' starts to look like the utmost madness, not to say childishness. So many of us have found in her grave outrage an uncannily accurate representation of our own feelings, as though she were revealing an intimate link between the child and political anger.

To insist on this link is not to characterize political anger as infantile. It is rather to suggest that to become meaningfully adult, we must retain contact with the child we were and remain. We become jaded and cynically indifferent at the point we silence the child in us, the voice that laments and revolts against the world's failure to hear our basic needs and deepest wishes. Thunberg unabashedly gives expression to both − the need for the species to survive, but also the wish for a future worth having.

The Italian psychoanalyst Massimo Recalcati suggests that the predicament of youth in our age of moral chaos, lawlessness and loss of meaning is not, as in the classical Oedipus complex, having to manage the desire to kill and replace the father. Instead, he suggests, younger generations are in the grip of a 'Telemachus complex'. Telemachus is the son of Odysseus, waiting on the island of Ithaca for the return of his father, twenty years absent from home.

In his father's absence, the Proci, menacing suitors of Penelope, have invaded and usurped the family home, rampaging through its halls, ransacking its food and raping the female servants. Telemachus must endure and hold off the attack while searching over the horizon for Odysseus to return and restore order and justice to the ravaged home.

Doesn't Recalcati capture precisely the nature of the anger animating Thunberg and her generation of climate protestors? Their demand is not murderous, not the expression of a drive to kill and usurp the older generation, but a desperate cry across the horizon to the parents who have gone quiet or missing while the planetary home has been violated and ransacked. The anger is directed toward not disposing of the parents but bringing them back to where they're most needed.

It is because of her unapologetic youth that we confer on Thunberg a licence to speak truths we feel too compromised to voice ourselves. She becomes a projection of the honesty and straightforwardness worn away in us by the shabby complicities of adulthood. She can express our sense of the wholesale betrayal of our political trust, and the demand it be regained by representing the most basic interest of humanity.

The protesting Telemachus of today doesn't so much refuse adult authority as demand that it become, and remain, worthy of its own status. Global public mistrust in the political class begins in the failure to listen to that demand.

Thunberg is such a potent embodiment of that mistrust because she tells a resonant story about it: in the face of an emergency that demands the unequivocal force of black-and-white thinking, she is endowed with an exemplarily black-and-white mind. Under her gaze, the politicians, pundits and lobbyists who obfuscate the urgency of global heating by raising doubts about the science or insisting on a 'balance' between environmental and economic concerns are exposed as a parade of naked emperors whose clothes the rest of us are pretending to see.

From this angle, Thunberg's years of hunger and school strikes look less like overblown adolescent rage than the proper reaction for anyone who perceives reality without the defensive filters of denial and complacency. Her anger is calibrated tightly to the scale of the outrage she is addressing.

Because anger follows the relentless logic of the drive, feeding off its own proliferating dissatisfactions, it is liable to have a numbing effect on its audience, as Gerard reminds me. Instead of a means to voice the specific sources of his unhappiness, anger had become Gerard's way of life, the air he breathed. From his first raging thought of the day to the arousal of the furies of his dreaming mind, his anger was frantically searching for, and failing to find, a form that would make it intelligible to himself and to everyone else.

'I want to give myself a rest from all this agitation,' he told me. 'Living in my head is hell, like playing an unending game of whack-a-mole.'

*

The role of a psychoanalyst is to help Gerard bring this hellish game to a stop. But what if the analyst chooses instead to use their privilege as the recipient of the patient's anger to manipulate and exploit it?

A particularly egregious version of this scenario played out in a thirty-year therapeutic relationship narrated by *The Shrink Next Door*, a hugely popular podcast of 2019 adapted for TV by Apple in 2021. The podcast was written and presented by journalist Joe Nocera, and begins in 2010, when Nocera and his wife were sent a formal invitation via the neighbour's handyman to tea at his neighbour's vacation home in the Hamptons.

The neighbour was Isaac 'Ike' Herschkopf, a New York psychiatrist evidently enamoured of high living and celebrity. The walls of his home were lined with rows of framed photographs showing Ike embracing Gwyneth Paltrow, Elton John, Henry Kissinger and O. J. Simpson alongside hundreds of other members of Hollywood, political and pop music royalty. Unimpeachably gracious hosts, Ike and his wife had the same handyman serve tea.

Only the following summer did Nocera discover that the handyman, Marty Markowitz, was in fact the house's owner – and Herschkopf's patient of thirty years. During the intervening year, Markowitz had ejected his long-term house guest and ended their intricately entangled therapeutic, social and financial relationship.

Nocera goes on to unfold a startling story of control and exploitation. At the time of his first consultation with Herschkopf in 1981, Markowitz had recently lost his parents, broken off an engagement and inherited ownership and control of their family business, a fabric supplier to theatres.

Overwhelmed by self-doubt and beset by familial rivalries over control of the inherited business, Markowitz was sent by his rabbi to the young psychiatrist, who ended the consultation proposing three times weekly psychotherapeutic sessions and assuring Markowitz he would (as Markowitz recalls it) 'take care of everything'. Over the three decades that followed, Herschkopf was as good as his word: he assumed near total control of Markowitz's personal and financial lives.

At Herschkopf's direction, Markowitz fired his sister from the company and severed relations with her, refusing all contact for twenty-seven years. He had Markowitz set up a charitable foundation to which he left his entire estate, with Herschkopf as sole executor of his will. Throughout the entire period, Markowitz was employed without pay as Herschkopf's effective personal assistant and house servant, including at the lavish, celebrity-studded annual summer parties Herschkopf hosted at the Hamptons house. Through all these extortive intrusions, Markowitz continued to pay outlandishly high fees for his sessions.

At least as disturbing as these brazen violations of the thera-peutic contract is the fact that Markowitz explicitly consented to them all. How could a psychotherapist effect such a radical and sustained surrender of a patient's personal autonomy?

The initial approach to a therapist activates a strange paradox. The adult patient makes a mature and reasoned decision to seek help for their suffering; but once they do so, the therapeutic situ-ation arouses feelings of intense dependency. The therapist has to receive and to bear this state of dependency. They cannot try to banish the patient's infantility and demand they grow up; but nor can they cynically enlist that dependency to their own advantage by assuring their patient that they'll 'take care of everything'.

Markowitz is clear on this point: the invitation to surrender mind and selfhood to his therapist was 'very comforting to [him]', an instantaneous provision of an ideal parent. Who could resist it? Like Faust, Herschkopf called up the occult powers of transference, conjuring into visibility the helpless infant ordinarily concealed in the adult's unconscious, and making it an instrument of his own self-interest.

But how did this surrender become so total for so long? It was only when Herschkopf failed to visit Markowitz in hospital following a hernia operation that the previously impregnable balloon of his idealization was popped, putting an end to his massive psychic investment in the fantasy of his therapist's curative benignity. It took a single thoughtlessly inflicted narcissistic injury to do what decades of cynical expropriation of mind and money could not.

The brazen and violent thefts and humiliations, it seems, could be integrated into a narrative of cure. And the longer they continued, the more Markowitz had to lose the moment he allowed the scales to fall. Herschkopf, one suspects, knew this and made it part of his bold gambit.

Herschkopf is the author of a number of self-help books, notably a self-published 2003 book on anger, *Hello Darkness, My Old Friend: Embracing Anger to Heal Your Life*, which may cast some intriguing if oblique light on his motives and methods. Its basic premise is that 'perceiving and appropriately expressing anger is healthy'. Herschkopf shows his readers how to maintain steadily controlled contact with their anger so as to ensure it serves their own interests and enhances good relationships. At the heart of this conception of anger management is a fantasy of full self-possession and mastery. Herschkopf's illustrative anecdotes, especially when they feature himself, are exemplars of the delicate tightrope walk between directness and control.

At a party, a friend's mother declares herself a member of an unnamed cult (likely Scientology) and tells Herschkopf, 'Psychiatrists are the lowest form of life. You're worse than a murderer.' Herschkopf feels outrage welling up in him, but his external response is to stand up and announce he's going to get some water. His friend praises his adroit handling of the situation.

However wild the horse of anger may be, Herschkopf is always confident of keeping it under his command. What, he asks, differentiates 'the healthy constructive expression of anger' from its 'unhealthy destructive expression'? Healthy anger, he answers, involves a focus on changing the future rather than ruminating on the past, and 'having a finite end point after which the anger ceases, rather than continuing interminably'.

But the spirit of the drive is precisely one of interminable continuation; as Freud reminds us, something in its nature doesn't admit of satisfaction. I'm reminded of this when I imagine the breathless seriality of the rows of celebrity selfies on the walls of the Hamptons house. Isn't this an expression of the drive's demand 'continuing interminably', forever seeking the elusive object that will bring its desire the resolution it craves? Someday, the wall seems to say, we'll display a photo here enviable enough to allow us finally to stop displaying photos.

The podcast reveals that both Herschkopf and Markowitz are children of Holocaust survivors. Herschkopf had written a column in a Jewish newspaper which described being beaten by his father. Markowitz grew up in an atmosphere of prohibition and silence around the trauma that conditioned his family's life. The experience of radical deprivation produced in one a raging hunger for recognition and compensation, in the other a sense of chronic insufficiency, where an abundance of material resources only amplified the bottomless lack of inner resources.

Herschkopf commends us to embrace anger as a fire that warms but used it as a fire that burns. He employed it to arouse the sleeping anger of his patient, who dutifully played out his repertory of resentments against his family, and to extract the vacation home and vast inheritance and glamorous celebrity friends, those fantasized debts that can never be settled.

It wasn't only Markowitz, we learn without surprise, that fell into the same relationship of deepest dependency with Herschkopf. Various patients disclosed their private injuries and vulnerabilities, which were enlisted by their therapist not in the service of self-understanding but for the aggrandizement of his own power. What made Herschkopf so dangerous was not that he didn't understand transference, but that he did. He had a confidence in its total power that might make any self-doubting, ordinarily neurotic analyst blush. This is what enabled him to capture his patient's minds and lives so completely.

Perhaps this drama of total control and submission can tell us a little about the major phenomenon of global politics of the last decade: the rise of the strongman leader. Just as Markowitz elected to consult Herschkopf and willingly participated in the latter's takeover of his rights and autonomy, so electorates in Russia, the US, Hungary, Brazil, Turkey, India and the Philippines chose leaders who explicitly promised to curtail freedoms and rights of dissent and normalize institutional discrimination against minorities. And, like Herschkopf, the leaders in question persuaded their subjects that these restrictions on their lives were in fact enlargements of them.

The strongman leader and the opportunistic psychotherapist employ the same method: identify the vulnerability of their subjects and pledge to protect it – from marauding migrants or envious family members, from a shady political elite or an assertive friend or lover – all the while exacerbating that vulnerability. The more insecure the citizen or patient feels in the face of these enemy forces, the more they will cleave to their idealized leader or therapist.

In his 1960 paper 'Aggressivity', the French psychoanalyst Daniel Lagache posited that a basic propensity to aggression drives human life and relationships. To live in a world of others is to be caught up in the knots of domination and submission.

The fundamental 'interhuman reality,' claims Lagache, is the conflict of each person's needs and desires (what he calls their narcissism) with everyone else's. We need only watch a toddler's meltdown when refused a favourite sweet, or two siblings fighting furiously over a plastic toy, to recognize the difficulty of tolerating the existence of demands or desires other than our own. At our narcissistic core, other people are just obstacles to us getting what we want, barriers in the way of our satisfaction, provocateurs of our aggression.

One key task of individual and social development is to tame that aggression by sending it underground, below the surface of consciousness, leaving it to bubble away and erupt to the surface in endless different guises, which may include criminality, violence and terror, greed, manipulation and exploitation, cruelty and humiliation – different ways of saying the same thing: I count, you don't.

It might seem as though this psychoanalytic picture of the human species, with its unmistakable echoes of Machiavelli and Hobbes, can only lead us to reactionary political conclusions: if liberty is only a spur to conflict, and equality and fraternity are naive delusions, surely the overriding political imperative is to maintain social order by whatever means necessary?

From the perspective of our primitive aggression, we are each surrounded by enemies, soldiers in Hobbes' 'war of all against all', uncompromisingly belligerent precisely because we are so helplessly vulnerable. The strongman intuits this paradox and exploits it. Having identified his angry, disenfranchised constituency, he names their enemies – the metropolitan elite, the deep state, the woke warriors and snowflakes – and promises their victimhood will soon be transformed into triumph.

'Embracing Anger to Heal Your Life' runs the subtitle to Herschkopf's book, a nice formulation for a strongman of the psyche. Herschkopf worked on his patient with the same manipulative skill that Trump roused his base, arousing and stoking Markowitz's anger by touching the sore spot of his anxieties and insecurities. The rage that was meant to repair the cracks in his self and relationships only widened and deepened them. Ordinary family disputes took on the dimensions of an epic battle for survival that could be won only by extreme measures – cutting off relations with his family; handing over his finances, his home and his very selfhood to his therapist.

Markowitz's ordinary frustrations with family and colleagues were harnessed by Herschkopf as an energy he commandeered to place the patient entirely in his power. But his astonishing political trick, so redolent of the authoritarian leader, was to pass off this total domination as Markowitz's personal liberation.

This demagogic manipulation of anger is often referred to as a form of cynicism. But how has cynicism become a byword for the calculated exploitation of others' vulnerability and credulity? In its first, philosophical forms, Cynicism meant something very different, almost the inverse of the sense we now give it. The first Cynic philosophers and our own cynical politicians see the human being as haunted by the same frailties. But they come to very different conclusions as to what to do about this problem.

Born around 410 BC in the Black Sea town of Sinope, Diogenes was the first proponent of Cynic (derived from *cyn*, the Greek word for dog) philosophy. As none of his writings survive, we learn of his teachings largely by way of reportage from later historians, and above all from Diogenes Laërtius' *Lives of the Eminent Philosophers*, written around six centuries later.

Much of Diogenes' teaching is distilled in the form of anecdotage; as the enemy of all propriety and conformity, he led a life of radical self-sufficiency, minimizing his needs for food, clothing and shelter, begging without shame when he needed to, respecting no hierarchies and bowing to no authority above him. The most famous vignette has him visited by a fascinated Alexander the Great, who asks him if there is anything he could do for him. In Plutarch's version of the story, Diogenes grunts, 'Yes, shift a bit out of my sun.'

Diogenes Laërtius writes that when asked why he would call himself a dog (*cyn*), he replied: 'I fawn on people who give me alms, I bark at them if they refuse me, and I snap at scoundrels.' As a dog snapping at scoundrels, Diogenes is the model for speaking truth to power. Defecating and masturbating in public on the example of his canine inspiration, he is free of the large burden of shame instilled by social training. Unencumbered by status or possessions, he has nothing to lose and therefore nothing to fear.

Diogenes wants to dispense with need and shame because it is these forces above all that make human beings vulnerable and fearful. Because we hate these feelings, we do everything we can to attain power over those around us. But, unlike Diogenes, we can't display our aggression openly for fear of retaliation and loss. Instead of making our minds and bodies stronger and more self-sufficient, we seek to wrap ourselves in defensive layers of power and luxury.

Power, in the form of money, high-placed allies and social status, assures us that we can't be harmed. Luxury, like high-thread-count linen, interposes layers of protection between ourselves and the hostile elements, allowing us to forget the infant self we once were, helpless against the depredations of hunger and cold. The problem with power and luxury, though, is that they beget a constant state of desire to maintain and enhance them, which is only exacerbated by the fear of losing them. This predicament is nicely outlined in 'The Cynic', a dialogue written in the Socratic style by the Greek writer Lucian, around 500 years after Diogenes.

Reading the dialogue, it's surprising to find in it an amusing homily often quoted by Freud, whose source wasn't Lucian but a series of Yiddish folk tales of the hapless everyman Itzig. Both versions of the story tell of a man who mounts a wild horse that straight away dashes off furiously. A pedestrian on the road asks him where he's going as the horse flashes by. 'That's up to the horse,' replies the man.

More intriguing still is that Lucian and Freud use the story to the same purpose – to show that the obscure desires that impel us forward, what Freud calls the drives, are carrying us to unknown and potentially dangerous destinations, even and especially when we think they are under our control. 'Now,' says the Cynic of Lucian's dialogue,

> if someone asks you where you're off to, if you're honest you will simply say that your desires will decide – the desires of pleasure, greed and ambition ... Then anger, or some other emotion like fear, seems to direct you. For you are on the back not of one but many horses, and different ones at different times – but all of them out of control, which is why you end up in ditches or falling off cliffs. And you have no presentiment that any such calamity awaits you.

Cynicism was a bid to put limits on the human drives, to forge a mode of life that wouldn't be plagued by perpetual dissatisfaction. Impelled by vanity and grandiosity, the breathless pursuit of happiness succeeds only in making us angrier and more fearful.

On this reading, should we not place Greta Thunberg squarely in the Cynic tradition? The adolescent who stands in a T-shirt before the world's richest and most powerful operators and mouths all the empty pieties of corporate green orthodoxy – 'innovation, cooperation and willpower', 'green jobs!', 'smooth transition' – before interrupting herself with mocking iterations of the same phrase: 'blah blah blah'. It is not just her fearless ridicule that places Thunberg in the Cynic tradition. In unmasking the 'solutions' of technocratic political and business leaders as disguised exacerbations of the problems, shifty ways of evading the effects of their own power, she is following the logic of Cynical argumentation.

We might say that Thunberg's 2021 speech in Milan pits her ancient Cynicism against the modern cynicism of the political and business classes. Like Diogenes, she starts from the premise that power today harbours within itself a fatal weakness, namely a phobic horror of questioning itself, a refusal to contemplate any brake on its own appetites. World leaders would rather risk humanity's survival than advocate lower levels of mass consumption. Ancient Cynicism proposes that if the satisfaction human beings are so haplessly and perpetually chasing can never be realized, they should stop running and seek instead to place strict limits on the scope of their desire. Modern cynicism takes this same perpetual dissatisfaction and enlists it in the service of power.

The modern cynic is concerned neither to remedy nor to eliminate dissatisfaction. Ancient Cynicism's interest in human dissatisfaction fed a disinterested inquiry into the conduct of life most conducive to rationality and spiritual integrity; the modern cynic (the politician, the advertiser, the lobbyist) realizes that the same insights into dissatisfaction can be leveraged to achieve their political and economic interests. Their interest is rather in maintaining dissatisfaction, in stoking his constituency's perpetual anger, for which the cynic politician becomes figurehead, directing it at corruptions and injustices being perpetuated in places too impenetrable and elusive ever to be reached.

Trump and his MAGA movement employ a language of calculated vagueness in naming their enemies: the deep state, the global elite, the woke army, interlocking networks of conspirators against the real America, injecting the nation with the insidious poisons of migrant hordes, vaccines, radicalism and godlessness while depriving it of jobs, guns and petrol.

The places from which these poisons are being administered become ever more diffuse and inaccessible, culminating in the fantasies of the QAnon movement, which trades on a story of a heroic Trumpist agent's imminent exposure and prosecution of the hidden satanic paedophile cabal running all governmental institutions. It is often remarked that by doing nothing to disconfirm this excitable nonsense, Trump and his acolytes facilitate its dangerous spread. But less remarked is their never having made any attempt to confirm it. This may seem obvious – to give explicit credence to QAnon's claims would surely be politically suicidal even for Trump. But more importantly, Trump's near silence creates the atmosphere most favourable to QAnon's spread and growth. To the movement's followers, it signals a tacit confirmation of the conspiracy's truth.

It also protects the story from fact-checking pedantry. By remaining silent on its specific claims Trump ensures they remain in an obscure outland, beyond the reach of all proofs, positive or negative. For true believers, every appeal to the discernible facts ('There is no Q!', 'The Democratic party is not a secret paedophile ring!') only confirms the nefarious concealment of the *real* facts.

Cynicism mobilizes conspiracy theory not to explain or enlighten, but to sustain and deepen mass dissatisfaction. The cynical politician makes a peculiar virtue of the fact that the injustices they decry are defined by the impossibility of obtaining any redress for them. You can't hunt down the paedophiles or expose election fraud because such crimes are defined by their perpetrators' capacity to cover their own tracks, because the systems that should be finding and punishing them are under their secret command.

This means that their followers are denied the satisfaction they crave and demand. The advantage of this denial is that it ensures they remain in a state of permanently unassuaged anger, providing the cynic with a precious and endlessly renewable resource. If anger is the political gift that keeps on giving, the trick is to keep it flowing; to achieve redress would risk switching off the tap.

But denied satisfaction is an ambiguous gift. Let's recall once more that for psychoanalysis, the human being can only endure so much dissatisfaction. Once the state of heightened tension induced by it reaches a certain pitch in us, we feel helplessly compelled to discharge it in one way or another. The January 6 attack on the Capitol was an instance of this compulsion.

The campaign of election denial waged by Trump and his team of slapstick litigants fuelled a mass rage too voracious and too extreme to be contained by mere words or sentiments. The nervous system cannot support tension on this scale indefinitely; it is impelled to find a way to discharge it in real-world action. As sexual arousal demands urgent discharge in orgasm, so anger eventually demands urgent discharge in aggression.

As the permanent threat of rebellion and the unrealized promise of retribution, anger is the cynical politician's lifeblood. In the aftermath of that day, it seemed as though by encouraging the passage from mass anger to mass violence, Trump had handled the cynical politician's kryptonite. For a while, the image of puddles and piles of excrement reportedly deposited by the insurrectionists in the Capitol hallways resembled an allegory of Trump's hubris: for as long as it spread unhindered through the immaterial conduits of the airwaves and internet, the stolen election narrative was political gold; once it invaded the physical centre of American power, it quickly turned to shit.

At least that is what liberals and leftists including myself, desperate as ever to consign Trumpian populism to the dustbin of history, told themselves the world over. This reverse alchemy, we insisted, began the moment Trump appeared not only to exploit the rumours of a stolen election, but to believe them. Instead of letting the election results float in the ether of doubt and ambiguity, he aggressively proclaimed their fraudulence. His press secretary appeared on TV brandishing random stacks of paper said to be irrefutable evidence of election fraud. His personal lawyer brought a farcical succession of failed legal challenges to the results, eventually telling an Arizona official, 'We've got lots of theories. We just don't have the evidence.'

Surely, I told myself as I watched these events unfold, there is no coming back from this. Surely as soon as political cynicism stakes itself on a claim to verifiable truth, it is deprived of one of its key resources: the unfalsifiability of its own claims. As soon as you say, 'This is true and I intend to prove it', you are no longer an authentic cynic. You are forced to operate in the relatively narrow confines of shared reality, against which your words will be tested. Febrile rumour can sustain popular anger while leaving just enough ambiguity to prevent it from spilling over into aggression. But once rumour has morphed into a claim to truth, anger is bound to shade into aggression. This is what happened at the Capitol.

Movements fronted by cynical leaders live off a diffuse, free-floating rage directed against nefarious and elusive enemies. Once that rage crosses over into actual aggression, the movement runs ahead of its leadership; as the insurrectionists stormed the Capitol,

Trump could only bear witness to them gormlessly on TV. His silence during those hours signalled not the wily ambiguity of the cynic, but the helpless panic of the cornered rat. The one thing he couldn't do was hide, either from his opponents or from his devotees.

When he was railroaded the next day into an unconvincingly presidential televised condemnation of the 'heinous attack' on the US Capitol, expressing his outrage at the 'violence, lawlessness and mayhem' and calling for a revitalization of 'the sacred bonds of love and loyalty that bind us together', there could have been very few, whether followers or opponents of Trump, who did not see through its phoney pieties.

What made the statement so transparently insincere was the knowledge of every viewer that Trump believed the election to have been stolen: and to one who believes, or indeed 'knows', that the American people were defrauded by a tightly concealed and concerted network of shadowy operators, the act of insurrection is as reasonable as it is proportionate. So why on earth would you condemn it?

Angrily denouncing the 'swamp' or the 'system', Trump, in the time-honoured manner of the cynic, likes to pose as a Cynic, speaking lies to the powerless under cover of speaking truth to power. The political problem for Trump was that for his followers, the increasing psychic effort of splitting off the lies was manageable only by way of escape to a fantasy world like QAnon. Living in a tightly conceived conspiratorial illusion in which your leader is the world's imminent saviour may be the only way to shield yourself from seeing the tediously rambling, shabbily opportunistic old man who bears his name. This seemed to be the conclusion of Trump's donors and voters in the two years following the insurrection as his political star slowly but inexorably faded.

What hopeful liberal commentators failed to anticipate was the supreme flexibility of Trumpian cynicism, the massive political advantage that accrues to the candidate freed from obligations to truth or consistency. Trump became increasingly mired in multiple state and federal indictments for his role in fomenting the January 6 insurrection, promising a fitting climax to his downfall. Those indictments have proved instead to be the motor of his revival.

Having let his base run ahead of him, Trump set about making up the lost ground, transforming the political dross of the insurrectionists' mass prosecutions and his own legal jeopardy back into electoral gold. He countered the irrefutable falsifications of all claims of election interference by leaning into them ever more aggressively. Under his Midas touch, established facts were remade as inventions of deep-state and Democrat enemies, with Trump self-cast as their martyr and avenging angel.

We have been returned to the world in which Trump's every claim is unfalsifiable and all documentary evidence unverifiable, to a soil perfectly primed for the sowing and eventual harvesting of infinite reserves of mass anger.

Over the last decade or so, Vladimir Putin has leaned increasingly on an openly autocratic rhetoric to justify the suppression of all opposition and dissent. Imprisoning and murdering political opponents at home and abroad, brutally putting down mass protests, shutting down media outlets that subject his regime to critical scrutiny, gazing down broodingly on adoring, flag-waving crowds, he edges ever closer to the model totalitarian ruler. Above all, of course, he has waged a war of murderous aggression on Ukraine in the name of a revived Russian imperialism, which as I write shows no signs of abating.

Trump's admiration for Putin and other autocratic rulers and regimes is likely rooted in envy of their freedom to override norms that fail to serve their interests. His predicament, shown most vividly by the broad comedy of his failed legal challenges, is that he is obliged to operate in democratic institutions, and so is subject to norms such as the burden of proof and political accountability.

It's worth recalling that Putin himself was democratically elected, that when his presidency started life he was feted as an economic and geopolitical ally by Tony Blair, George W. Bush and many other Western leaders. The Western political establishment saw Putin building and cultivating the institutional and legal structures of a democratic state. Hindsight shows us that he was presiding over something closer to a cynical pastiche of democracy, an ingenious mimicry of its basic mechanisms and conventions. When the clothes of democracy are so thin, it is much easier to shed them and reveal the naked autocracy that's always lurked beneath.

When he emerged from political obscurity in 1999 to be anointed Boris Yeltsin's successor by a closed circle of oligarchs and Kremlin insiders, Putin had somehow to ride the wave of free-floating, disorganized mass rage manifesting in the noisy convergence of nationalist, neo-fascist and Communist revivalist protest against the chaos-inducing market reforms of the previous decade.

It would not be enough for Putin merely to weather the storm of this rage; if he was to sustain his power in Russia, he would need to harness it, to make himself its champion and representative. But how to appease a populace traumatized and enraged by poverty and lawlessness? Sincere appeals for patience and endurance will have little effect on the hungry, as we saw from Revolutionary France.

Politicians like Trump and Putin harness anger by driving

cynicism to its outer limit. They hit on a deep seam of anger that has no agreed upon cause or object. This anger is directed instead to a conveniently plastic range of essentially fictive provocations – immigrants, 'paedophiles', the Radical Left, 'abolitionists' of gender, the EU, the US, the West. Mass rage is dispersed, a floating resource liable to capture by the highest bidder, for whom it serves as an endlessly renewable reserve of political capital. The conjuring up of imaginary enemies is central to the cynical project. It creates a political atmosphere in which reality itself is fictive, in which the world is described not in accordance with the finite field of facts but with the infinitely malleable stuff of fantasies and wishes.

What could be a more efficacious path to political domination than to manage the hard matter of reality as though it were the airy, weightless stuff of art? To preside over a political territory as though it were one's own imaginary playground – that may be the definition of total sovereignty.

In his 1949 essay, 'Literature and the Right to Death', Maurice Blanchot presents the French Revolution in just these terms. 'Revolutionary action,' he writes, 'is in every respect analogous to action as embodied in literature: the passage from nothing to everything.' What Blanchot means is that just as literature can make a living reality out of weightless marks on a blank page, the Revolutionary Terror did the same in reverse – it took living reality and turned it back into 'pure abstraction', making reality unreal.

Specifically, the Terror turned individual human beings into empty abstractions, transforming them instantaneously from living, breathing citizens into anonymous ciphers whose substance consisted solely in whether they were perceived as allies or enemies of the Revolution. Under the terms of the Terror, a citizen could be casually decapitated because the Revolution had already deprived them of their life by killing the individuality that defined them as alive; they could be killed with the novelist's breeziness in killing off a character.

Every totalitarian regime seeks for this reason to bathe itself in the ether of the aesthetic, to turn society into a total work of art, an artifice to be made and remade at will. From this perspective, Trump's failure to capture the machinery of the state looks like a kind of aesthetic indiscipline. His breathless excitability was incompatible with the ruthless auteurist mastery required for the task.

Were he given to learning, he might glean a lot from a man who executed this capture with startling success for over a decade: Putin's chief 'political technologist' Vladislav Surkov, who, beginning in the late 1990s, conjured up a model of fictive governance he called (not without irony) 'sovereign democracy'. Like Trump after him, Surkov's feat was to identify a bottomless political resource in the disorganized rage that was overwhelming Russia. Occupying a succession of high offices until his first political excommunication in 2012, Surkov 'directed Russian society like one great reality show', as writer and propaganda expert Peter Pomerantsev puts it. Surkov oversaw the effectively permanent installation of the ruling United Russia party while creating its 'opposition', nominally independent parties of the left and right whose policies and votes he micromanaged to best serve the interests of the Kremlin.

Surkov's sovereign democracy centralized all political speech and activity; movements and parties financed by the Kremlin would then be in permanent political debt to it, bound by its interests, subject to its instruction. He became an artist on Blanchot's model of the revolutionary; nationalist or communist parties that appeared to carry an inheritance of history and ideology were reduced by him to mere simulacra of real political entities whose speech and activity were fed harmlessly back into the order they appear to contest.

Central to Surkov's painstakingly curated mythology is his literary and theatrical education and links to Russia's bohemian art circles. In a 2021 interview with Henry Foy, he recounts his training in the *commedia dell'arte* tradition as a kind of metaphorical apprenticeship in political management: 'People need to see themselves on stage . . . In this masked comedy, there is a director, there is a plot. And this is when I understood what needed to be done.'

Commedia dell'arte involves a limited range of stock characters replaying plots and routines whose course is known at the outset. Similarly, the Russian opposition, along with the roiling mass discontent they were meant to represent, are now prisoners inside a playscript whose occasional variations only underscore the inevitability of the outcome. In modelling it on the imaginary worlds of art and literature, Surkov turned political life into an empty spectacle, imprisoning its actors in an airless hell of repetitious illusion.

In his pseudonymously published 2009 novel *Almost Zero* (*Okolonolya*), Surkov extended and further confused this traffic between literature and reality. His protagonist Yegor, an amoral PR man who traffics in underground literature, is invested in books for their capacity to break rather than make links between words and world. 'Yegor,' Surkov writes, in a passage that might be channelling Blanchot, 'was interested in the adventures of names, not people.' To be a name rather than a person is to be reduced to a de-corporealized abstraction in a world without differences, where the lines marking one thing off from another dissolve. What remains is reality as raw matter to be perpetually made, unmade and remade by whoever seizes hold of it. And as Blanchot's Revolution showed us, the paradox of this new 'egoless', incorporeal perspective is that it prepares the way for limitless violence.

Surkov first fell out of favour with Putin in 2012, when the strings of his marionette theatre seemed to slip through his fingers; the oppositional groups he had seamlessly directed and controlled finally assumed a life of their own, turning on his stage management and breaking through his fourth wall.

When thousands of protestors broke with his script and took to the streets of Moscow, Surkov declined to order a crackdown. Rumours proliferated of his covert sympathy for the opposition. At very least, he seemed to see the protests as the inevitable breakdown of his rule of illusion. Surkov's consequent dismissal paved the way for Putin's regime to drop its contrived façade of plural democracy and expose the brutal autocracy that had always lurked behind it.

But that was by no means the end of Surkov. In 2014, he resurfaced in Ukraine, as historian Timothy Snyder recounts in *The Road to Unfreedom*, to foment violence against the Maidan opposition and stir up pro-Russian separatist agitation in Crimea. The day after his arrival on February 15, 'live ammunition was distributed to Ukrainian riot police'. While awaiting the outcome of a parliamentary discussion of constitutional compromise, 'Protestors on the Maidan were surprised by massive and lethal violence.'

In November 2021, after six years leading covert operations to destabilize Ukraine and presiding over the self-styled separatist 'republics' in the Donbas, Surkov wrote an article conceptualizing these operations as the simple logic of 'physics', specifically the law of entropy famously formulated by James Clark Maxwell.

In 1999, Surkov writes, Putin inherited a country and system running headlong into entropic decay and chaos and stabilized its economy and governance. 'But,' he continues, 'if the second law of thermodynamics is true (and it is true)', then entropy can never be conjured away; it is in the nature of every closed system to generate entropy, raising the question of what to do with it. Surkov's answer is, as he openly acknowledges, the cynical recourse of every struggling empire: export the chaos elsewhere. The 'socially toxic' entropic energies aroused by and against Putin's regime have been diverted to Ukraine in a new iteration of a venerable imperial strategy: 'Exporting chaos is nothing new. Divide and Conquer is an ancient recipe ... Rally your own + divide others = you will rule both.'

Three months later, Russia invaded Ukraine.

But cynicism doesn't merely exploit popular anger; it gives it a façade of sneering invulnerability, perfectly concentrated in an unofficial slogan that appeared during the Trump 2020 campaign: 'Fuck Your Feelings'. The irony of the slogan is that right-wing populism draws all its force from feelings; the MAGA movement's appeal is to the anger and bitterness of constituencies afflicted by industrial decline and its attendant effects of lost economic security, as well as declining social and cultural prestige.

Trump promised a magical reversal of these losses, famously assuring a rally in 2016, 'We're going to win so much, you're going to be sick and tired of winning.' But lurking in that sentence is the present reality it inverts – that you're losing so much, you're sick and tired of losing. The alchemy by which losing turns into winning is as much emotional as it is political; it transforms depressive feelings of inadequacy and vulnerability into a state of total triumph.

One of the most striking revelations of *Men Who Hate Women*, Laura Bates's anatomy of contemporary forms of misogyny, is the extent to which the leadership of online male supremacist groups is conditioned by deep contempt. Alongside the predictably vicious bile directed against women, we see a smirking disgust for the smallest hints of weakness in men.

Paul Elam is a leading light of the men's rights awareness (MRA) movement, a network of mostly online groupings pathologically hostile to feminism, not to mention to women in general. When he received hundreds of contacts from men claiming to have been 'screwed over' or 'ruined' by some or other aspect of our 'anti-male' society, he didn't respond with the assuring solidarity his correspondents might have expected. Instead, he wrote a blog post titled, 'An open response to troubled men', in which he told these embittered victims to 'go fucking bother someone else with your problems'. It seems it is not enough to hate feminism or even actual women; the true MRA warrior hates the smallest intimation of 'feminine' tendencies – above all an openness to painful or difficult feelings – in all human beings and works tirelessly to eliminate all traces of them in himself.

This turns out to be a common feature of an array of militantly anti-feminist movements across the web. The stamp of authenticity in such groups is a tone of snarling mockery towards any member who shows any hint of weakness or self-doubt. As the saying goes, fuck your feelings.

This slogan was no flippant joke. It was a precisely calculated rhetorical move, distilling the essence of the MAGA movement. It is hardly a surprise to discover just how much crossover there is between the leading figures of online Trumpism and of militant anti-feminism. They are interlocking parts of a single vision of a world over which hardened alpha men preside, ruthlessly coercing women and weaker men into the service of their needs and desires. This is the context in which online groups boasting tens of thousands of members share their convictions in the natural justice of the domestic abuse and rape of women. The aim here is to be angry in a particular style, what American writer Andrew Marantz aptly calls 'mirth with a base note of rage'.

The mirth has a paradoxical effect of at once amplifying the rage and calling it into doubt. It is amplified because laughter and jokes license levels of aggression in the speaker that are impermissible in ordinary conversation. It is called into doubt because it's 'just a joke', and failing to laugh along reveals not how cruel the joker is but how humourless you are.

Take a vignette told by Marantz about Gavin McInnes, alt-right provocateur and founder of the Proud Boys. Marantz followed a crew of alt-right semi-celebrities, led by McInnes, to the DeploraBall, a celebration of Trump's impending presidency, the night before Trump's inauguration in January 2017. On his way in, McInnes punched an antifa protestor in the face, later on telling a news crew, 'I think that when I punched him, my fist went into his mouth and his teeth scraped me on the way out . . . now I might get loser AIDS.'

The 'joke' is set up to neutralize the outrage of the listener in advance. Its cruelty and crassness are so brazen, so overblown as to imply that no one should take it seriously. And this is the point: on the alt-right web, to take words or ideas or even policies seriously, to commit yourself to them, to have *strong feelings* about them, is to make yourself laughable. The notional ideal of the alt-right man is to treat political ideas largely as he treats (or likes to claim to treat) women, as expedient instruments for serving the needs of the moment.

The cynic politician, like the cynic therapist, has discovered anger as a resource to master and exploit. They both offer the dubious solace of an invulnerable father and a community united in shared rage. This may bring into focus why so much of this shared rage orbits around women and sexuality. The Right populist leader promises a world of perfectly rigid paternal control, in which all insubordination receives a casual punch in the face and everyone and everything is in, and knows, its place. Mirth in such a set-up is a way of signalling that you are in full command of your own rage, that your power consists precisely in your capacity not to care, not to succumb to the weak-willed sentimentality that afflicts women.

This in turn makes sense of how so many of the mirthful provocateurs of the alt-right are also tricksters and trolls disseminating manifestly delusional conspiracies like Pizzagate. The two roles share the same relationship to truth: only weak-stomached women and womanish men are still credulous enough to care about it. The authentically strong man can say anything without needing it to be true.

Before and during Trump's presidency, many of these alt-right figures were writing and broadcasting for Russian media outlets, the avant-garde of 'post-truth' politics. As Surkov's career showed us, with enough ingenuity and effort, factual truth can be effectively eliminated from the political sphere, creating a vacancy to be filled instead by the story Putin wants told. Insofar as the entire space of politics is commandeered by one regime, Russia is very different from the US, perhaps enviably so for the MAGA extremists forced to share political space with those who think differently. Rageful mirth is a means of compensating for this unfortunate circumstance; unlike Putin, MAGA warriors don't enjoy the privilege of imprisoning or killing their opposition. Instead, they can create an atmosphere which annihilates the human significance of their opponents, turning them into nothing more than the butt of a joke.

Putin certainly likes to mock from on high, but he doesn't deign to clown or joke. With the entire state machinery at his disposal to crush all dissent, he doesn't need to. He presides over a population fed a steady diet of state propaganda, starved of all alternative sources of information and cowed into submission by the threat of arrest should they publicly question or protest his rationale for the so-called special military operation in Ukraine.

This near total power over the citizenry undergirds Putin's portrayal of Russia as sole bulwark against the decadence of the West, expressed above all in its obsessional hatred for the gender and sexual equality movements. Timothy Snyder notes that Putin's regime has long been gripped by an obsessive hostility towards Western sexual permissiveness and its threat to 'traditional values'. As Russian troops mobilized to invade Crimea in 2014, Foreign Minister Sergei Lavrov published an article presenting Russia as the real victim of the conflict with the West: according to Lavrov, the true aggressors were 'the international gay lobbyists'.

In a screed of 2021 presenting Trump as a hero of the war against globalist technocracy, Putin's court philosopher and obscurantist neo-fascist Alexander Dugin proposes that the real aim of the movement for gender rights is to dehumanize the individual by divesting them of any distinctive biological characteristics. In fact, Dugin claims, progressive gender politics is a central plank of an elaborate 'Western' scheme 'to replace humans, albeit partially, by cyborgs, artificial intelligence networks, and products of genetic engineering. The optional human logically follows optional gender.'

One of the finely honed traits of Putinist and Trumpian rhetoric alike is the perpetual inversion of the positions of victim and aggressor. It is Putin, leader of a regime now unambiguously fascist in its philosophical lineage and its practice, who perpetually labels his enemies and victims fascists. It is Dugin who proposes banishing women to the home and gay people to the closet; but somehow it is the feminist and LGBT movements who are accused of dehumanization. This is the advantage of abolishing a shared reality; it enables the speaker to bend reality, now weightless and pliable, to their will.

The MAGA movement and Putin regime share the same wish to restore a fixed order of gender and sexual power. This aspiration isn't confined to the conspiratorial inventions of Democrat-run paedophile rings. American conservative groups have in recent years forged a concerted strategy to reverse the teaching of sexual equality, including gay and trans rights, in schools by attacking school board members with the noxious slur of 'groomer', equating an inclusive sex education with child abuse.

Why this obsessive recurrence of these fantasies of the enemy's pathological sexuality? These projections of extreme perversity and aggression emanate from the deep unconscious of the conspiracy-mongers themselves. The imputations of the other's degeneracy, the ideals of a 'traditional' gender and sexual hierarchy cleansed of all deviations, the contemptuous mockery of weak men and strong women all speak to a terror of sex as a force of internal danger and chaos that must be brought under control.

It's this terror, and the rage it arouses, that a cynical politics seeks to exploit, promising to restore order to a world disordered by sexual equality and freedom. But such promises are risky, for like the 'Stop the Steal' protests, they depend on arousing and nursing an anger that can easily tip over into aggression. While the rage of the incel against women for declining to service his sexual needs is discharged in online rants, it remains a political resource. But once that rage impels him to shoot actual women, the rage is no longer usable.

Bates notes that Trump's long-time adviser, alt-right guru Steve Bannon had identified the potential political value of incels in 2016, enlisting the services of Cambridge Analytica to target them as a constituency that 'could have a massive impact in swing states'. But it's essential that relationships like this remain ambiguous and plausibly deniable. Bannon is too canny an operator to make an explicit endorsement of incel and MRA groups. By drawing them into a quiet alliance, keeping them close enough to use and far enough to disavow, he is able to draw on their rage as a political resource, as the Trump campaign did with a diverse range of hate groups and far-right leaders.

Keeping such relationships ambiguous effectively allows Bannon to harness the anger of such groups while repudiating their aggression. As we saw in relation to the January 6 insurrection, when anger passes into real-world aggression, disappointment and bitterness are bound to follow, because the action that is supposed to effect the desired change fails to do so. The incel shooter excitedly imagines he'll terrorize women into submission to male authority, but his actions produce only grief and horror. The utopia of straight white male supremacy he and his online cheerleaders hope for is never achieved. The cynic's promises are revealed in all their craven emptiness.

It strikes me that Gerard's rage fuelled a kind of one-man war against the cynicism he saw all around him. The dating apps and the politicians drew so much of his fury because they preyed on human vulnerability, especially his own. In his mind, he was perpetually at the edge of some new humiliation, of being exposed as stupid, naive, desperate.

I suspect that without quite knowing it, he approached me with the same wish that Markowitz brought to Herschkopf: that I would 'take care of everything'. But Gerard and Markowitz both carry histories that make this wish very complicated.

As a child, Gerard had been in awe of his father, ascribing to him an intellectual brilliance, ready wit and debonair sophistication that made him the object of both bottomless, yearning admiration and an impossible remoteness. As a child, he had felt he could never gain his father's attention, interest, concern or curiosity. If he tried to show his father some creative work, or confide in him about problems at school, or ask him questions about the world, he was met with a look of glazed distraction, which would reliably turn into irritability if Gerard pressed his case: 'Gerard, you can see I'm very busy. We can discuss this later,' he'd respond, audibly gritting his teeth.

Gerard quickly learned that 'later' would never arrive, that the moment of paternal recognition he craved would only be deferred once again. He would take some of his questions and concerns to his mother, who was at least warm and responsive. But she too was invested in her husband as the one who knows, the ultimate stamp of authority and approval, next to which anything she could say meant very little. 'Oh dear Gerry,' she replied when he revealed he was being bullied, 'That's too awful, you poor thing. We'll talk to your father about it tonight, he'll know what to do!'

Gerard and his mother formed a kind of implicitly abandoned family, passively awaiting the return of a patriarch to direct and instruct them. The problem was that the patriarch had never left, but neither had he ever really been there. The desperate hope that his presence would become more than a kind of ghostly physical apparition, that he would see them and affirm for them that they really existed for him, could never be realized. This sense of indefinite hiatus meant that Gerard lacked any conviction that he could act for himself. It seemed never to occur to him to get angry with his father, or to conclude that if his father was never going to show interest in him, he would need to show interest in himself. What had prevented him from letting his father see his disappointment and anger was the terror that his father would retaliate by rejecting him permanently, cutting off any possibility that Gerard might finally make real contact with him. It was this possibility that held both Gerard and his mother together; without it, they might just unravel.

In other words, Gerard was left suspended indefinitely in the hope that someone would take care of everything. He was burdened by the unconscious fantasy that his father's near total emotional neglect would be transformed into its opposite, an enveloping and inexhaustible love. It was inevitable that this hope would be transferred onto me from the moment he came to see me.

But by the time he started to work with me, around the age of forty, this hope had been so long unfulfilled that it had come to express itself as a kind of permanent, weary anger. At our first meeting, I asked him what he hoped for from our work. 'Isn't it obvious?!' he replied testily, 'I'm in a bloody mess and I'm furious and embittered and terribly tired and I want it to stop before it ruins the rest of my life. Do you think that's even possible? Because if it isn't, let's not waste my time or yours.'

Perhaps it would have felt like a huge relief for me to have replied, like Herschkopf, that I'd take care of everything. It's not uncommon for a person to come to psychoanalysis secretly hoping for a promise like this, which is why it's so dangerous to make it. In pledging to reverse all the pain and damage of another's life, a therapist is only ensuring it will continue. I replied instead that I could hear how much he was suffering; I offered to work with him to try to understand why, and to think about how things might change for the better.

As therapeutic aims go, I'm aware these might sound deflatingly vague. For many critics of my profession, the unwillingness to set clear and defined goals only points to the cynicism of psychoanalysis. After all, with all that 'trying' and 'thinking about' and 'might', aren't I just stringing him along, dangling phantom carrots, drawing him into a vortex that sucks up time and money and hope while achieving nothing tangible? Am I not, like the cynic politician, harnessing Gerard's rage to my own advantage? It may be that the only honest answer to this question is maybe. It may well be that we work together and that months and even years will pass and he will feel no less furious and embittered and tired.

But as I see it, it's precisely the absence of a guaranteed outcome that prevents psychoanalysis from shading into cynicism. In the face of feelings as overwhelming and debilitating as Gerard's, it would be pure hubris to claim you can tame them and bring them under control. These would be just fine-sounding words masquerading as action.

Whereas, paradoxically, to tell someone in the grip of a tormenting fury that you're willing to receive and listen to it and think with him about it for as long as necessary is closer to a real action with real effects. It creates a world for him which didn't previously exist, in which someone else recognizes and is curious about his inner life and wants to help reflect it back to him, to give it shape and meaning. This, after all, is what has been so profoundly missing from his life from the beginning and has condemned him to the despair of a permanent and irremediable state of rage.

Gerard no longer feels condemned to this state. He remains angry, but those images that used to assail me of his fury physically filling up the room, depriving me of any space to move or breathe, have gradually abated. His rage is as real as ever, but it no longer feels like some elemental force of which no questions can be asked, about which no curiosity is possible.

Instead of being overwhelmed by his rage, Gerard has slowly developed a capacity in our work to represent it; that is, to understand both its source and its object. In defining the who and the what of his anger, he has come closer to perceiving not only who he is, but who he *isn't* angry with. His anger no longer seems to spread inexorably from one target to the next, accusing everyone and therefore no one.

It isn't the case, of course, that Gerard didn't know he was angry with his father. The problem was that the father had mutated in his mind into a figure of mythically large dimensions, a judging and punitive god before whom his son could only cower and abase himself. When he began to talk about his actual father, he recovered a man with an emotional history of his own. Gerard's father did not come into the world a fully formed monster of emotional neglect and spiky contempt. He was carrying over the legacy of his own childhood neglect; his father, a shadowy figure who spent much of his time on unspecified government business abroad, had been an object of uneasy veneration for his children.

In one session, Gerard recalled an exchange from around age eleven, when he'd asked his father about the grandfather he'd never known. Rather than snapping back with a dismissive non-answer, as so often happened, his father stared into the middle distance, caught in a silence that felt genuinely reflective.

'A look came over his face which I felt like I'd never seen,' said Gerard. 'I realized he was sad, and I think I found that over-whelming. I suspect I had some secret belief my father had no feelings, other than irritation. He stared for a long while, then said, "When I was your age, all I knew about my father was that he was a man of great importance to his country. I didn't know what that meant at the time, only that whatever he was doing meant far more to him than me."'

Gerard continued: 'Only now do I see what he was trying to tell me – that he'd never had a sense of mattering to his own father. All that prickliness and contempt he showed me . . . well, it still hurts, but it somehow takes on a new complexion. I can see he's no demigod. He's a very damaged man.'

For as long as he could remember, Gerard had carried within him an amplified, exaggerated version of a punitively disdainful father, a father who spurned his child's love and need. Perceiving this other father, too hurt and too defended against his own need to be able to take the risk of loving his child, enabled the anger he felt towards the father he had to be slowly assuaged by grief for the father he couldn't have.

In encouraging and stoking popular rage while offering no hope of meaningful redress, cynical politics deprives its followers of this grief. Like Quixote before the windmills, the devotees of conspiracies and mass hatreds can only ever tilt at hopelessly elusive targets. The cynic invests their followers in illusory aims and objects – a leader who saves the world and purges the nation of all unwanted others – so heavily that they can never give them up.

'Fuck your feelings' is the slogan of this refusal to mourn. It is the battle cry of those condemned to stay angry, unable to mourn what they can't have and equally unable to turn their energies and desires to what they could have.

Chapter Four

Usable Rage: Love, Justice, Creativity

For many years, every student, colleague or friend seemed to be urging me to read Elena Ferrante. I'd be hooked from the start, they would assure me. No writer was as brave, as wrenching, as startlingly truthful about the perils of human intimacy. Much as they piqued my curiosity, they also aroused that peculiar wariness that comes with being told what to read, watch or listen to. Besides, there is always too much to read, always another author threatening to wedge herself into the tottering pile of good intentions. I figured I'd get to her at some point.

As it happened, she got to me instead, one late November weeknight in 2021. I was already in bed and reading someone else, when my wife returned home and looked at me with an unseeing stare that unsettled me enough to ask her if she was all right.

She furrowed her brow, an inch or two off direct eye contact. 'Yes,' she said, 'fine'. She reminded me that her filmmaker friend had taken her to a screening of the new movie with Olivia Colman, *The Lost Daughter.*

'Hmm. The Ferrante thing.'

Sat at the opposite edge of the bed, she stared into the night. Then, abruptly breaking the shared, dense quiet, she said, 'Yeah. I think I need to read that book.'

Two days later, she was pressing that book into my hands. '*You* need to read this,' she said. 'You're writing about anger. You can't . . . not read it.'

Of course I'd read it, I thought to myself, grateful for this live interest in my mind and projects. Besides, it was invitingly slim, nothing like the forbiddingly thick Neapolitan novels everyone went on about. And it was Friday so I could read as late as I liked. Still, as I turned to the first page, I was aware of some slight disturbance at the periphery, some sense of being not quite sure what kind of gift this was. *You need to read this.* But why, and what would happen if I didn't?

The question became more real as the novel sucked me in to its vortex of female and maternal anger, with Leda, its narrator, 'screaming with rage, like my mother, because of the crushing weight of responsibility, the bond that strangles', until *You need to read this* began to feel like an inextricable dimension of the book itself, another front in its violent ambush on my nerves.

When I finished the book the next morning, my mind was bubbling with anxious questions: What did you need me to read? Did you mean the fearless anatomy of female discontent that would nourish the book I was writing on anger? Or did you want me, finally, after twenty-two years raising three boys, to hear you *screaming with rage*, at them, at the world, but mostly at me: 'Do you get it? *DO YOU GET IT NOW?!*'

Time flies when you're having fun. A watched pot never boils. Folk psychology reminds us that all moods have their own peculiar temporality. Joy seems to vaporize the passing hours, while boredom sadistically elongates the seconds.

For its part, anger wrenches us out of the continuum of time, cancelling out both past and future and locking us into the suffocating cell or 'red mist' of the present moment. In an instant, we wipe out any history (friendly, loving or indifferent) with the object of our rage, and burn all bridges to any relationship to come.

This helps explain why anger can be so corrosive to long-term relationships. As the consulting room has often shown me, rage has a way of wearing away a marriage's durability, that sense of a containing structure persisting above and beyond the vicissitudes of one or the other's passing feelings. When it runs sufficiently long and deep, anger attacks our emotional hold on what a loved one has been and can be for us, reducing them to the hostile or hateful object of the immediate present.

Perhaps the most extreme instance of this tendency can be found in the narrative that frames *One Thousand and One Nights*, the tale of the Sasanian king Shahryār and his bride Scheherazade. As the story has it, having earlier discovered the faithlessness of one of his wives, the king has her executed. Believing all women to be the same at heart, he marries a succession of virgins, each of whom he puts to death the following morning before she too can dishonour him.

Shahryār's royally licensed serial killing issues from a narcissistic wound which each marriage threatens to reopen, and which each execution sews up a little more tightly. He is executing not merely the brides but the possibility of passing time, of a future whose emotional risks he cannot predict. Murdering his brides protects him from the pain of what hasn't yet happened, but at the hellish price of sealing himself inside the same, obsessively repeated act of violent rage.

When the vizier's daughter Scheherazade hears of the king's murderous campaign against the adulterers of the future, she boldly offers herself up as the king's next bride. On their wedding night, she entertains Shahryār with a tale only to suspend its climax, compelling him to postpone her execution if he wishes to hear its end. Once she has brought it to a close, she begins another, only once again to hold off concluding it. The postponement of the execution is repeated over the next thousand nights, during which time she has borne the king three sons. By the time Scheherazade tells the king she's finally run out of stories, he is too much in love with her to go through with the endlessly postponed execution, and so makes her his queen instead. While told by a single character, the stories in *One Thousand and One Nights* were collected over centuries across different regions of Asia and Africa and compiled in Arabic by Islamic scholars. Many are iterations of tales that go back to the very earliest civilizations and have been translated into new languages and cultures.

Scheherazade, in other words, releases her bridegroom from the grip of his rageful Groundhog Day by inducing him to hear other, unknown voices, stories and worlds. It may not be merely narrative suspense that ensures her survival, but the space and time she creates to make these unknown people and landscapes sensible to the king, pulling him out of his claustrophobic certainty and into new regions of strangeness and curiosity.

As an association to my wife's one-off gift, Scheherazade's tales may appear both wildly overblown and off the mark, not least because Ferrante's novel seemed to be signalling my wife's rage more than postponing mine. But I stand by its salience here, for Ferrante, Scheherazade and my wife address anger, whether their own or their partner's, in the indirect form of someone else's story. Stories, after all, unfold in language and narrative, which is to say over time. If they express rage, they do so not in in concentrated explosions of accusation and insult but in the intricately crafted creations of other voices, of characters and situations that we have to get to know.

In handing me *The Lost Daughter*, wasn't my wife at once communicating and displacing intimate personal truths about her experience of marriage and motherhood, sending a message from, and about, both herself and someone else to, and about, both me and someone else? Anyone who has been in, or even around, a long-term couple will be aware that marital rows are most destructive when their salvos are delivered in tones of self-certainty, or what I earlier called the knowledge of being right. If it didn't sound like an unintentionally hilarious parody of middle-class domesticity, I might propose that instead of trading wounding barbs, couples exchange novels.

Less concretely, I would suggest that lurking inside Scheherazade's storytelling ruse is the key to the problem of how to live with our anger. If anger is to serve as more than the emotional prelude to aggressive action – executing one's wives, say, or political opponents or deporting refugees or denying elections – then it must be disarmed of the self-certainty that propels it.

The affliction of the rageful person is that they are deprived of all voices but their own, which drowns out and excludes all others from the mind's ear. We need to find ways to make those voices audible, and to carve out the time and space to listen to them.

This fine-sounding proposition becomes questionable the moment we ask how we go about achieving this goal. If drowning out the other's voice is the essential logic of anger, it may not make much sense simply to propose we stop doing it.

A recent *Guardian* article compiled a helpful list of techniques for managing anger, among them the time-honoured hacks of counting to three, punching a pillow and walking in nature. Some techniques involve a temporary suspension of our anger, some a hydraulic discharge of it, others still a complete diversion away from it. But not even the most enthusiastic booster for these techniques is going to claim they can actually dispel anger; at best they can insert a pause, slow its momentum, perhaps bring some passing relief from the pressure it exerts on us.

Since there is no reliable method, psychoanalysis not excluded, for dispelling anger, only different ways of living with it, why should we object to hacks? If counting or yelling or breathing can shield us from the most reckless and destructive consequences of our rage, it would be hubris to disparage or dismiss them.

If there's a problem with such practical psychology, it arises not in its individual uses but in the internal relationship it sets up between ourselves and our angry feelings. Behavioural solutions, because their aim is to make us feel less angry, put us at odds with our anger, make an enemy of it. Put a brake on it or expel it or try to forget it, they exhort us; but at any rate, break off contact with it.

Scheherazade uses allied techniques, delaying and diverting her husband's anger until it finally exhausts itself, but what she doesn't do is try to coax him out of his anger. On the contrary, as dawn arrives each morning, she presents him with a choice which demands he listen to his own state of feeling: discharge your anger against women and put me to death, or spare me another day so you can hear the end of my story. At each of these moments, Shahryār is forced to measure his anger against his desire by listening to both, to ask himself whether his accumulated rage against women trumps his curiosity and excitement.

We can cast a little light on the nature of this dilemma by turning to the Italian psychoanalyst Eugenio Gaddini, whose paper of 1972, 'Aggression and the Pleasure Principle', develops a psychoanalytic theory of aggression. This involves distinguishing between two different kinds of human energy. The first, which he calls aggressive energy, is 'linked to the concept of *action*'. It serves the biological aim of achieving homeostasis, or the lowest and most even possible distribution of stimulus around the organism, by means of 'an *external* discharge of energy, through the motor apparatus'. The model for this discharge is set up at the beginning of life, namely the baby's 'muscular sucking apparatus', which serves as 'the first and complete model of coordinated action'.

In sucking at the mother's breast or a bottle, the baby is discharging through the muscles around his mouth and jaw the tension accumulated by his rising hunger. Directing his bodily 'motor apparatus' — the limbs and organs and muscles that work in concert to satisfy our bodily demands — to serve his nutritional needs, he is mounting his first aggressive action in the external world. Aggressive energy is primarily directed towards meeting vital needs in the name of survival. In this sense, its quality is essentially impersonal, oriented towards one's development not as an individual but as a member of the species. Put more crudely, it is more concerned with what I need than with what I want.

This is in direct contrast to Gaddini's second kind of energy, much more familiar in the context of psychoanalysis — libidinal energy. If aggressive energy tends outwards towards action, libidinal energy tends inwards towards *affect*, or feeling. It is the medium of desire, of the conduct of the individual rather than the member of a species. Feelings, as the word hints, disturb our internal equilibrium, arousing us to passions we may be unable to understand or to bring under our control. Our individuality is defined in and through our feelings; without feelings, we are interchangeably functional units permanently stuck in the loop of our own blind survival. Aggression, we might say, anonymizes me, where libido personalizes me.

For aggressive energy, discharge is imperative and the baby can't tolerate its postponement for long; the longer he remains unfed, for example, the more liable he is to become psychically as well as somatically dysregulated. Libidinal tension, on the other hand, is generally easier to bear; indeed, children and adults alike know that the gratifications of pleasure – gustatory, sexual or otherwise – can often be enhanced by being postponed. As Gaddini has it, 'Libidinal tension . . . is less rigid and more plastic and, inasmuch as it is a source of pleasure, it can be prolonged.'

We can see the tension between these two kinds of energy at work in the Scheherazade story. Shahryār's serial execution of his brides is a bid to kill off the possibility of homeostatic disturbance (in this case, the humiliation of an unfaithful wife) before it can even arise. It has the urgency and impersonality of blind action taken in the name of survival. Shahryār won't literally die if his bride lives, of course, but the possibility of her betrayal is felt by him as an intolerable threat to his basic sense of personal integrity and cohesion.

The impersonality Gaddini ascribes to aggressive energy operates here at its furthest extreme. How true, loving and desirable an individual bride may be doesn't matter to Shahryār; each one exists only as an abstract representative of the hated category of 'woman', and it is as such rather than as a singular person that he executes her. There is also, to be sure, an element of libidinal energy at work in his murderousness, for the threat he feels from female sexuality hints at quantities of anger and desire in him that he cannot keep under control. But this libidinal charge is enlisted in the service of his aggressive bid for mastery over the other.

In snaring her husband in the web of her stories, Scheherazade rebalances the distributions of aggressive and libidinal energy. As long as he's dominated by aggression, Shahryār cannot allow action to be postponed; he must kill the next bride before she can expose him to any further humiliation. But under the spell cast by Scheherazade, he can begin to bear the 'more plastic' tension of libido, to live more for desire than for survival.

Scheherazade's position in the network of royal power and

prerogative doesn't allow her to express anger; we see only her charm, wit and deference, those attitudes and traits she is licensed to display in the royal court. But it isn't hard to imagine her story-telling scheme being tacitly informed by a kind of angry urgency to stop the flow of femicides and bring to heel the unrelenting violence of her husband's will. To the rigid, unyielding aggressive energy of Shahryār, she opposes an adaptive and flexible libidinal energy.

An excess of aggressive energy tends to foster the illusion that I am, to use Winnicott's term, an 'isolate', an integral being sealed off from all other beings, with whom I must compete for life's necessities. Libidinal energy signals, on the contrary, that my existence is inextricably bound up with and dependent on others. It is much easier to cut yourself off from feelings about others if you can convince yourself you don't depend on others.

This dependency, as Shahryār so starkly reminds us, is apt to make us feel very angry and humiliated, even to the point that, rather than bear these feelings, we might prefer to kill the person who arouses them.

Every patient I've seen leaves an indelible sensory impression, some quality of their voice or walk or dress or smile. When I recall Stella's face, delicate, oval and pale, it is caught forever in mid-eyeroll, as though there could be no escape, even for a moment, from life's crushing irony. So defining was the gesture, it seemed to spread from her face into the insouciant rhythms of her speech and movement, as though one could eyeroll with one's whole body.

Literary theorists note that irony, saying something other than what we mean, can be used both to unsettle meaning and to fix it in place. Stella's irony was very much of the latter variety. Whatever she might say, I was rarely left in doubt as to how she really felt. The fluency of her speech never wavered, nor the soft and even pitch of her voice, nor the easy grace with which her open hand sliced the air as she spoke. Yet she made no pretence of concealing the sheer rage lurking behind her languid elegance.

I had first seen her in March, when she told me her marriage was becoming intolerable. When I asked her why, she told me it was because Max, her husband of nine years, was 'irredeemably useless' as a husband, father and lover, for all his talent as a consultant cardiologist. 'He knows all about hearts,' she said, her voice lilting gently upwards as she arched her eyebrow, and added, 'with the mysterious exception of mine.'

From our first meeting I was aware and wary of the temptation to be recruited to her psychic team, to enjoy too readily the gleeful precision with which she dispatched her targets. Most people come to me for the first time in a state of palpable anxiety and confusion, unable to make sense of what they are feeling or why. Stella seemed peculiarly clear on both counts; she was feeling the exasperation and despair of being married to a man of acutely low emotional intelligence.

Those early sessions quickly became exercises in remote evisceration, brutal yet forensically precise dissections of Max's manifold incompetencies. He would put their little girl's skirt on her back to front or drone tediously at dinner parties about the latest advances in coronary medicine. He could go a week without asking a single question about herself or her life, but come the weekend he could be relied upon to signal sexual desire 'by way of this ludicrous grin, which he seems to delude himself is a seductive smile, asking me if "I . . . you know . . . fancy a bit of fun upstairs?" "Like what, Max," I feel like replying, "chasing diazepam with a bottle of vodka?"'

At the edges of these performative assassinations I could feel a hint of seduction, as though relaying these shaming details of Max's inadequacies were a way of marking me off from him, placing me as the adult man to his outsize boy and letting me know she was sure *I* knew how to soothe a crying child, load a dishwasher or locate a clitoris.

I would dutifully remind myself I was the object of an idealizing transference, that such ostentatious love was only ever the obverse of an unconscious hate. But perhaps I was only paying lip service to these cautions, unconsciously setting them aside so I could continue to enjoy the dubious narcissistic pleasure of triumphing over a phantom husband.

A few weeks later, Stella returned to the first session after Easter break noticeably pale and downcast. She lay still for a couple of minutes before flatly announcing, 'He's left me.'

'He's . . . left you?' I said.

'That's what I said, wasn't it?' she replied. 'He's. Left. Me.'

I remained silent, too disorientated to speak.

'Well, I'll say one thing for him – he's surprised me. And you too, by the sounds of it.'

I said nothing.

'Nope, didn't see that one coming,' she continued, 'but then, neither did you. And you're the shrink. Can't help thinking there was a big miss somewhere along the line.' Then, for the first time, a furious break in the breezily ironic tone: 'Yes, a big, expensive fucking miss PROF! *YOU ARE THE PSYCHOANALYST! Why didn't you say something?*'

The Greek word *anagnorisis* describes the point in a story when a key character makes a discovery that casts his previous experience in a new and transformative light. The most famous example is also a *locus classicus* for psychoanalysis: the discovery by Oedipus that he's murdered his father and married his mother. The word came to me unbidden in that moment, alongside the startling realization that I hadn't said something for all that time because, while I'd been listening, I'd not picked up what I needed to hear, namely that when she had talked about her useless husband, *she had been talking about me.*

Every analyst in every analysis draws a transference to themselves. I had lulled myself into believing that I stood for some version of her father, a successful and dominant man who treated her mother with the same reflexive impatience Stella showed towards her husband. I hadn't wanted to notice that the man she'd been talking about and eyerolling all those weeks, the man who knew neither how to listen nor how to communicate, who might have a good enough reputation but was clearly no use to her, this man, whatever name she may have called him, was me.

Perhaps this interpretation sounds like too wild a stretch, an instance of the psychoanalyst's annoying habit of making everything about themselves. Only when I put it to Stella, she paused and seemed to recover her seamless composure. 'Hmm,' she said, 'yes. That sounds about right.' She paused again. 'Even a stopped clock, blah blah blah.'

This first stage of work with Stella serves as a cogent reminder that psychoanalysis is a way of thinking about the strange knots of time. One of Freud's most enigmatic and productive concepts, developed especially in his 1918 'Wolf Man' case, is *Nachträglichkeit*, literally 'afterwardsness'. The rendering of the term by James Strachey, Freud's English translator, as 'deferred action' is misleading, connoting as it does the idea of an event or experience whose meaning is deferred – that is, which can only be understood at a later date.

This isn't exactly wrong, but it's unhelpfully linear, as though it were simply a matter of waiting for the real meaning of the earlier event to come into focus later. French psychoanalysis in the mid-twentieth century, under the influence of Jacques Lacan in particular, proved more adept at coaxing out the deeper and more unsettling sense of Freud's term, coining the rendition now widely used even in Anglophone psychoanalysis: *après-coup*.

Après-coup, literally 'after-blow', captures the essential non-linearity of psychoanalytic time. Retrospection doesn't simply clarify or explain earlier events in our lives; throwing time out of joint, it can bring those events into being, as though the later experience preceded the earlier one. When Oedipus discovers the truth of his origins, he doesn't merely learn something new about his past; he undergoes a kind of shattering transformation of his whole life and self. In an experiential sense, we could say, Oedipus commits patricide and maternal incest decades after he kills his father and beds his mother.

In fact, tragedy is almost always shaped by an *après-coup* logic for the simple reason that it portrays human beings in the grip of forces they cannot comprehend in the moment they're at work. And for that reason, when comprehension comes it always comes too late. As he visits the ultimate retribution on himself for his wife's murder, Othello asks to be remembered as 'one that loved not wisely, but too well; / Of one not easily jealous, but, being wrought, / Perplexed in the extreme'. Othello's *anagnorisis* involves not merely the discovery of previously unknown facts – the unaccountably malign stratagems of Iago – but of unbearable truths about himself. He realizes too late that he was vulnerable to his ensign's manipulation because his passions exceeded him. Loving 'too well' means loving not too generously but too *much*, to a point where he is mastered by, and not master of, his love.

Recall Itzig on the wild horse, so often invoked by Freud to figure the ferocious momentum of the drive. 'Where are you going?' shout the peasants on the road. 'Do I know?' he replies, 'Ask the horse.' This is Othello's *après-coup*, the sudden awareness that his passion has ridden him into regions too dark to see where he's gone or what he's done. Iago's diabolical subtlety lies in his intuition of the precise quantum of doubt required to turn Othello's over-abundant love to rageful jealousy.

We might also say, following Gaddini, that Iago transforms the energy driving Othello's passion. When we meet Othello, he speaks with a rare refinement of feeling and emotional insight of how he and Desdemona fell in love. At her father Brabantio's house, having regaled her with stories of war and savagery, 'She loved me for the dangers I had passed, / And I loved her that she did pity them.' In these lines we hear a voice turned inward, tuned into the life of feeling, attending to the subtleties of emotional exchange: she falls in love listening to him, he falls in love with her listening. This is the delicately personal quality of relating that characterizes libidinal energy. Iago captures that energy and spikes it, injecting a poisonous suspicion into the abundant stream of Othello's love and turning it into an ungovernable excess of blind aggression. He brutally depersonalizes Desdemona for Othello, who comes to see her like one of Shahryār's virgin brides, an interchangeable exemplar of feminine evil, fit only to be killed.

In the light of the *après-coup*, ignorance is revealed not as an unfortunate contingency of psychic life but as its essence. Ironically enough, this ignorance is something of which we prefer to remain ignorant. Confronted with their own vulnerability, Louis Trevelyan, Shahryār and Othello choose the destructive consequences of false certainty rather than bear the inevitable pain of not knowing.

To trust the one you love is indeed a terrible risk; the meaning of trust implies the possibility of its betrayal. Once awakened to this possibility, none of these three men can live with it. They prefer the conviction their lover is false to ignorance of whether she's true, even as this preference consigns them to their own personal hell.

For the man caught in this hell of his own making, anger becomes his reliable friend, a comfort blanket swaddled tightly round himself, the assurance, even as he suffers at the extremities of isolation and self-hatred, that he's right. Anger serves as a talisman against doubt, against having to go through life knowing very little, either about ourselves or anyone close to us.

For Trevelyan and Othello, the *après-coup* can only be a disaster, forcing them to reckon with a truth they've spent most of their lives furiously denying. We might say that both die of the *après-coup*, of the knowledge that clinging to their rightness has cost them their own and another's lives.

Rightness runs on aggressive energy; it is defensive, automatic and will not take the risk of listening to the self or to another, which is to say the risk of being led by desire. This is the chance we take when we let ourselves be guided by the flows of libidinal energy, by the feelings that animate and unsettle body and soul alike. Perhaps it's here that we start to edge towards a sense of what it would be to have a positive and meaningful experience of our own anger. Aggressive anger stakes itself on the premise that if we already know we're right, we never have to get up close to our angry feelings, to listen to what they're saying, to what unknown anxieties and desires might secretly be driving them.

How might a more libidinally driven anger be different? To invoke the Itzig analogy, it wouldn't mean allowing the wild horse of rage to hurtle towards blind action; nor would it mean wielding the riding crop of anger management to force the horse to a premature halt. To recall Antonio Damasio, it would involve the experience of feelings rather than mere emotions. Where emotions in Damasio's sense are essentially reactive stimulus responses (the realm of aggressive energy), feelings involve the internal mapping of those immediate stimuli, listening to and making sense of what they're telling us, raising our trigger responses to a higher level of consciousness.

This isn't to imply that feelings are serene and contemplative, looking down from an Olympian height at our hardwired primitive reactions. The transition into feeling means that emotion finds a footing in ideas and words, a mode of expression beyond reaction. In anger management, the idea is to stop feeling angry; in psychoanalysis, the aim is more to start feeling angry rather than merely being angry.

The Hulk, recall, *is* angry, is anger itself, but this manifestation of anger comes at the explicit price of radical dissociation from the speaking human being in whom he originated. Having lost all contact with words and ideas, the Hulk's only expressive vehicle is violent action. In anger management, he would be enjoined to calm down, as though his anger were a toddler whose waywardness must be brought under control by the finger-wagging parent called reason.

Psychoanalysis would instead be interested in bringing the Hulk back into contact with the man from whom he's split off, in finding ways for the man, whose anger is trapped on the inside, and the monster, whose anger is trapped on the outside, to give voice to one another. Simply calming him down and getting him to speak reasonably would ensure that his anger was never heard *as anger*, as felt experience, but as a temporary bit of madness from which he's now moved on.

The difference between suppressing and listening to our anger has significance far beyond the confines of the consulting room and the individual. Its broader implications are made evident in the ways our political masters respond to the anger of its citizens. In 2022 the UK government passed the Police, Crime, Sentencing and Courts Act (PCSCA), which instituted a major expansion of the state's power to regulate protest, giving the police discretion to ban or curtail public protests and to impose massive fines and prison sentences on activists deemed to be obstructing highways or other public areas.

The following year saw the passage of the Public Order Act (2023), which has added to the PCSCA new provisions to expand police stop and search powers for individuals suspected of plans to commit protest-related offences, as well as specifically criminalizing 'locking on' and other obstructive tactics used by climate activists to interfere with fossil-fuel-based infrastructure and transport systems.

Under these provisions, two Just Stop Oil activists, Marcus Decker and Morgan Trowland, received two-year prison sentences for climbing the cables of a suspension bridge in Dartford, where the London Orbital Motorway (M25) crosses the Thames. It is difficult to avoid the suspicion, which its recent abandonments of key environmental commitments on transport, energy and forest protection have only amplified, that the current Conservative government's aim is to silence not merely anger but the urgency and anxiety that fuel it. Even as it dismantles projects to address the climate emergency and suppresses the voices that call attention to it, it continues its gaslighting insistence that it is meeting its green pledges.

The government points to the availability of other avenues of protest such as petitions and letter-writing, forms of representation that corral anger into the narrowest and most innocuous channels, licensing their recipients to pay lip service to them if not ignore them altogether. In other words, it seeks to create a kind of hostile environment for public anger.

This hostility, however, is notably selective. As the government was preparing to pass the Public Order Bill, the former

Conservative leader and MP Iain Duncan Smith publicly backed pro-motorist activists who vandalized Ultra Low Emission Zone (ULEZ) cameras monitoring polluting car emissions in London. It turns out there is a much more congenial environment for obstructing or destroying infrastructure that challenges fossil fuel interests than for infrastructure that supports them.

We saw in the previous chapter that contemporary populism harnesses a diffuse anger that it mobilizes for the protection of the existing order and against the threat of any change or disturbance to it. This is the anger generated by aggressive energy, which leaps to action that will buttress power and silence any voices which unsettle or question it. Its primary enemy is libidinal energy, which is concerned not with maintaining homeostatic comfort but with asking what it is that we desire, individually and collectively. From the perspective of power, the problem with desire is that it might induce us to refuse what's on offer and demand something new.

Psychoanalysis differentiates itself from behavioural therapies above all in listening for the unpredictable flows of libidinal energy, even if this means putting in question ourselves and our lives. In this sense, it has an essential affinity with art, with which it shares a capacity to unsettle our assumptions about who we are and what we want.

When my wife handed me *The Lost Daughter* with that peculiar urgency, she was letting me know that this was one of those works of art that intrude into the most private and vulnerable spaces of a person's interior and lodges there. She was signalling a kind of disturbance at the border between fiction and reality, a sense that this novel might be carrying truths too violent for reality to bear, things unsayable in the medium of ordinary conversation, even the most intimate. Sometimes the strangest and most difficult feelings can be made audible, to ourselves and each other, only through the detours and displacements of fiction.

Or, in Ferrante's case, potboilers: dizzyingly paced sagas rich in conflict, crisis, scandal, carnality, in all the narrative pleasures and enervations of 'low' cultural forms – teen photo-romances, women's magazines, soap operas – she avowedly draws on. But in borrowing from these subgenres, she divines in them concealed horrors they themselves can never disclose, and stretches them to excess, threatening their structure and coherence.

The spark that lights the touchpaper of Ferrante's stories is typically a breakdown, which becomes not only the motor of the narrator's plot, but the event that induces her to write in the first place. Namely the novels portray events whose force and meaning can't be contained in the minds of those to whom they happen. This is where they exceed soap opera: the disaster they dramatize is less the objective experience of loss, betrayal, abandonment or violence than the shattering of any means of representing it, the unravelling of any story that could tell it.

Leda, for example, the narrator and protagonist of *The Lost Daughter*, connects Nani, the doll she has stolen from a little girl, to her second pregnancy. In her own mind, Leda's first pregnancy was a period of intense pleasure, a transcendent experience of carrying a life 'purified of humors and blood, humanized, intellectualized, with nothing that could evoke the blind cruelty of live matter as it expands'.

The doll reminds her that her second pregnancy was very far from this airy, near disembodied experience. As she empties from the depths of its inert body a viscous stream of grainy brown liquid, she recalls carrying the foetus that would become her daughter, Marta:

She attacked my body, forcing it to turn on itself, out of

control. She immediately manifested herself not as Marta but as a piece of living iron in my stomach. My body became a bloody liquid; suspended in it was a mushy sediment inside which grew a violent polyp, so far from anything human that it reduced me, even though it fed and grew, to rotting matter without life. Nani, with her black spittle, resembles me when I was pregnant for the second time.

Living iron, bloody liquid, mushy sediment, violent polyp, rotting matter, black spittle – the pile-up of imagery is a delirious mimesis of the body's, and the novel's, 'out of control' attack on itself. The controlled beauty of the 'humanized, intellectualized' novel sinks sickeningly into a formless, overlapping mass of bodily symptoms and redundant synonyms. 'The real breakdown for me,' Leda comments, 'was that: the giving up of any sublimation of my pregnancy'. Not the pregnancy itself, but her inability to give it creative or intellectual form – this is the misfortune afflicting Leda.

The passage places us in the region Ferrante calls *frantumaglia*, a Neapolitan dialect word meaning 'jumble of fragments'. For Ferrante, this is the sudden and incomprehensible revelation of the self to itself as 'an infinite serial or aquatic mass of debris', a pure disorder or incoherence lurking just under the surface of the discrete, integral *I* we present to the world. It is also the state of psychic and linguistic chaos lurking just under, and forever threatening to break through, the precise and efficient surface of Ferrante's prose.

My wife gave me *The Lost Daughter* as a husband and father, as a writer, but also, and again ambiguously, as a psychoanalyst. Ambiguously because she was fully aware of passing on a book that seems to affirm some of the most basic psychoanalytic insights about maternal ambivalence, but also a book that ought to make a man, even and especially a male psychoanalyst, wary of understanding it too quickly.

You, husband and father and analyst, *need to read this* because your life at home and your training and your daily work may lead you to think you know something about what motherhood does to a woman, which may even be right but which is also fatally wrong, wrong in a way that this book makes fully apparent.

In fact, this is just where Ferrante locates her suspicions about psychoanalysis, that is, in its tendency to 'organize into universal representations what in the individual, beyond any system, beyond any analysis, remains pure specific inner disorder, irreducible flashes of ectoplasm, a jumble of fragments without any chronology'.

Put more simply, what troubles Ferrante above all about psychoanalysis is its orientation towards understanding, which often enough tends also to be the orientation of husbands and fathers and analysts towards mothers. Ferrante loves Freud, she says, because he perceived more perspicuously than his followers that 'psychoanalysis is the lexicon of the precipice' – its concepts are too dangerous, too resistant to our efforts to know and understand, to be assimilated to 'expert' knowledge. It's not surprising, then, that in another interview from 2015 for *The Paris Review*, Ferrante remarks that, she has, from the beginning, 'produced a writing that is dissatisfied with itself'. Her narrators, and the stories they tell, are driven by a dissatisfaction that is only exacerbated by all their restless and ultimately vain attempts to resolve it.

Dissatisfaction is the motor of her writing, and its expressive medium is rage. Each of her protagonists is afflicted at the outset by some wound – a humiliation or betrayal – to which they will not reconcile themselves, which they insist on protesting, resisting, lamenting, thus consigning themselves to an anger ever deeper and more irremediable. The Neapolitan Quartet begins with the narrator Lenù's rage at her best friend Lila's decision, at the age of sixty-six, to withdraw herself wholesale from the world and 'eliminate the entire life she had left behind'. In her most recent novel, *The Lying Life of Adults*, the narrator's aunt Vittoria is a teeming volcano, permanently enraged at her brother for having broken up her affair with a married man. And in Ferrante's second novel, *The Days of Abandonment*, Olga, the protagonist and narrator, becomes an increasingly angry polemicist against explanation, specifically the trite rationalizations offered to her when her husband Mario leaves her for another, much younger woman.

Mario's colleague tells her, 'It's that age. Mario is forty – it happens.' Olga finds it particularly unbearable to be told Mario is simply conforming to expected behavioural patterns, as though merely knowing this should salve the gaping wound of her abandonment and humiliation. But the expectation of resigned equanimity is all around her, not least in herself: 'The reasonableness of others and my own desire for tranquility got on my nerves.'

Despite her anger, Olga imposes a code of good behaviour on herself – she will not intrude on Mario's friends, she will not be hateful – a code that derives from the longstanding and deeply internalized imperative to conceal the 'clamorous life' within. Over the years, she has taught herself to speak in gentle tones, to subordinate all instinctual reactions to thoughtful delay, 'to wait patiently until every emotion imploded and could come out in a tone of calm, my voice held back in my throat so that I would not make a spectacle of myself'.

Described thus, this struggle between impulses to express and to withhold emotion starts to look more complicated than a straightforward conflict between instinctual violence and civilized self-control. Freud, after all, reminds us that repression draws its energy from the forces of lust and rage it wants to repress, employing their violence against them. To tell someone, yourself or another, in the grip of rage to stay calm, that these things happen, that you'll get over it, is as likely to be felt as an attack as a reassurance, a denial of what you're feeling and a demand to feel otherwise.

Read in this light, Ferrante's entire corpus starts to reverberate with the same conflict between two kinds of anger. The first is the rage of the afflicted, the neglected, the betrayed, of the pent-up accumulations of dissatisfaction and demand we hear in the voices of *Troubling Love*'s Delia, in Leda, Olga, Lenù, Lila, and in *The Lying Life of Adults*'s Vittoria, as well as in the protests of exploited factory workers whose voices intrude into the febrile chorus of everyday life in the Neapolitan Quartet.

This rage – searching, vulnerable, uncertain of what it wants – aligns with the libidinally driven anger I've described above. Set alongside it, the second kind of anger is rooted in fear of this first kind. It is the rage of men against women, rich against poor, fascists and Camorrists against ordinary citizens, mothers against daughters. And it's the rage of individuals, especially women, against themselves.

Who was Stella raging against? Against her husband certainly, at times her mother, and eventually, as we've seen, against me. For weeks, she sustained a cold fury towards me for my failure to call out her unrelenting criticism and denigration of her husband. Wasn't it obvious that he wasn't going to put up with it indefinitely, that at some point his rope would fray irreparably?

'I'm aware,' she said, 'of your professional duty to remain neutral, refrain from directing me and all of that, but I was telling you daily that I made him feel useless and unwanted and you just *sat* there, like you were witnessing a car barrel full speed into some poor oblivious pedestrian without so much as a warning shout.'

Who was she in this analogy, I asked her, the car driver or the pedestrian?

'What?' she replied, raising her voice. 'This is the problem, I tell you something urgent and you give back pedantry. Who was I, I don't know! The driver I suppose. God knows that's what Max would've said.'

'I'm not sure the question is pedantic. I think your analogy is more telling than you realize. It was you I didn't shout a warning to. That surely makes you the poor oblivious pedestrian.'

'Fine,' she said irritably, then paused. 'So who's the driver then? I'm not aware of anyone having rammed me with a car, real or figurative.'

'Except perhaps for you.'

The impact felt palpable in the silence that followed, as though she had indeed been hit by a figurative car. For perhaps the first time since we'd started, I felt like I had some sense of where her mind was. I said we both seemed to be contemplating a scene of helplessness in the face of disaster; a driver who can't stop the car, a pedestrian who can't see it coming, a witness who can't shout a warning.

In a tone of deep sadness and quiet, she said, 'You're describing my life.'

When I'd been hit by the *après-coup* realization that the useless man she'd been railing against was me, a question had continued to trouble me: why had she needed me to warn her? Wasn't it obvious to her what she was doing? The analogy with the imminent accident gave me a kind of answer: the scene cast her as driver, pedestrian *and* witness, watching herself fall under her own speeding car and unable to run out of the way, hit the brake or shout a warning. Her complaint now was that she had needed me to be the witness she couldn't be to herself, to shout loud enough to startle her out of her self-destructive rage.

Psychoanalysis frequently reproduces or (to use the technical term) enacts the scenarios the patient creates outside the consulting room. This is what had happened here: Stella rendered me, the person she most needed to help her, helpless. Although to put it this way gives the misleading impression that I was her victim. It would be more accurate to say that I was complicit with her, that like so many of the people around her, I fell in with the idea that she was the safe and confident driver of her own life. I didn't let it occur to me that she was unable to get out of the way of her own car, that even as she could see she was heading for the collision she couldn't tell herself to stop.

Yes, the useless person concealed by Max was me; but the useless person concealed by me, and the ultimate object of her rage, was Stella herself. Here the word 'useless' takes on a poignant resonance. In his seminal paper of 1969, 'The Use of an Object', D. W. Winnicott suggests that in earliest life, a child needs to develop the capacity to use others.

Using another person has an overwhelmingly negative connotation for us, connoting an instrumental if not cynical way of relating to them. Winnicott's point is that we're able to use someone only when we recognize that we need them, that is, when we see in them something they can offer and that we don't already have. This requires us to perceive the other as separate from us rather than, as Winnicott has it, 'a bundle of projections'.

When the other is a mere bundle of our projections, we reduce them to versions of ourselves. Instead of being seen for who they are, they become embodiments of our own anxieties, beliefs and desires. This was Stella's predicament, the source of her malaise. Everyone she cared about sooner or later became a bundle of her projections, an iteration of the inadequate, disappointing self she saw in the mirror. Her husband was indeed 'useless', but only because she lacked the means to use him.

What might happen in early life to prevent us from developing this capacity? A child can only learn to use an adult who can let themselves be used. Behind her soft and affectionate persona, Stella's mother had concealed a profound depression. A year after she had first come to see me, Stella began to talk to her mother about her early years. Her mother, reluctant at first to 'rake over the past', seemed to feel some relief in talking about a period experienced in such lonely isolation.

Stella's mother had given up her work as a GP to raise Stella and the sister that came after her. Stella's father ran a successful medical publishing company that frequently kept him at the office into the evenings. Having assumed she would take to childrearing with ease and pleasure, her mother was in some shock, as well as feeling overwhelmingly guilty, at the sheer boredom and nervous exhaustion motherhood induced in her. Her husband would only exacerbate his wife's sense of inadequacy and self-hatred, telling her that her negative feelings 'weren't natural', that she had nothing to complain about, she should try doing his job for a few days – that'd give her reason to grumble.

'I was wary of her,' Stella told me. 'I can't remember her ever having shouted at me, and only a few explicitly cross words. But from the youngest age I was aware of how close she seemed to unravelling – forever asking us with that pitiful imploring look to stop running, laughing, arguing, forever at the edge of migraine or swallowing the lump in her throat.' Stella found herself perpetually tiptoeing around her mother, all the while quietly accumulating and suppressing her own resentments and tensions.

It wasn't difficult to see the traces of this history in Stella's adult personality. Her brutally high-handed irony was rooted in a repudiation of her mother's neediness and sensitivity, ensuring that everyone around her was useless, meaning they could never make her feel dependent on them. She cultivated an aggressive rage that helped shore up her invulnerability and confirm no one could give her anything – love, interest, pleasure, care – she really needed.

She had married out of an unconscious wish to prove she had no need of a husband, and entered psychoanalysis from an unconscious wish to prove she had no need of an analyst. If she now wanted her husband back and needed an analyst to understand herself, then who was she? She had wanted to believe she was her father's daughter, emotionally self-sufficient and in command of the world around her, only to find herself living the lonely and precarious inner life of her mother.

How was she to discover an anger she could use?

The maternal relationship is the primary source of rage for Ferrante's characters. Most of her narrator-protagonists are both mothers and daughters, caught in a pincer movement of the generations above and below. Leda recalls her mother dragging her from the sea trembling with cold:

> When she saw that my teeth were chattering she became even more furious, yanked me, covered me from head to toe in a towel, rubbed me with such an energy, such violence that I didn't really know if it was worry for my health or a long-fostered rage, a ferocity, that chafed my skin.

Rage blurs the boundaries between love and hate. The unbearable burden of love that stirs Leda's mother to such alarm is felt as a ferocious resentment and a wish, rubbed violently into her daughter's skin, to be free of its overbearing demands. In becoming a mother herself, Leda will fall into the same trap.

Recalling a day when her daughter got lost on the beach, she takes up the perspective of a frightened child with rare empathetic insight: 'A child who gets lost on the beach sees everything unchanged and yet no longer recognizes anything.' But when Leda finally finds her, the empathy instantly gives way to rage, as she screams at her daughter 'with rage, like my mother, because of the crushing weight of responsibility, the bond that strangles, and with my free arm I dragged my firstborn, yelling, you'll pay for this, Bianca, you'll see when we get home . . .'

Leda is still the little girl reeling under the blows of her mother's raging love, even as she becomes the mother, dispossessed by the incomprehensible intensity of her own rage. What becomes insupportable in that moment is the sense of loss and abandonment conveyed by Bianca's tears, inducing in Leda a pain so excruciatingly close to her own childhood experience, she can only drown it out in furious threats.

For Ferrante, a mother can never avoid transmitting to her child the same state of unconscious self-division inherited from her own mother. The mother's wish to redeem the privations and cruelties of her own childhood comes into tension with a resentment towards the daughter enjoying the freedoms and possibilities she lacked. In *Those Who Leave and Those Who Stay*, Lenù's mother Immacolata, deprived from childhood of any educational or commercial exit paths out of poverty, menaces her daughter, now a published novelist and fiancée to a distinguished young professor, with the injunction not to forget that 'I who carried you in here am just as intelligent, if not more, and if I had had the chance I would have done the same as you, understand?'

Immacolata fights her own desire to realize through her child the future denied herself, the wish described by Freud in his essay on narcissism to 'fulfil those wishful dreams of the parents which they never carried out'. In *The Story of the Lost Child*, the last of the Quartet, Immacolata from her sickbed speaks to Lenù of her life as an unending series of dissatisfactions: marriage to a man she can't recall ever having given her pleasure, a lack of feeling for the children she bore after Lenù ('a sin for which she would go to Hell'), and finally the disappointment of Lenù herself, now the scandalous woman who has left her respectable husband for a pathological philanderer.

For Immacolata, Lenù is her eldest and 'only true child', the moment of her birth 'the only good thing in my life', which only makes her refusal of Immacolata's narcissistic projections all the more unforgivable. Lenù, for her part, is caught in a peculiar bind; without the self-assertive anger that has enabled her to escape the confines of the neighbourhood, she could not have fulfilled her mother's deepest wish, namely that she live a different and better life. But the same anger has led to an irremediable separation that her mother has felt as violently hostile. Immacolata carries an anger sufficiently fierce to disrupt the existing order, but which has been diverted into shoring it up. Thus does libidinal anger become aggressive.

This conflict between a disruptive libidinal anger and a reactive aggressive anger haunts Ferrante's novels, frequently manifesting in conflagrations – marital breakdowns, generational clashes, labour disputes – that leave behind only a patch of scorched earth. But there are also sporadic hints of an anger that can be channelled and employed creatively. Indeed, the explicit impetus for Lenù to write Lila's and her own story is the rage she feels when Lila disappears and erases from the world all traces of herself. Instead of cancelling itself out, Lenù's rage finds a home in writing.

The Quartet explores the ways anger can be marshalled as a source of creative energy. The most memorable instance might be an incident in the second volume, *The Story of a New Name*, in which Lila, now unhappily married to local entrepreneur and Camorrist Stefano Carracci, strikes out at her abusive husband by creating a work of art. Lila takes an old advertisement featuring her photo, resplendent in her wedding dress and shoes, and subjects it to artful deformation.

With 'glue, scissors, paper and paint', the materials of the children's art room, Lila's destructive rage channels and transforms itself through play. Using pinned strips of black paper, she erases herself from the image, leaving only bodily traces: an eye, a mouth, a strip of bust, a line of leg, the shoes. The effect is conveyed through the impression of a dramatic change in Lila's mood, as Lenù writes:

> Lila was happy, and she was drawing me deeper and deeper into her fierce happiness, because she had suddenly found, perhaps without even realizing it, an opportunity to *portray* the fury she directed against herself, the insurgence, perhaps for the first time in her life, of the need . . . to erase herself.

In this moment, creative and destructive expressions of anger meet each other not in a mutually annihilating fight to the death but in a paradoxical and productive collusion. Lila erases herself, but this erasure becomes a portrait, a way of giving body to her wish to disappear.

The story of the defaced photograph, like the Quartet, like all of Ferrante's writing, reminds us why anger needs art. In art, anger finds a home for itself, a mutual accommodation in which the house isn't burnt down and the fire isn't extinguished. Perhaps this is what makes the gift of a book such an effective way to convey a secret rage. Pressed into the receiver's hands, it transmits to them a ferocious heat that somehow, miraculously, doesn't burn them.

Sarcasm, exasperation, contempt: ways of expressing anger that defend against really feeling anger, which was surely why Stella made such liberal use of them. The contemptuous person places herself above the object of her contempt, but equally above herself. She makes a show of her low opinion of the other but betrays nothing of how hurt or vulnerable she may feel before them, or of her need for their love and care. The need disgusts her, for it makes her feel as weak and useless as the person she disparages.

Within a couple of weeks of his leaving her, Stella discovered Max had been having an affair with a junior doctor in his department. In the previous few sessions, I'd sensed with some hopefulness the quality of perfect, high-handed superiority she always conveyed giving way to a more ordinary, emotionally layered anger infused with sadness, perhaps even a hint of regret.

Anger becomes less rigidly defensive at the point it makes contact with neighbouring emotions like sadness and anxiety. As Gaddini implies, this is where it shifts from expressing itself in the impersonal form of aggression to its more libidinal manifestation of felt inner life. Simply put, it is the difference between insulting the other person and telling them honestly why you feel hurt and angered by them.

Stella seemed to be leaning into her feelings of hurt and loss in the days following Max's abrupt departure. She was under no illusion as to how much cause she'd given Max to leave, only in shock at his finding the will to do so. 'I suppose I thought he'd resigned himself to being a punching bag. And being who he is, he never caught on that I secretly wanted him to stand up to me. Now he's run away instead.'

But once she discovered the affair, her contempt went into overdrive: 'I gather she's about twenty-eight,' she said. 'What a pathetically sad cliché, high-flying middle-aged consultant taking up with simpering little Miss Junior.' She switched into a breathy, high-pitched comedy voice, 'Oh Mr Max, can I *pleeease* sit in on your stenting consultation?' And then back to herself, 'It'd be funny if it weren't so crushingly sad.' And then, addressing me, 'I expect any man would leave his family for a decent blow job and a tighter cunt. How about you, *Prof*? Surely even you couldn't resist a pretty young girl on her knees?'

At first it all sounded like a reversion to a reassuringly familiar register. But it was impossible not to catch, under the surface of her unforgiving mockery, the rage and pain of abandonment, of an entire, intricate system of defence breaking down inexorably.

Recalling the tremor of barely controlled ferocity in her voice, it is hard not to think of Ferrante's Olga in *The Days of Abandonment* catching sight of her husband Mario strolling the streets with his young lover Carla, her ears bearing family heirloom earrings that had once belonged to Olga. After ramming Mario's face into a glass window, throwing him to the floor and kicking him, she makes to rip the earrings from Carla's lobes and 'tear the flesh':

> So she thought she had full rights to take my place, to play my part, the fucking whore. Give me those earrings, give me those earrings. I wanted to drag along her beautiful face with the eyes the nose the lips the scalp the blond hair, I wanted to drag them with me as if with a hook I'd snagged her garment of flesh, the sacks of her breasts, the belly that rapped the bowels and spilled out through the asshole, through the deep crack crowned with gold.

I would hear similarly violent urges towards Max's young lover from Stella, albeit not graduating to actual physical attack. But for a few days at least, it felt like that same level of aggressive rage was seething in her, lacking any outlet beyond her sessions. I let her rant uninterrupted, discharge her fury in an avalanche of increasingly unbound hate replete with hair-raising Ferrantean imagery.

What did that cunning little bitch want with a sad old pot-bellied pig like Max? But of course, she was probably slipping his credit card out of his inside pocket while her other hand played the decoy down his pants. What a colossally deluded, narcissistic prick he was, believing her interest could have any other motive.

Those sessions were draining and distressing, for her as well as for me no doubt, but also very necessary. Stella drove her aggression to the point of collapse, until one Tuesday morning she wept silently for thirty minutes and then, in a whisper redolent with sleeplessness and pain, said 'Who wouldn't leave me? I am the worst. The very worst.'

Over the months that followed, Stella entered regions of herself she'd always avoided, most of all the child abandoned to her yearning for a mother's curiosity and attention, and her rage at the failure to provide it. Abandoned too to the crumbs of cheery goodwill her physically and emotionally absent father occasionally sprinkled her way. Max had married her believing her caustic aggression was just a front, that the tenderness he sometimes glimpsed would win through eventually.

In fact, Stella had said yes to him believing something similar, that her anger would gradually dissipate under the loving gaze of this kind, clever young man. What she hadn't seen until it was too late was how fragile he was emotionally, how inadequately set up to withstand her attacks. 'He would sulk and pout when I was mean to him, which only spurred me to be meaner still. I don't know why.'

'I think you do,' I said. 'You wanted him to ask you what the hell was wrong with you, speaking to him like that. To stand up to you, yes, but also really to wonder what was wrong, why you were so angry. You wanted someone different from your parents.'

'But that seems so unfair. It wasn't *his* job to work out what was wrong or why I was so angry.'

'No.'

There was a long silence. 'I should have come to you years earlier. I might still be married.' She paused. 'Probably not. We were never right for each other. But the parting could have been much kinder.'

Six years after her separation from Max, there was a much kinder parting with me. There was no new love, no Hollywood sunset. She wondered whether she wanted another long-term relationship. 'Perhaps one day,' she said towards the end, 'I'll be able to choose someone because I want to be with them rather than to escape from myself.'

While she was frequently and, no doubt, entertainingly wicked, she was never again blindly vicious, towards me or anyone else. Instead of incinerating her humour, her rage gave it just enough heat. Being angry, she realized, could be a way of feeling rather than annihilating her feelings.

As we moved towards ending our sessions, she began writing a novel based on her marriage. It would be a way to make sense of the work she'd done with me. 'I don't know what, if anything, I'll end up doing with it, but I feel like it needs the mask of fiction to make the work we've done here fully real. The difficult bit will be to avoid either exonerating myself or making myself a monster.'

I agreed. 'Either option would be an easy way out.'

'Well, maybe you'll end up in it. The tricky bastard who denied me an easy way out.'

In a meditation on different forms of human conversation, the French writer and philosopher Maurice Blanchot reflects on the pause, the interval between one speaker and another, as the condition 'that alone permits speech to be constituted as conversation'. The pause signifies the recognition of an interlocutor, someone to whom I'm both addressing myself and listening to. It signifies

a limit to my power of speech and a basic receptivity to the voice
of someone else.

Speech without pause, Blanchot continues, raises the spectre of
the worst persecutory terror: 'Let us recall Hitler's terrible monologues. And every head of state participates in the same violence
of this *dictare*, the repetition of an imperious monologue, when
he enjoys the power of being the only one to speak.'

To dictate is literally to possess 'the power of being the only
one to speak', and therefore to exclude and negate the possibility
of other voices, other ways of perceiving, feeling and thinking.
Blanchot's allusion to Hitler is in this sense more than an example; he is the end logic of this violent tearing away of speaking
from the pause and so from listening. In effectively abolishing
the other's voice, Hitler's raging monologues are a concentrated
expression of his murderousness.

Blanchot's observation, I suggest, captures the essence of racism
both as a personal attitude and as a social structure. Racism is a
way of systematically excluding the other from conversation, from
the possibility of human recognition and contact. As Hitler's monologues remind us so viscerally, the anger mobilized by racism is
indistinguishable from aggression. Even as 'mere' speech, racism's
function is to injure, humiliate and reduce the other.

Racism has been the unfortunate occasion for a range of
modern writers and thinkers not only to make sense of politically
inflected rage of this kind, but to imagine ways of resisting and
defeating it, of enlisting anger in the service of love and justice
rather than fear and hate. Few writers pursued this task more
consistently and substantially than the Black American novelist
and essayist James Baldwin. For Baldwin, the relation of Black
Americans to America could not be reduced to that of 'oppressed
to oppressor, of master to slave'; indeed, this relationship cannot
be understood at all, he writes in his 1951 essay 'Many Thousands

Gone', 'until we accept how very much it contains of the force and anguish and terror of love'.

Baldwin points the way here to a different mode of anger, one that breaks out of the sterile rage of the unhearing monologue or rant, placing anger instead on the plane of love, albeit a love heavy with turbulence and ambivalence. The problem, as Baldwin conceives it, is that the grim realities of racial inequality and injustice have trapped Black Americans in the malign projections of American mass psychology, in which Black Americans typically manifest as ticking time bombs of dangerous and vindictive resentment, while their tormented and ambivalent love for America – the only country they have – remains unperceived. Under such conditions, relations between Black and white Americans can only perpetuate mutual fear and suspicion, a point echoed in the writings of his equally celebrated contemporary Frantz Fanon. Writing out of the lived experience of colonialism and the terrible ravages of the Algerian War, the Algerian psychiatrist anatomized the pathological effects of racism on both oppressed and oppressor.

As we saw in Chapter Two, Fanon today is often invoked for his advocacy of violent resistance as a 'cleansing force' that, as he writes in *The Wretched of the Earth*, his seminal 1961 book published shortly after the end of the Algerian War, 'frees the native from his inferiority complex and from his despair and inaction; it makes him fearless and restores his self-respect'. But the broader context of his writing gives us reason to question this apparently unequivocal sanguinity towards violence. Violence for Fanon more often appears as the expression of a deep-rooted social pathology in which human relationships are distorted at the outset by the psychic and institutional structures of racism.

As a psychoanalytically oriented psychiatrist, Fanon was especially concerned with the ways racism infiltrated the bodily lives of native Algerians. He notes, 'The dreams of the native are always of muscular prowess . . . of action and of aggression. I dream I am jumping, swimming, running, climbing; I dream that I burst out laughing'. This unconscious life of unrestricted bodily freedom is in direct contrast to a daily life in which 'the native's muscles are always tensed'.

Muscular tension becomes the body's way of expressing life under siege, at once the fear induced by the police, the military and the whole apparatus of the colonial order, and a coiled preparedness for action against it: 'The native is an oppressed person whose permanent dream is to become the persecutor.'

In his clinical discussions later in *The Wretched of the Earth*, of the pathologies of oppressor and oppressed under colonialism, he notes that 'a generalized muscular contraction' had become an established symptom of native Algerians long before the War. Fanon describes this contraction as 'the expression in muscular form of his rigidity and his refusal with regard to colonial authority'. It can often result, he writes, in a kind of permanent inhibition of release, a stiffening that can find no relief; as one patient puts it, 'You see, I'm already stiff like a dead man.'

Racism creates a perpetual state of internal alert, a deadening feeling of psychic and bodily constriction that infects oppressor as well as oppressed. We meet a police inspector tormented by the urge 'to hit everybody all of the time', which he visits on his young children and wife, and which is aroused against anyone offering the slightest resistance to his will. I find it hard not to hear an oblique echo of Blanchot's dictator here, a kind of allergenic defence against awareness of any voice, desire or will not his own, as well as a violent denial of his own vulnerability, embodied in 'the baby of twenty months' whom he hits 'with unaccustomed savagery'.

We see here the effects of racism above all on the feeling life of those who live in its oppressive grip. The automatic reaching for aggressive action, a kind of spring-release of the tightly bound musculature, is a way of evading the feelings of pain, injury and humiliation that afflict oppressor and oppressed alike. The colonial police officer, unable to bear the excessive burden of guilt and shame inherent to his role, begs Fanon 'to help him go on torturing Algerian patriots without any prickings of conscience, without any behaviour problems and with complete equanimity'.

Fanon also records the case of two Algerian schoolchildren of thirteen and fourteen who stab to death one of their European schoolfellows. Under Fanon's questioning, both acknowledge the boy was a friend who had done nothing to harm either of them, and both appeal to an abstract logic of redress for the unpunished murder of countless Algerians by the French. When one of the children tells Fanon that 'they kill children too', Fanon counters that this is no reason to kill their friend. 'Well, kill him I did,' the child replies. 'Now you can do what you like.'

These studies in the psychopathology of colonialism and racism reveal a society whose capacity for contact with their own and others' psychic states has been fatally corroded. Under these conditions, it is very difficult for anger to take any form other than pure aggression, blind action dissociated from desire or intent, or from any feeling at all beyond a compulsive pressure to kill the other.

It's no accident that Baldwin's discussion of the psychic life of Black Americans centres on Richard Wright's seminal 1940 novel *Native Son*, a book whose central character, Bigger Thomas could serve as an exemplary case study in this kind of dissociated aggression. In the novel, the impoverished Bigger, seething with rage and envy towards wealthy white society, flees the scene after killing, apparently by accident, the daughter of the rich white family who have just employed him as a chauffeur. While in flight, he rapes and then kills his girlfriend Bessie before finally being captured, tried and sentenced to death. Baldwin's essay is an appreciative but ultimately unsparing critique of the novel, and in particular what he sees as the one-dimensionality of Bigger's inner life, which comes perilously if inadvertently close to confirming some of the most pernicious tropes of white racism. The difficulty, argues Baldwin, is that Wright's portrayal is emphatically not without truth. There is, he writes,

> no Negro living in America who has not felt, briefly or for long periods, . . . hatred; who has wanted to smash any white face he may encounter in a day, to violate, out of motives of the cruellest vengeance, their women, to break the bodies of all white people and bring them low, as low as that dust into which he himself has been and is being trampled.

Setting aside the conflation of Black Americans with Black men, Baldwin here confirms the truth of that same dissociated rage we see in Bigger or in Fanon's cases studies. But this is a partial truth that loses sight of what this dissociated rage is dissociating itself from, namely 'the force and anguish and terror of love'. This troubled love is an equal part of the Black American experience; as long as it goes unseen and unfelt, the likes of Bigger can only exist as a horrifying 'warning' to the frightened hearts of liberal America. 'To present Bigger as a warning is simply to reinforce the American guilt and fear concerning him, it is most forcefully to limit him to that . . . social arena in which he has no human validity, it is simply to condemn him to death.'

Under Wright's gaze, Bigger's rage is too thoroughly saturated with hatred of both himself and others to admit of any other possible end than punishment by death, unforgiving and unforgiven.

Racism, the novel seems to conclude, has deprived him of an inner life which might have afforded him enough contact with his rage to facilitate the stirrings of love and justice. Racist society gives birth to his blind murderousness, and so racist society must kill him.

In his later book *The Fire Next Time* (1963), Baldwin asks how we might break out of this cyclical violence which is endemic to a racist world. The first and much shorter of the book's two sections is a letter to his nephew, also named James, 'on the one hundredth anniversary of the Emancipation'. His nephew may have the moody temperament of his late grandfather, Baldwin's preacher father, who died defeated 'because, at the bottom of his heart, he really believed what white people said about him'.

For all that one was a preacher and the other a delinquent youth, there is in this regard an unsettling affinity between Baldwin's father and Bigger. Both are trapped in the projections of racism; if he is to escape this fate, the young James must see what they could not, that what white people believe of him 'does not testify to your inferiority but to their inhumanity and fear'. Without this insight, words like 'acceptance' and 'integration' are meaningless, for they rest on 'the impertinent assumption that *they* [white people] must accept *you*'. On the contrary, Baldwin tells James, '*You* must accept *them* . . . and accept them with love.' What does it mean to accept white people with love? It is to see what Baldwin calls, with simultaneous sincerity and irony, their 'innocence', their entrapment inside a history they don't understand, one which has bound them willy-nilly to an ingrained and unquestioned belief in their own superiority.

While white and Black Americans tacitly collude in this belief, they are bound together in the same deathly fate. White people will continue to delude themselves that the 'imprisonment' of their Black brothers and sisters in ghettos has 'made them safe', and Black people will never allow themselves 'to go behind the white man's definitions'. 'Integration' on these terms means merely that 'you try to become like white people'.

But there is a different and deeper sense of integration: 'that we, with love, shall force our brothers to see themselves as they really are, to cease fleeing from reality and begin to change it'. What this task of love means can be interpreted many different ways; the sense that may be most relevant to us is of acknowledging 'fleeing from reality' as first of all a state of dissociation, not only from history but from feeling.

White identity, Baldwin suggests, and its assumption of the normativity against which all other identities are judged and measured, is based on an unacknowledged dependence on the history of violence and exclusion it prefers to deny, because to acknowledge that history would be to unsettle reality at its core: 'The black man has functioned in the white man's world as a fixed star, as an immovable pillar: and as he moves out of his place heaven and earth are shaken to their foundations.'

But this assumed normativity has come at a psychic and bodily cost to white as well as Black Americans. It has required them to become insensible to centuries of suffering and rage, to all the passions that have shaped American history, and this insensibility, as the word itself suggests, has come to impact white people's relationship to their own sensuality.

By sensuality, Baldwin is not conjuring the racially charged spectres of 'quivering dusky maidens or priapic black studs' but 'something much simpler and less fanciful': 'To be sensual, I think, is to respect and rejoice in all the force of life, of life itself, and to be *present* in all that one does, from the effort of loving to the breaking of bread ... Something very sinister happens to the people of a country when they begin to distrust their own reactions as deeply as they do here, and to become as joyless as they have become.'

When Baldwin observes caustically that 'white Americans seem to feel that happy songs are *happy* and that sad songs are *sad*', he is describing an abstracted psychic state in which the borders of feeling are forever being policed, rigorously if unconsciously, so that if I'm experiencing one feeling I can't be experiencing another. This artificial marking off of feelings from one another is bound to render feeling itself bloodless and thin.

This, perhaps, is the problem with the way Black anger circulates in American culture, as a fixed and discrete force without contamination from other, perhaps quite contradictory feelings – like love. Perceived in this reduced, unambiguous way, anger takes on the status of a 'warning', a fearful harbinger of aggression and violence that must be ignored or, when necessary, punished.

An anger this one-dimensional cannot really be *felt* in the sense in which I've tried to put across in this book; whoever expresses it is out of contact with themselves. The problem with Bigger as a character, and indeed the way in which 'he is most American,' writes Baldwin, is that he 'has no discernible relationship to himself, to his own life, to his own people, nor to any other people'. His is precisely a non-sensual anger, an anger that is discharged in aggressive action before it can be contacted and listened to by the self who is feeling it.

Aggressive anger, I suggested earlier, depersonalizes the self. Verbal and physical acts of aggression tend to turn the person who performs them into an interchangeable instance of a generalized feeling. When I yell pointlessly through my windscreen at a driver who's just cut me up with a reckless right turn, I'm secretly and unhappily aware that I'd rather hide behind the comical stock figure of a middle-aged road rager than endure the momentary feeling of humiliation hovering unwanted at the edges of my consciousness.

If I didn't default so quickly to yelling, in other words, I might be forced to feel something more than a reflexive anger. Lurking beneath that reflex would be, perhaps, feelings of impotence and anxiety, some resentment and even envy at the how readily available such aggression is to other, especially *younger male* drivers, in contrast to the distance and unease I feel in relation to my own aggression, not to mention the sadness I feel at no longer being young.

There is, I'm suggesting, a rich but disavowed personal history of feeling that is concealed even beneath the trivial, unseen event of my yelling at a person who can't hear me. Baldwin vastly expands this insight, asking us to see what depths and rich complexities of feeling are hiding inside us all, unheard and unfelt. How transformative might it be for relations between people of different races if those depths could be sounded and heard and received?

Baldwin implies that two conditions must be in place to enable such an encounter. There must be a readiness among Black Americans to open their white fellow citizens to the reality they've been fleeing from. And there must be white persons able to renounce the wilful deafness of the dictator endowed with the sole right of speech, and listen to this other voice.

There can be no ideal iteration of this kind of encounter because both parties involved will come to it carrying the internalized distortions of racism – this, of course, is what makes the encounter necessary and meaningful in the first place. With that proviso in mind, I turn to the unfolding relationship, in 1930s Johannesburg, between a Russian Jewish psychoanalyst and a medicine man of the Manyika tribe of eastern Zimbabwe, narrated in Wulf Sachs's remarkable 1947 book, *Black Anger*, with the thought that it might offer a version of Baldwin's imagined encounter.

Black Anger is the revision of a book published ten years previously under the tellingly different title of *Black Hamlet*. The revisions and change of title attest to a subtle but decisive change in the book's understanding of its own aims and intentions. Where *Black Hamlet* signals the reading of an African man through a psychoanalytic narrative grid, *Black Anger* makes audible the feeling voice of the man himself.

Born in Lithuania in 1893, Sachs studied psycho-neurology under Pavlov in St Petersburg and took a further degree in Cologne, before qualifying as a doctor in London in 1922. Soon after, he emigrated to South Africa with his family, where he became a pioneer of psychoanalysis, publishing an introductory book in 1934 with an approving foreword from Freud.

Sachs was an energetic participant in South African left politics, in large part informed by his Jewishness. 'Didn't I myself,' he reflects in *Black Anger*, 'belong to a people ceaselessly driven from pillar to post?' He edited a socialist journal, *The Democrat*, from 1943 and was instrumental in founding the SA Psychoanalytical Training Institute in 1946 before his sudden death in 1949.

As the South African historian Saul Dubow notes, *Black Anger* covers a period between the early thirties and the Second World War, during which time racial segregation had become increasingly 'entrenched in law and fact'. John Chavafambira, the Manyika medicine man at the centre of the book, was part of a large migratory movement of rural southern Africans seeking work in rapidly expanding cities.

The initial meeting between Sachs and Chavafambira was informed by a fair share of self-interested motives on both their parts. Sachs was introduced to Chavafambira by 'a woman anthropologist' whom Dubow identifies as Ellen Hellmann, a fellow participant in Sachs's political and intellectual circles. His aim in making his acquaintance was to understand 'the black man's mind in its normal state' as a way of testing the cultural generalizability of psychoanalysis. This required a subject willing to meet regularly, to free associate and so reveal 'the wide range of desires, conflicts, strivings, contradictory and confusing', without which we cannot hope to understand 'the depths of the human mind'.

For his part, Chavafambira hoped to learn something of the European doctor's techniques for treating the human mind and body, to develop his own practice as a *nganga* or medicine man. Inevitably, his curiosity about Sachs was hedged by ambivalence and a suspicion, hardly unjustified, about his motives. Added to this was the inhibiting effect of Sachs's whiteness on the 'freedom' of his free associations. Free association is bound to run up against the roadblock of inhibition in any analysis, but Sachs was made to recognize 'how much more difficult it was for John to talk about me and the white people he hated and feared'.

Sachs is perceptive enough to recognize that these profound differentials in power, added to the cultural and linguistic distance between them, prevent him from conducting anything like an orthodox analysis of Chavafambira. He is flexible enough clinically to do away with some of the most basic features of the psychoanalytic setting, including payment, abstention from self-disclosure and confinement of contact to the consulting room. Sachs visits all the locales of Chavafambira's working and domestic life and history, and as their intimacy deepens, shares his thoughts and feelings, while intervening increasingly concretely in Chavafambira's life problems and dilemmas.

And Sachs is sufficiently self-examining to recognize that his 'native' subject's suspicion of him is all too well founded: 'He mistrusted every white man, for he fully realized that a white man always wanted to get something out of a black . . . The truth is, he was quite right in that respect; for a long time John was to me merely an object for psychological study.'

There is an anticipation here, directed towards himself, of Ferrante's criticism of the psychoanalytic tendency towards understanding, the temptation to render the disordered reality of the inner life as a coherent narrative. Sachs's admission of his incapacity to see Chavafambira as other than 'an object for psychological study' hints at the temptation to squeeze his subject's life into the confines of a particular narrative grid.

The admission is also implicit in the change of title from *Black Hamlet* to *Black Anger*. The earlier title had placed the emphasis on Chavafambira's 'Hamletism', a variation on the Oedipus complex identified by Freud in *The Interpretation of Dreams*. Like Hamlet, the young medicine man is filled with a murderous resentment towards the uncle suspected of poisoning his father and usurping his place, and is afflicted with the same 'indecision and hesitancy in situations requiring direct action'. But in forging these striking parallels, Sachs passes over the many ways Chavafambira's story eludes and exceeds the tight bounds of the Hamlet narrative. In changing the title, Sachs shifts the book's emphasis from his interpretation of the man to the man's own feeling life, from a ready-made explanation of Chavafambira's anger to listening to it on its own terms.

The book Sachs intended to write, a psycho-anthropological study of the mental effects of an African medicine man's migration from a rural *kraal* or village to a major city, morphs as he writes it into a story of the transformative effects on his own mind of his relationship with Chavafambira. The ambition to 'find out the workings of the primitive unconscious mind', which involves examining that mind from a conceptual distance, gives way to a realization of how he and Chavafambira are each being changed by their relationship.

The pivotal moment here comes when Sachs notices the correlation between Chavafambira's increasing self-destructiveness and his 'abrupt severance from me' (their meetings had become infrequent as Chavafambira was building his practice). Sachs notes that with a conventional analytic patient, he would have been fully aware of the risks of breaking off contact while the patient was in 'the state of so-called positive transference' to the analyst. But he failed to account for this danger when it came to Chavafambira because, 'I had to confess again – John had been to me only a subject of experiment, and the whole analysis nothing more than a case of psychic vivisection.'

By providing regular confirmation of his psychoanalytic intuitions, the medicine man had long been an abundant source of narcissistic gratification for Sachs. But faced with the prospect of real risk to Chavafambira's well-being and safety, Sachs begins to discern the emergence of a 'new man' – not the case study but 'the human: the real John'.

It isn't a matter here of Sachs throwing off at a stroke all the prejudices and distortions of a racialized way of seeing. In fact, he continues to betray these prejudices in ways he isn't always aware of. He can be patrician and high-handed in his dealings with Black men and women, and never questions his assumptions of European superiority in intellectual and aesthetic judgement. When Chavafambira becomes infatuated with a young woman in his *kraal*, Sachs expresses admiration for her 'exceptional beauty, judged even by European standards'.

But Sachs's continued and unavoidable embeddedness in the racism which conditions his daily life is an important element in the story of his faltering transformation. A Jew growing up during the twilight of Tsarist Russia, he bears within himself both the historical legacy of antisemitism and the social, economic and legal privileges of whiteness in southern Africa. His Jewishness attunes him to the rage and fear aroused in his Black interlocutors by his whiteness.

Through all his years of dialogue with Chavafambira, Sachs is continually honing his receptivity to what his informant is telling him, above all about Black anger. He comes to see that something in its force and intensity can't be contained inside the standard psychoanalytic frame. Immersing himself in the various communities Chavafambira moves between, he learns more of the rage and humiliation accrued by Black South Africans in the course of their daily lives.

When Sachs visits Chavafambira in the impoverished 'Blacktown' settlement (a pseudonym for the Orlando neighbourhood in Soweto), the medicine man tells the assembled company about going to buy a train ticket at Benoni station one hour in advance of travel to allow himself a little time to rest beforehand. 'You Kaffirs get enough rest, lazy bastards,' the vendor tells him, slamming the window shut. When Chavafambira returns an hour later, he is made to wait while white customers buy their tickets and so misses his train.

It is an incident to set alongside a story of Chavafambira's educated friend Tembu: a response to Sachs's question as to whether Tembu considers him to be 'a real friend of the Africans'. Tembu relates his visit to a wealthy white liberal's house to hear him declaim against the New Native laws depriving Africans of their last vestiges of human rights. Following the talk, Tembu asks for the toilet, only for the white speaker to direct him past the house toilet to one in the servants' quarters, 'a dirty, foul-smelling latrine . . . I ask you. Doctor, what are we to think?'

Bearing witness to the sheer relentlessness of such unthinking racism in everyday Black life, Sachs comes to see that the humiliation related in Tembu's story is structural rather than incidental. The assumption of Black inferiority is woven into the texture of daily life, unquestioningly assumed by whites, resentfully suffered by Blacks.

This is why he can't in any conventional sense conduct an analysis of Chavafambira. The power differential intrinsic to the relation between analyst and patient is operative only within the consulting room. Psychoanalysis tacitly assumes the social and legal equality of the two participants outside the room; if this is absent, as we've seen, it erodes the possibility of free association and of the development of a transference, that is, of anxieties, beliefs and fantasies about the analyst based in psychic rather than external reality.

When Sachs accompanies Chavafambira to his *kraal* in Manyikaland, 'the fortnight of sharing the intimacies of daily living' – a sleeping area, meals, social visits – breaks down the barriers between them. But their return to Johannesburg and its 'conventions regulating black-and-white relationships' quickly restores them. They can no longer be companions, nor 'psychoanalyst and subject'.

Chavafambira, Sachs concludes, was never a patient. He cannot be said to suffer from 'characterological deficiencies', but only from 'his whole life situation ... produced by the society in which he lived. John's greatest need was not to know more of his repressed unconscious, but to know the society he lived in, to recognize its ills and to learn how to fight them.'

The key finding of a book by a white psychoanalyst on *Black Anger* is that Black anger can't be psychoanalysed, that its sheer quantity and force overwhelm the psychoanalytic conceptual grid. It is as though Sachs and Chavafambira have together executed the painful and difficult task formulated sixteen years later by Baldwin: 'that we, with love, shall force our brothers to see themselves as they are, to cease fleeing from reality and begin to change it'.

What is it about this record of a relationship forged over eight decades ago that speaks so resonantly to our own moment?

Prejudice and oppression today no longer require a cumbersome legal apparatus. Apartheid has ended, civil rights have been advanced, states and institutions may be slowly and falteringly coming to terms with their racist and colonial histories. Waves of feminist activism, up to and including the #MeToo movement, have shaken the legal and institutional foundations of sexism. We can point to similar achievements in the movements for gay and trans rights, not to mention the fight for a liveable planet. In each of these fields of activism, we have seen anger successfully mobilized in the service of love and justice.

And yet our civil societies are being torn asunder in new ways by forces intent on unleashing on the world a reactive rage against these social and political advances. So-called populist parties, candidates and movements harness their massive monopolies of attention across conventional and social media to arouse and disseminate paranoia and hate against the enemies who have dared to question and agitate against existing social and political arrangements.

The ultimate imperative of these populist movements is to insulate their constituencies from other voices, to ensure that every one of their followers internalizes the dictator who alone has the right to speak. The result is an effective prohibition on listening to anyone or anything who questions their entrenched and immovable rightness.

In an atmosphere like this, speaking anger from across an apparently unbridgeable divide to an ear that tries to receive it seems like at once the quietest and most transformative event imaginable.

Philip Guston
The Studio 1969

Oil on canvas
121.9 × 106.7 cm / 48 × 42 inches
Promised gift of Musa Guston Mayer to The Metropolitan Museum of Art
© The Estate of Philip Guston, courtesy Hauser & Wirth
Photo: Genevieve Hanson

Coda

Under the Hood

At the tail end of 2023, I forced myself to leave the house to go to Tate Modern's Philip Guston show. I was off work and grieving my father, who four weeks earlier had died suddenly of a massive stroke. I was averse to the prospect of going out, to the flood of strangers on the Tube, to the exhibition crowds and their earnest curiosity or poorly concealed boredom. I preferred to stay at home and nurse my grudge against the world.

But I also knew that I would be back at work in a few days, and if I didn't go soon, I'd miss it. During the first weeks of mourning, every little dilemma of this kind aroused in me a wave of resentment, as though daily life was holding me to ransom like an unimaginative parent: No X for *you* if you don't do Y! *I don't want to*, I wanted to scream back. But who was I going to scream at now? I got on the Tube instead.

The abstract canvases of the first rooms, each one a vortex of painterly intensity, cast a deep spell over me. They culminated in the ghostly heads of paintings made in the mid-sixties, which peered out from inside square cages of thick, compacted black, staring into the dark inside of my own.

These pictures paved the way for the figurative explosions in Guston's work that followed over the next few years. But nothing prepared me for this muted orgy of colours and things, and especially not for Guston's notorious hood paintings, the hapless stooges in Klan cloaks idling, driving and painting their way through the world, the smears and scraps of their evildoing just perceptible behind or around them.

The museum label informed me that thirty-three of these paintings were shown in a major exhibition at the Marlborough Gallery in New York between October and November 1970. This was the month of my birth, I noted, as though the paintings were a kind of bespoke commentary on the state of the world at the point of my entry into it. Grief can feel like being shrouded in narcissistic fog; everything seems to be about you.

The New York art world received these paintings in bafflement and disgust. With a few exceptions, artists and critics reacted with sneering distaste to the comic-strip reductionism, lurid palette and Klan imagery, wondering how Guston could have gone from the sublime abstractionist of a decade ago to these shambolic tableaux of chromatic and political chaos. Some friends, notably the avant-garde composer Morton Feldman, cut off contact with him altogether after leaving the gallery.

One painting snared my gaze and held it at a standstill: *The Studio* (1969). Against a trademark candy pink wall muted by the greys and whites pressing through it, and surrounded by the clutter of the painter's studio, a hooded Klansman presses a brush to the canvas with his oversized blood-red right hand. Splotches of red – blood, or paint – spatter the lower fold of his white cloak. The image forming on the canvas is himself.

The painting speaks to us from a moment fraught with violence and menace in America and the world beyond. Guston painted it as war was raging in Vietnam, a resurgent Klan had been terrorizing Black communities in the South for decades, and Martin Luther King Jr had been assassinated in April of the previous year, sparking riots in cities across the country.

Robert F. Kennedy was assassinated in June, while in August police had brutalized crowds outside the Democratic National Convention in Chicago.

Looking at the painting, it reminded me of the mire of our own moment of spreading violence and authoritarian zeal. The previous and perhaps next US President is a revered icon of the KKK, mainstreaming white supremacy in ways they could only have dreamed of. As global heating and war drive larger and more urgent streams of mass migration, the UK and many of its European neighbours cultivate a 'hostile environment' for migrants and asylum seekers, deliberately engineering their destitution.

Guston's words from the period of *The Studio*, printed on another wall label, resonate today: 'So when the 1960s came along I was feeling split, schizophrenic. The war, what was happening to America, the brutality of the world. What kind of man am I, sitting at home, reading magazines, going into a frustrated fury about everything – and then going into my studio to adjust a red to a blue.'

What kind of man am I? I felt like I couldn't move, a physical stuckness both vertiginous and distressing, a disorientation at once physical, emotional and moral. The picture seemed to speak my own frustrated fury and inability to find a usable outlet for it. The flouting of perspective amplified this sense of inadequacy, as though making visible my own difficulty in mapping the world and my place in it.

Freud writes that in the unconscious, two contradictory realities can sit alongside one another, 'exempt from mutual contradiction'. This phenomenon is familiar to us from our dream life, where we can be simultaneously in one place and another, where people can be both themselves and someone else ('it was my Dad, only not my Dad'). Guston's late paintings look like snapshots of this landscape of the unconscious. Instead of a stable perspectival space in which one thing is clearly marked off from another, all differentiations collapse into the chaotic flatness of the canvas. 'Painting,' wrote Guston 'is really . . . this metaphysical plane where the condition exists of no finish, no end, but infinite continuity.' In the space of *The Studio*, the lightbulb appears to hang at once in front of and beside the clock, just as the grey plume of cigarette smoke in front of the painting could double as a stain on the back wall. Is that a curtain of red fabric hovering from the top of the canvas, or just a different colour on the wall? The spatial regime of the world of the painting looks flimsy and vulnerable, on the verge of caving in. In psychoanalysis that regime, conferring structure and coherence on the world, is known as the paternal order.

If I had to go to an exhibition in the first flush of grief for a father, this felt like the one to choose. Or possibly the one to avoid at all costs.

The painter painting himself painting, a classic *mise en abyme* in the centre of the canvas, but also spilling out of it; the first, invisible link in this chain of self-painters is the painter of *The Studio*, into whose perspective the painting railroads us, inserting us into its infinite play of mirrors. You don't get to see this scene from a comfortable distance; if you really want to look at it, you have to get inside it. You have to look under the hood.

'In the beginning the canvas is empty and you can do anything, and that's the most frightening experience,' said Guston in a 1980 interview. Glossing this remark, the critic Mark Godfrey notes that Guston paints not from the observation of an existing reality but as the creator of a new reality, summoning images into existence 'as Genesis describes God bringing into being the parts of a world'.

The point here is that you cannot navigate this created world by reference to the world you already know. You can only enter it on the terms set by the paintings themselves, and this enforced compact with them makes you feel queasy and angry. How many paintings have made me want to turn away in relief, as though the real world were preferable?

Entartete Kunst, 'degenerate art', comes to mind, the Nazi term for the distortions and contortions of modernist lines and colours, its products exhibited to the German public in 1937 to warn of what happens when the degenerate Jewish spirit is left free to contaminate and pervert the ideal rectitude of classical Aryan order and morality.

Had my own gaze been infiltrated by this Nazi spirit? Was I looking away in disgust from these degenerate images, reaching for the paternal order corroded by the ugly horrors of this Jewish artist's perverse imagination? Was I looking at the paintings from under a hood, feeling somewhere the furious urge to burn them?

There is a Guston painting of 1970, *Flatlands*, in which two hooded figures float blankly across the middle of a flat white desert, a wasteland of abandoned objects which are recurrent motifs of the whole series of paintings – a child's orange sun on the same undifferentiated plane as clocks, hanging blank canvases, a tree stump, but also an amputated foot, a pair of shoed human legs clad in what look suspiciously like striped concentration camp pyjamas.

The traumatic historical reference is overlain disturbingly by a pop-culture reference: legs poking out horizontally from the edge of a comic-strip frame, known as the 'plop take', denote a comedy pratfall. I was reminded that when actors start laughing uncontrollably on stage, they call it corpsing. The more I looked around, the more I noticed these mutual adulterations of laughter and horror.

In another 1970 canvas, *Caught*, a gloved hand unsettlingly like Mickey Mouse's descends from the sky to point accusingly at a pair of hooded Klansmen sat in their jalopy, who stare at it like frightened rabbits, little red bullets of sweat pouring down their cloaks. The same hand is appended to a black forearm bursting through the right edge of the frame in *Courtroom* (also 1970), its finger of judgement pointed squarely at the Klansman, who stares at it in 'Who, me?!' bewilderment from under his blood-stained cloak, even as the stripe-trousered legs of an upside-down corpse poke out of the dock behind him.

The gag ruins the gravitas of moral horror and lamentation, just as the intimations of hate and murder ruin the gag (although it's equally true that they *are* the gag). Guston is another child of Jewish refugees from Tsarist Russia, born twenty years after Wulf Sachs, the South African psychoanalyst who found himself entangled in, and seeking to shed light on, Black anger.

Like Sachs, though by very different means, he comes to see that he will get nowhere in this task unless he turns his gaze critically on himself. 'White Americans seem to feel that happy songs are *happy* and that sad songs are *sad*', Baldwin had written six years previously. Guston's paintings put paid to this emotional complacency.

Adapting Baldwin's formulation, we might say that Guston emphatically doesn't feel his angry paintings are *angry*. He declines to take refuge in the cosy knowledge of being right. There is no moral vanishing point from which to view and judge the actors in these paintings. The finger-pointing hand of *Caught* and *Courtroom* is intruding from outside the frame, as though haughtily refusing to implicate itself in the picture. Rather than orienting and organizing our gaze, it's just another element in the chaos.

The slapstick Klansmen of these paintings are not stock

embodiments of pure evil. Their bodily comportment suggests sadness, loneliness, vulnerability. Stare at the vertical black slits through which their eyes peer and you might see uncertainty, guilt, embarrassment and desolation staring back at you.

These are certainly paintings to make you feel angry, but they will make you feel a lot of other things as well. Anger is most rigid when it's *angry* to the exclusion of other feelings, and most alive and creative where it dares to make contact with other feelings.

That afternoon in the Tate, I didn't just see the Klansmen's feelings, I inhabited them, wore them like a cloak I couldn't take off. I was furious at the paintings for exposing me to places in myself I wanted to avoid. I was grateful to the paintings for speaking my rage at the fact that nothing had changed between the moment of my birth and this one, for screaming my infantile rage at my father for leaving this world without having fixed it. I trembled with anger, but also with laughter, and also with tears, and it was difficult to tell the difference.

Notes

Introduction

p. xiv   *gestures that 'represent more or less plainly . . .'*: Charles Darwin, *The Expression of Emotion in Man and Animals* (London: Penguin, 2009), p. 76

p. xv   *Freud categorized the drives*: Freud develops and revises his theory of drives throughout his writings, but the key texts in this regard are *Three Essays on the Theory of Sexuality* (1905), 'On Narcissism' (1914), 'Drives and Their Vicissitudes' (1915) and *Beyond the Pleasure Principle* (1920). All quotations from Freud are from *The Standard Edition of the Complete Psychological Works of Sigmund Freud*, trans. J. Strachey, ed. J. Strachey and A. Strachey (London: Vintage, 2001). *Three Essays* is in Volume 7, 'On Narcissism' and 'Drives' in Volume 14, *Beyond the Pleasure Principle* in Volume 18.

p. xvi   *caught in the grip of an 'infinite wrath'*: Sigmund Freud, 'The Moses of Michaelangelo' (1914), *Standard Edition*, Volume 13, p. 215

p. xvi   *'which in the next instant . . .'*: ibid., p. 215

p. xvii   *'without conscious knowledge of the undertaking'*: Antonio Damasio, *Looking for Spinoza: Joy, Sorrow and the Feeling Brain* (London: Vintage, 2003), p. 79

p. xvii   *'the possibility of creating novel, nonstereotypical responses'*: ibid., p. 80

p. xviii   *the sobbing 'stopped as abruptly as it had begun'*: ibid., p. 68

p. xviii   *'Emotion-related thoughts came only* after . . .': ibid., p. 69

p. xviii   *transformation of drives into 'psychic phenomena'*: Hans W. Loewald, 'On Motivation and Instinct Theory' in *Papers on Psychoanalysis* (New Haven: Yale University Press, 1980), p. 132

p. xix   *and is 'suddenly aroused to wrath' when told*: Freud, 'The Moses', p. 232

p. xix   *'the giant frame with its tremendous physical power . . .'*: ibid., p. 233

p. xx	*he reveals that he's been 'living through the scene . . .'* : Sigmund Freud and Josef Breuer, 'On the Psychical Mechanism of Hysterical Phenomena: Preliminary Communication', *Standard Edition*, Volume 2, p. 14
p. xx	*'the scene in the law-court . . .'*: ibid., p. 14
p. xxi	*'an experience of satisfaction'*: Sigmund Freud, *Project for A Scientific Psychology*, *Standard Edition*, Volume 2, p. 318
p. xxi	*the startling inference that 'the initial helplessness . . .'*: ibid., p. 318
p. xxiv	*Arthur Janov's 'primal therapy'*: See Arthur Janov, *The Primal Scream* (1970) (London: Penguin, 1987)
p. xxiv	*as documented by* Guardian *writer Gaby Hinsliff*: Gaby Hinsliff, '"Lift the lid and there's a well of rage": why women are mad as hell (and not afraid to show it)', *Guardian*, 4 March 2023, https://www.theguardian.com/lifeandstyle/2023/mar/04/lift-the-lid-and-theres-a-well-of-rage-why-women-are-mad-as-hell-and-not-afraid-to-show-it
p. xxv	*a drive, on the other hand, is 'always a* constant *one'*: Sigmund Freud, 'Drives and Their Vicissitudes', *Standard Edition*, Volume 14, p. 118
p. xxv	*lies 'on the frontier between the mental and the somatic'*: ibid., p. 122
p. xxvi	*The French psychoanalyst Jean Laplanche points out*: See especially Jean Laplanche, *Essays on Otherness* (London: Routledge, 1998)
p. xxvii	*A second, more surprising feature*: Sigmund Freud, 'Female Sexuality', *Standard Edition*, Volume 21, p. 231
p. xxvii	*that the patient's mother 'did not give her enough milk . . .'*: ibid., p. 234
p. xxvii	*the more likely explanation is that 'the greed of a child's libido'*: ibid., p. 234
p. xxix	*God is 'grieved at heart'*: Genesis, Chapter 6, Verse 6, *The Pentateuch and Rashi's Commentary: A Linear Translation into English*, trans. A. Ben Isaiah and B. Sharfman (New York: S. S. and R. Publishing Company, Inc., 1949), p. 55
p. xxix	*'I will blot out man whom I created from the face of the earth . . .'*: ibid., Chapter 6, Verse 7, p. 56
p. xxix	*Abraham intercedes on behalf of Sodom and Gomorrah*: ibid., Chapter 18, Verses 24–32, pp. 161–4
p. xxix	*'the Lord caused to rain upon Sodom and upon Gomorrah brimstone and fire . . .'*: ibid., Chapter 19, Verse 24, p. 175

p. xxx   *ten of them return and 'spread an evil report'*: Numbers, Chapter 13, Verse 32, *The Pentateuch*

p. xxx   *swallowed by a 'mouth' that opened and sealed them in the earth*: ibid., Chapter 16, Verse 32

p. xxxii   *Jonah's defiant response is to 'flee unto Tarshish . . .'*: Jonah, Chapter 1, Verse 3, *The Twelve Prophets,* ed. A. Cohen (London: Soncino Press, 1948), p. 138

p. xxxii   *God 'turns away His fierce anger'*: ibid., Chapter 3, Verse 9, p. 147

p. xxxii   *'for I knew that Thou art a gracious God . . .'*: ibid., Chapter 4, Verse 2, p. 148

p. xxxii   *'Are you greatly angry for the gourd?' God asks him*: ibid., Chapter 4, Verses 9–11, pp. 149–50

p. xxxiv   *by Jon Ronson in* So You've Been Publicly Shamed: Jon Ronson, *So You've Been Publicly Shamed* (London: Picador, 2015)

p. xxxv   *the 'accursed anger', of Achilles*: Homer, *The Iliad,* trans. M. Hammond (London: Penguin, 1987), p. 51

p. xxxvi   *'great defence against the horror of war'*: ibid., p. 57

p. xxxvi   *for the 'savagery in his breast'*: ibid., p. 179

p. xxxvii   *bringing to a halt the 'endless pendulum of hit and retaliation'*: Peter Sloterdijk, *Rage and Time: A Psychopolitical Investigation* (London: Polity, 2010), p. 49

p. xxxvii   *'banking' the rage of the 'humiliated and offended'*: ibid., p. 115

p. xxxviii *' . . . the imaginative elaboration of somatic parts . . .'*: D. W. Winnicott, 'Mind and Its Relationship to Psyche–Soma', *Through Paediatrics to Psychoanalysis: Collected Papers* (London: Routledge, 1975), p. 244

p. xxxviii *dialogue with our own body that 'is felt by the individual . . .'*: ibid., p. 244

p. xxxix   *'violent head-banging appeared as an attempt to produce a blackout'*: ibid., p. 251

p. xxxix   *'constantly engaged in immediately dispersing in action'*: Joyce McDougall, *Theatres of the Body* (London: Karnac, 1989), p. 94

p. xxxix   *'feeling empty, misunderstood or out of touch with others'*: ibid., p. 96

p. xl   *'What it damages are the feelings of security and trust . . .'*: Will Davies, *Nervous States: How Feeling Took Over the World* (London: Jonathan Cape, 2018), p. 20

Chapter One: Righteous Rage

p. 2   *'Once you have a reason to be angry . . .'*: Agnes Callard, 'On Anger', *On Anger*, ed. A. Callard (Boston: MIT Press, 2020), p. 18

p. 4   *In her 2023 book* On Marriage, *the writer Devorah Baum*: Devorah Baum, *On Marriage* (London: Hamish Hamilton, 2023)

pp. 8–9   *'The key element to Hulkness is the rage-to-strength feedback loop . . .'*: Joel Aschenbach, 'All the Rage: The Hulk in Us All', *Washington Post*, 19 June 2003, https://www.washingtonpost.com/archive/lifestyle/2003/06/19/all-the-rage-the-hulk-in-us-all/fbf12212-e7da-4406-b78a-c8aa05a7a838/

p. 9   *'What if violence is precisely the kind of phenomenon . . .'*: Judith Butler, *The Force of Non-Violence* (London: Verso, 2020), p. 14

p. 18   *in a community in which 'everybody lies about everything of importance'*: Hannah Arendt, 'Truth and Politics' (1967), *Between Past and Future* (London: Penguin, 2006), p. 247

p. 18   *'turning "facts" into precisely the type of hot political issues . . .'*: Will Davies, *Nervous States*, p. 24

p. 22   *'the familiar egoism of the sick person'*: Sigmund Freud, 'On Narcissism', *Standard Edition*, Volume 14, p. 82

p. 24   *'With a flashing eye and an angry tone . . .'*: Anthony Trollope, *He Knew He Was Right* (London: Penguin, 1994), p. 15

p. 24   *'he was one to whose nature the giving of any apology was repulsive'*: ibid., p. 16

p. 24   *'a lipless, unfeatured blank'*: Herman Melville, *Moby-Dick* (1851) (London: Penguin, 1986), p. 672

p. 24   *'This whole act's immutably decreed . . .'*: ibid., p. 672

p. 25   *'As I have done, and doing what I think to be right'*: Trollope, *He Knew He Was Right*, p. 48

p. 26   *'He had almost come to have but one desire . . .'*: ibid., p. 378

p. 26   *'Patience . . . your mind perhaps may change'*: William Shakespeare, *Othello*, Act 3, Scene IV, *The Works of William Shakespeare*, Volume 6 (New York: Peebles International Press, 1970), p. 284

p. 26   *'Like to the Pontic Sea . . .'*: ibid., p. 284

p. 27   *'rather a bore to his friends'*: Trollope, *He Knew He Was Right*, p. 163

p. 27   *'behaved with such indiscretion . . .'*: ibid., p. 279

p. 28   *private detective Bozzle, 'whose business it is'*: ibid., p. 243

p. 28   *'Let it once be conceded from all sides that he had been right . . .'*: ibid.,
           p. 660

p. 29   *not from 'belief in her infidelity' but from 'an obstinate determination to*
           yield nothing': ibid., p. 816

p. 30   *'He was as wretched a being to look at . . .'*: ibid., p. 579

p. 30   *'not quick in deciphering such stories'*: ibid., p. 579

p. 32   *'The direction of the French Revolution . . .'*: Hannah Arendt, *On*
           Revolution (1963) (London: Penguin, 1990), p. 92

p. 33   *'speculators and monopolists' over the economy, 'bloodsuckers of the*
           people': Jacques Roux, 'Manifesto of the Enragés'. All quotes
           from Roux's 'Manifesto' taken from https://www.marxists.org/
           history/france/revolution/roux/1793/enrages01.htm

p. 34   *'The* malheureux *changed into the* enragés *. . .'*: Hannah Arendt,
           On Revolution, p. 110

p. 34   *'Suffering,' she writes, 'whose strength and virtue lie in endurance . . .'*:
           ibid., p. 111

p. 34   *Once 'necessity invaded the political realm'*: ibid., p. 114

p. 35   *effectively abolishes the assessment of whether they work*: For an
           incisive critique of *enragés'* policy of price controls, see Simon
           Schama, *Citizens: A Chronicle of the French Revolution* (London:
           Random House, 1989), pp. 710–14

p. 36   *In April 2014, Elliot Rodger drove into and shot students*: Laura Bates,
           Men Who Hate Women: The Extremism Nobody is Talking About
           (London: Simon and Schuster, 2020), p. 39

p. 37   *'a loser, rejected by society'*: ibid., p. 44

p. 37   *'collective treachery'*: ibid., p. 46

p. 39   *'the repudiation of femininity'*: Sigmund Freud, 'Analysis
           Terminable and Interminable', *Standard Edition*, Volume 23,
           p. 250

p. 40   *a celebrated short poem*: Yehuda Amichai, 'The Place Where We
           Are Right', *The Selected Poetry of Yehuda Amichai* (Berkeley:
           University of California Press, 1996), p. 34

Chapter Two: Failed Rage

p. 48   *'It's because we're men like them . . .'*: Robert Antelme, *The Human*
           Race (Evanston: Northwestern University Press, 1998), p. 219

p. 55   *'All who desire something and cannot obtain it . . .'*: Aristotle, *The*

Art of Rhetoric, trans. J. H. Freese (Cambridge, MA: Harvard University Press, 1967), p. 179

p. 55   *'rage seems built into an infant's scream'*: Michael Eigen, *Rage* (Middletown, CT: Wesleyan University Press, 2002), p. 4

p. 56   *Freud generalized this insight*: Sigmund Freud, *Civilization and Its Discontents*, Standard Edition, Volume 22, pp. 57–60

p. 61   *'GET RID OF NEGATIVE PEOPLE . . .'*: Barbara Ehrenreich, *Smile or Die: How Positive Thinking Fooled America and the World* (London: Granta, 2009), p. 55

p. 63   *'Logic defeats anger, because anger . . .'*: 'Control anger before it controls you', APA website, https://www.apa.org/topics/anger/control

p. 65   *'billions of things such as key turnings . . .'*: Timothy Morton, *Humankind: Solidarity with Nonhuman People* (London: Verso, 2017), p. 73

p. 68   *'Their eyes blaze and sparkle . . .'*: Seneca, *De Ira*, trans. A. Stewart (London: G. Bell and Sons, 1900), Book 1, Section I, https://en.wikisource.org/wiki/Of_Anger/Book_I

p. 68   *'Let it rather be locked . . .'*: ibid., Book 3, Section XIII

p. 70   *'most frightful to behold . . .'*: ibid., Book 2, Section XXXV

p. 71   *'for, while anger is the foe of reason . . .'*: ibid., Book 1, Section III

p. 72   *'The lower the status . . .'*, Arlie Russell Hochschild, *The Managed Heart: Commercialization of Human Feeling* (Berkeley: University of California Press, 2003), p. 270

p. 72   *'Cuss. Want to hit a passenger . . .'*: ibid., p. 25

p. 72   *'If you think about the* other *person . . .'*: ibid., p. 196

p. 73   *In 2014, notes William Davies, the UK government*: William Davies, *The Happiness Industry: How the Government and Big Business Sold Us Well-Being* (London: Verso, 2015), p. 111

p. 75   *'The ego,' writes Reich, 'the exposed part of the personality . . .'*: Wilhelm Reich, *Character Analysis* (London: Vision Press, 1950), p. 342

p. 78   *'the risk here of a very small minority of very activist civil servants . . .'*: 'Tensions rise after Dominic Raab claims he was targeted by "unionised officials"', *Guardian*, 21 April 2023, https://www.theguardian.com/politics/2023/apr/21/tensions-rise-after-dominic-raab-claims-he-was-targeted-by-unionised-officials

p. 79   *André Green's 'passivation'*: see, for example, 'Passions and Their

Vicissitudes', *On Private Madness* (London: Karnac, 1986), pp. 247–9

p. 81   '*But if destroying fences . . .*': Andreas Malm, *How to Blow Up a Pipeline* (London: Verso, 2021), p. 159

p. 84   '*undeducible, like the storm and the sunlight*': Peter Sloterdijk, *Rage and Time*, p. 7

p. 85   '*Rage undergoes a metamorphosis . . .*': ibid., p. 60

p. 85   '*All history . . . is the history of rage applications*': ibid., p. 62

p. 85   '*bank of rage*' that '*draws its force from . . .*': ibid., p. 56

p. 85   '*an active mass of value and energy*': ibid., p. 59

p. 85   '*none of the political parties . . .*': ibid., p. 206

p. 87   '*bust the entire carbon budget . . .*': George Monbiot, 'I back saboteurs who have acted with courage and coherence, but I won't blow up a pipeline. Here's why', *Guardian*, 28 April, 2023, https://www.theguardian.com/commentisfree/2023/apr/28/saboteurs-how-to-blow-up-a-pipeline-climate-crisis-direct-action

p. 88   '*Something in the nature of the sexual drive . . .*': Sigmund Freud, 'On the Universal Tendency to Debasement in the Sphere of Love', *Standard Edition*, Volume 11, pp. 188–9

p. 89   '*Police, we love you . . .*': Andreas Malm, *How to Blow Up a Pipeline*, p. 115

Chapter Three: Cynical Rage

p. 98   '*The individual,*' *says Winnicott*: D. W. Winnicott, 'Birth Memories, Birth Trauma and Anxiety' (1949), *Through Paediatrics to Psychoanalysis*, p. 188

p. 102   *Machiavelli's core teaching in* The Prince: Niccolo Machiavelli, *The Prince*, trans. G. Bull (London: Penguin, 2003)

p. 102   *But as Hannah Arendt reminds us, a ruling class's reliance*: Hannah Arendt, 'What Is Authority?', *Between Past and Future*, p. 97

p. 103   *the autism she calls her 'superpower'*: Alison Rourke, 'Greta Thunberg responds to Asperger's critics: "It's a superpower"', *Guardian*, 2 September 2019, https://www.theguardian.com/environment/2019/sep/02/greta-thunberg-responds-to-aspergers-critics-its-a-superpower

p. 104   *The Italian psychoanalyst Massimo Recalcati*: Massimo Recalcati, *The Telemachus Complex* (London: Polity Press, 2019)

p. 108   *'perceiving and appropriately expressing anger is healthy'*: Isaac Stephen Herschkopf, *Hello Darkness, My Old Friend: Embracing Anger to Heal Your Life* (New York: Xlibris, 2003), p. 119

p. 108   *'Psychiatrists are the lowest form of life . . .'*: ibid., p. 167

p. 109   *'having a finite end point . . .'*: ibid., p. 120

p. 111   *The fundamental 'interhuman reality'*: Daniel Lagache, 'Aggressivity' (1960), *The Work of Daniel Lagache: Selected Writings*, trans. E. Holder (London: Karnac, 1993), p. 212

p. 113   *'Yes, shift a bit out of my sun'*: *The Cynic Philosophers: From Diogenes to Julian*, ed. and trans. R. Dobbin (London: Penguin, 2012), p. 31

p. 113   *'I fawn on people who give me alms . . .'*: ibid., p. 41

p. 114   *'Now . . . if someone asks you where you're off to . . .'*: ibid., p. 18

p. 115   *The adolescent who stands in a T-shirt*: Damina Carrington, '"Blah blah blah: Greta Thunberg lambasts leaders over climate crisis', *Guardian*, 28 September 2021, https://www.theguardian.com/environment/2021/sep/28/blah-greta-thunberg-leaders-climate-crisis-co2-emissions

p. 122   *'Revolutionary action,' he writes, 'is in every respect . . .'*: Maurice Blanchot, 'Literature and the Right to Death', *The Work of Fire*, trans. L. Davis (Stanford: University of Stanford Press, 1995), p. 319

p. 123   *Surkov 'directed Russian society like one great reality show'*: Peter Pomerantsev, *Nothing Is True and Everything Is Possible: Adventures in Modern Russia* (London: Faber, 2017), p. 77

p. 124   *'People need to see themselves on stage . . .'*: Henry Foy, 'Vladislav Surkov: "An overdose of freedom is lethal to a state"', *Financial Times*, 18 June 2021, https://www.ft.com/content/1324acbb-f475-47ab-a914-4a96a9d14bac

p. 124   *'Yegor,' Surkov writes, in a passage*: Vladislav Surkov, *Almost Zero*, trans. N. Gojiashvili and N. Valentine (New York: Inpatient Press, 2017), p. 29

p. 125   *'live ammunition was distributed to Ukrainian riot police'*: Timothy Snyder, *The Road to Unfreedom: Russia, Europe, America* (London: Vintage, 2018), p. 137

p. 126   *'But,' he continues, 'if the second law of thermodynamics is true (and it is true)'*: Vladislav Surkov, 'Where has chaos gone? Unboxing stability', originally published in *Актуальные комментарии*, 20 November 2021, http://lobo.lu/unboxing-stability/

p. 127   *Instead, he wrote a blog post*: Laura Bates, *Men Who Hate Women*, p. 199

p. 128   *'mirth with a base note of rage'*: Andrew Marantz, *Antisocial: How Online Extremists Broke America* (London: Picador, 2020) p. 39

p. 128   *'I think that when I punched him . . .'*: ibid., p. 36

p. 130   *according to Lavrov, the true aggressors*: Timothy Snyder, *The Road to Unfreedom*, p. 137

p. 130   *'The optional human logically follows optional gender'*: Alexander Dugin, *The Great Awakening vs The Great Reset* (Budapest: Arktos Media, 2021), p. 13

p. 131   *'could have a massive impact in swing states'*: Laura Bates, *Men Who Hate Women*, p. 217

Chapter Four: Usable Rage

p. 140   *the narrative that frames* One Thousand and One Nights: *The One Thousand and One Nights*, trans. E. W. Lane, ed. E. S. Lane-Poole (London: Chatto and Windus, 1912), https://www.gutenberg.org/files/34206/34206-h/34206-h.htm

p. 142   *A recent Guardian article compiled a helpful list of techniques*: Laura Potter, 'Punch a pillow, hug your pet, write to your MP: 22 ways to deal with your anger', *Guardian*, 8 December 2023, https://www.theguardian.com/lifeandstyle/2023/dec/08/how-to-deal-with-anger-expert-tips-techniques

p. 143   *'linked to the concept of* action*'*: Eugenio Gaddini, 'Aggression and the Pleasure Principle', *A Psychoanalytic Theory of Infantile Experience*, trans. S. G. Morelli (London: Routledge, 1992), p. 37

p. 143   *'an* external *discharge of energy, through the motor apparatus'*: ibid., p. 37

p. 144   *the baby's 'muscular sucking apparatus'*: ibid., p. 37

p. 144   *'Libidinal tension . . . is less rigid and more plastic'*: ibid., p. 40

p. 146   *the illusion that I am, to use Winnicott's term, an 'isolate'*: see D. W. Winnicott, 'Communicating and Not Communicating Leading to a Study of Certain Opposites', *The Maturational Process and the Facilitating Environment* (London: Routledge, 1984)

p. 149   *developed especially in his 1918 'Wolf Man' case*: Sigmund Freud, *From the History of an Infantile Neurosis*, Standard Edition, Volume 17, pp. 57–60

p. 150   *'one that loved not wisely, but too well'*: William Shakespeare, *Othello*, Act 5, Scene II

p. 151   *'She loved me for the dangers I had passed'*: ibid., Act 1, Scene III

p. 154   *Under these provisions, two Just Stop Oil activists*: Damian Gayle, 'Just Stop Oil protestors' jail sentences potentially breach international law, UN expert says', *Guardian*, 20 November 2023, https://www.theguardian.com/environment/2023/ nov/20/just-stop-oil-protesters-jail-terms-potentially-breach- international-law-un-expert-says

p. 154   *Iain Duncan Smith publicly backed pro-motorist activists*: Rachel Burford, 'City Hall faces wave of ULEZ camera destruction as Tory MP says he "understands frustration" at fines', *The Standard*, 30 August 2023, https://www.standard.co.uk/news/politics/ london-ulez-camera-tory-mp-vandalism-police-iain-duncan- smith-b1103720.html

p. 156   *'purified of humors and blood . . .'*: Elena Ferrante, *The Lost Daughter*, trans. A. Goldstein (London: Europa Editions, 2008), p. 122

p. 156   *'She attacked my body . . .'*: ibid., p. 123

p. 157   *'jumble of fragments'*: Elena Ferrante, *Frantumaglia*, trans. A. Goldstein (London: Europa, 2016), p. 99

p. 157   *'an infinite serial or aquatic mass of debris'*: ibid., p. 100

p. 158   *'organize into universal representations . . .'*: ibid., pp. 123–24

p. 158   *'psychoanalysis is the lexicon of the precipice'*: ibid., p. 122

p. 158   *'produced a writing that is dissatisfied with itself'*: ibid., p. 286

p. 159   *'eliminate the entire life she had left behind'*: Elena Ferrante, *My Brilliant Friend*, trans. A. Goldstein (London: Europa, 2012), p. 23

p. 159   *'It's that age. Mario is forty – it happens'*: Elena Ferrante, *The Days of Abandonment*, trans. A. Goldstein (London: Europa, 2005), p. 25

p. 159   *'The reasonableness of others . . .'*: ibid., pp. 25–6

p. 159   *'to wait patiently until every emotion . . .'*: ibid., p. 12

p. 162   *'a bundle of projections'*: D. W. Winnicott, 'The Use of an Object and Relating Through Identifications', *Playing and Reality* (London: Routledge, 1991), p. 88

p. 164   *'When she saw that my teeth were chattering . . .'*: Elena Ferrante, *The Lost Daughter*, p. 39

p. 164   *'A child who gets lost on the beach . . .'*: ibid., pp. 41–2

p. 165   *'I who carried you in here am just as intelligent . . .'*: Elena Ferrante, *Those Who Leave and Those Who Stay*, trans. A. Goldstein (London: Europa, 2014), p. 47

p. 165   *'a sin for which she would go to Hell'*: Elena Ferrante, *The Story of the Lost Child* (London: Europa, 2015), p. 151

p. 167   *'glue, scissors, paper and paint'*: Elena Ferrante, *The Story of A New Name*, trans. A. Goldstein (London: Europa, 2013), p. 122

p. 169   *'So she thought she had full rights to take my place . . .'*: Elena Ferrante, *The Days of Abandonment*, p. 71

p. 171   *the condition 'that alone permits speech . . .'*: Maurice Blanchot, 'Interruption as on a Riemann Surface', *The Infinite Conversation*, trans. S. Hanson (Minneapolis: University of Minnesota Press, 1993), p. 75

p. 172   *'Let us recall Hitler's terrible monologues . . .'*: ibid., p. 75

p. 172   *'until we accept how very much it . . .'*: James Baldwin, 'Many Thousands Gone', *Notes of a Native Son* (London: Penguin, 2012), p. 42

p. 173   *'frees the native from his inferiority complex . . .'*: Franz Fanon, *The Wretched of the Earth*, trans. C. Farrington (London: Penguin, 2001), p. 74

p. 173   *'the dreams of the native are always of muscular prowess . . .'*: ibid., p. 40

p. 174   *'The native is an oppressed person . . .'*: ibid., p. 41

p. 174   *'the expression in muscular form . . .'*: ibid., p. 235

p. 174   *'You see, I'm already stiff like a dead man'*: ibid., p. 235

p. 174   *the urge 'to hit everybody all the time'*: ibid., p. 215

p. 174   *'the baby of twenty months'*: ibid., p. 215

p. 175   *'to help him go on torturing . . .'*: ibid., p. 217

p. 175   *'they kill children too'*: ibid., p. 219

p. 175   *Richard Wright's seminal 1940 novel*: Richard Wright, *Native Son* (London: Penguin, 2000)

p. 176   *'no Negro living in America who has not felt . . .'* James Baldwin, *Notes of a Native Son*, p. 39

p. 176   *'To present Bigger as a warning . . .'*: ibid., p. 41

p. 177   *'because, at the bottom of his heart . . .'*: James Baldwin, *The Fire Next Time* (London: Penguin, 1963), p. 13

p. 177   *'does not testify to your inferiority, but . . .'*: ibid., p. 16

p. 177   *'the impertinent assumption that they . . .'*: ibid., p. 16

Coda: Under the Hood

Acknowledgements

My thanks as ever to Bella Lacey, for the sharp precision and insight she brought to editing this book, as well as for the unfailing warmth and encouragement she's shown me and my writing over the last (gulp) two decades. Thanks also to Christine Lo, George Stamp, Lamorna Elmer and all the Granta team. From the moment she took me on, my agent Rebecca Carter has been a tireless champion, dealing with enquiries and responding to work in progress with miraculous efficiency, kindness and curiosity. Jack Alexander's copy-editing proved as exceptionally thoughtful and well-informed as it was thorough.

Abigail Schama remains the loving and inspiring interlocutor and reader she has always been, while Ethan, Reuben and Ira Cohen continue to offer their own singular and wonderful forms of love and inspiration. I am grateful too to Bonjella, for her dogged conviction that there is no creative frustration that cannot be alleviated by aggressively licking my face.

I've benefited from numerous discussions with and responses from Devorah Baum, Peter Pomerantsev, Leo Robson, Will Rees and Adam Phillips, as well as my clinical discussion group colleagues, Megan Virtue, Francois Louw and Helen Johnston. Marina Benjamin at *Aeon* commissioned and expertly edited the piece which served as this book's seed-kernel. Jim Surowiecki gave invaluable editorial feedback on two pieces on Vladislav Surkov and Elena Ferrante, which reappear in somewhat different form in this book. My thanks to Megan O'Rourke and *The*

Yale Review for the commissions and for permission to reproduce them here. The same goes for Jonathan Beckman at *1843*, who edited an earlier version of the section on passive aggression, which is reproduced here, with kind permission, in significantly different form.

This book is dedicated to the memory of my father, Edward Cohen, who died as I was finishing it, and who was asking after it (as with every other book) in every conversation, right up to what turned out to be our last. I feel the terrible ache of his loss daily, along with gratitude for the unquestioned love, pride and curiosity he bestowed on everything I did.

Index